Con[ten]ts

ABOVE: BULLEID West Country light Pacific No. 34027 *Taw Valley* made its comeback after nearly a decade when it hauled the luxury Belmond British Pullman along the Severn Valley Railway in the latest in a series of high-profile celebrations to mark the line's 50th anniversary year. The one-off visit, organised by UK Railtours, saw the luxury Pullman train, a sister to the Venice-Simplon-Orient-Express, travel from London Victoria to the SVR behind Class 55 Deltic D9009 *Alycidon* to Bewdley. There, it handed over its duties to *Taw Valley*, resplendent in its new livery and carrying the 'Golden Arrow' headboard, all ready for its first revenue-earning trip since its comeback. It was nearly 30 years ago, in August 1985 that the Severn Valley took delivery of the partially restored ex-Barry scrapyard locomotive. JOE CONNELL/SVR

FRONT COVER MAIN PICTURE: GWR 2-8-0 No. 2857 passes Bewdley South signalbox carrying the Severn Valley Railway Golden Jubilee headboard on May 16, 2015. As in the picture above, the wreath was carried in memory of locomotive engineer Bert Hitchen, who restored No. 34027 *Taw Valley*. JED BENNETT

FRONT COVER RIGHT: The Severn Valley Railway's first four main line engines line up on April 6, 1969. See page 44. DAVID WILLIAMS

FRONT COVER LEFT: Princess Anne visits the Severn Valley Railway on April 13, 2015. BOB SWEET/SVR

BACK COVER: LMS Stanier mogul No. 42968 breaks through the early-morning mist as it approaches Arley on December 16, 2012. ALAN CORFIELD

SEVERN VALLEY RAILWAY
50 GLORIOUS YEARS

AUTHOR: Robin Jones

DESIGN: atg-media.com

PRODUCTION EDITOR: Sarah Palmer

COVER DESIGN: Mike Baumber/Kelvin Clements

REPROGRAPHICS: Jonathan Schofield

MARKETING MANAGER: Charlotte Park

PUBLISHER: Tim Hartley

COMMERCIAL DIRECTOR: Nigel Hole

PUBLISHING DIRECTOR: Dan Savage

PUBLISHED BY: Mortons Media Group Ltd, Media Centre, Morton Way, Horncastle, Lincolnshire LN9 6JR. Tel. 01507 529529

PRINTED BY: William Gibbons and Sons, Wolverhampton

MORTONS
MEDIA GROUP LTD

Introduction

Welcome to the Severn Valley Railway, which in 2015 celebrated its 50th anniversary, with a string of high-profile events, not least of all was a visit by the Princess Royal, who, no stranger to steam, drove a locomotive from Bewdley to Kidderminster to mark the occasion.

It was fitting that she became the latest member of the royal family to visit this magnificent heritage line, for it is a great British achievement in every sense of the word, and its tale is a truly remarkable one.

We have all heard stories about ideas written on the back of a beermat changing the world. I presume that there must have been beermats in the Coopers Arms, a fairly unremarkable modern pub on a housing estate on the outskirts of Habberley, Kidderminster, which hosted a remarkable meeting in July 1965.

It was then that a group of like-minded railway enthusiasts met to see if they could emulate the success of the Bluebell Railway in Sussex, and in the wake of the closures of the Fifties and Sixties start a private line in the West Midlands on which steam trains could run, long, long after they had been replaced by diesels and electric locomotives on the national network.

After some deliberation, these preservation pioneers chose a superbly scenic section of the 40-mile cross-country route between Shrewsbury and Hartlebury Junction.

The original Severn Valley branch, as it was known, like so many railway schemes, failed to live up to its backers' revenue expectations. Occasionally used as a diversionary route, it was predominantly a local line doing what it said on the tin, serving the settlements along the valley of the longest river on the British mainland. Its latter days were rather slumberous and it was a ripe early target for closure on the recommendation of cost-cutting British Railways' chairman Dr Richard Beeching.

Yet that meeting in the Coopers Arms went on to create something very special for the once under-used Severn Valley branch.

The new Severn Valley Railway was up and running over its first 4¼ miles within five years, making what had been a sleepy Shropshire backwater of a route the centre of national and even international attention.

Since those early days, the line has gone from strength to strength. Carrying the best part of 250,000 passengers each year, it is a mainstay of the local tourist economy and widely recognised as one of the finest heritage railways in the world.

Once the haunt of humble Great Western Railway pannier and prairie tanks, there are now very few of the illustrious preserved big-name British steam locomotives that have not run over it at some time. Sixteen miles of pure steam heaven.

Yet setting up the railway was no by means plain sailing, and depended not only on hundreds of thousands of man hours of hard slog and fundraising by volunteers, but also simple good fortune.

Closed in 1963, the year after the route celebrated its centenary it seemed a matter of time before the demolition contractors ripped up the line south of Bridgnorth station just as they had done to the track to the north.

However, in the wake of that pub meeting, a telephone call was made to British Railways urging a temporary halt to the demolition. By pure luck, that call went straight through to a sympathetic ear who set the wheels in motion. Had that not been the case, it would probably have been the end of the story.

Back in the Sixties, there was no Heritage Lottery Fund or other sources of major grant aid available, but with the demise of steam on the nation's railways there was mountains of goodwill. There were people who would give up their spare time to keep the redundant track clear of weeds, repair and maintain the abandoned Victorian railway buildings, shake raffle tins and even save Green Shield stamps to buy essential tools.

BELOW: Newly repainted British Railways' black-liveried GWR prairie No. 4566, with historically appropriate carmine-and-cream coaches, and typical of a class which worked the Severn Valley branch, passes beneath a double rainbow at Severn Lodge on March 22, 2014, during that year's spring steam gala. DUNCAN LANGTREE

ABOVE: LMS Ivatt 2MT mogul No. 46443 skirts Trimpley reservoir south of Arley on April 12, 1987. BRIAN SHARPE

Two years after that meeting in the Habberley pub, the first steam locomotive arrived on the line. That alone was a remarkable achievement, bearing in mind that while railway preservation accounts for a significant slice of the UK tourist market today, it was hardly proven then, and largely dismissed as "enthusiasts playing trains".

Times have changed, however, and the Severn Valley has become a byword for the modern steam age.

That first short length from Bridgnorth to the village of Hampton Loade was opened in 1970, and four years later, the line was able to again run town-to-town services when Bewdley was placed back on the railway map. A decade later, and an even bigger town was added, in the form of Kidderminster, where a new station was built on the old goods yard.

With each mile added, more volunteers joined up, more shareholders invested and more passengers paid to ride the trains of yesteryear today.

Not only did the Severn Valley become a living museum of the steam age, but a much sought-after film set for period dramas as well as a linear stage on which a phenomenal variety of events could be successfully staged, from Forties weekends to classic car and bus shows and other themed festivals. Today you can learn how to drive a steam or diesel locomotive, and even get married there.

ABOVE: Resident Southern Railway Battle of Britain 4-6-2 No. 34053 *Sir Keith Park* crosses Oldbury viaduct on March 22, 2015 during the 50th anniversary gala. BRIAN SHARPE

Today, two stupendous railway museums are to be found along the line, the state-of-the-art Engine House visitor centre at Highley, and the Kidderminster Station Museum, with its unrivalled collection of local artefacts.

The railway's facilities are the envy of every other heritage line in the country, and possibly the world. At Kidderminster, it has a carriage shed a fifth of a mile long to protect its priceless collection of historic vehicles from the ravages of the elements.

Its boiler shop at Bridgnorth not only helps overhaul the huge fleet of steam locomotives based on the line, but also undertakes contract work for other heritage railways, bringing in much-needed revenue.

The railway now runs its own training academy, passing on vital skills to a new generation of apprentices, and again leading the field in its sector.

The subtitle of this book is 50 Glorious Years, but, you might ask, should it be 49?

In the summer of 2007, two freak rainstorms washed away sections of the line north of Bewdley, leaving the railway with a colossal rebuilding task. It was not a happy time.

However, grant aid was forthcoming, the public again rallied to the cause after a nationwide appeal, and other heritage railways across Britain helped out by loaning plant, equipment and rolling stock. The railway was back up and running by the following spring – yet another monumental achievement, and so, yes, 50 is correct.

A DAY NEVER TO BE FORGOTTEN!

THE Severn Valley Railway became a trunk route for the day, when it carried the Olympic Torch during the build-up to the 2012 Summer Olympics in London.

Pictures of a train carrying the torch stopping by the West Midlands Safari Park being greeted by a pair of flag-waving female African elephants appeared in worldwide media.

On May 26, day six of the torch relay, Kidderminster athlete, Christopher Stokes, carried the torch from Bewdley to Kidderminster aboard GWR 4-6-0 No. 7812 *Erlestoke Manor*,

ABOVE: The Severn Valley will never forget May 26, 2012, the day it carried the Olympic Torch. Elephants Five and Latabe give a trunk salute as the 'Worcestershire Express' carrying the torch and headed by GWR 4-6-0 No. 7812 Erlestoke Manor stopped alongside their West Midlands Safari Park home. SVR

hauling the 4.05pm eight-coach 'Worcestershire Express'. The name was chosen to avoid blatant advertising for the railway, which would have been barred by the Olympic organising committee.

The elephants, Five and Latabe, gave a 'trunk salute' as the train stopped. Five also waved a union flag to mark the occasion. The feat was successfully completed following a fortnight of intensive training when trains stopped alongside their enclosure for 'trial runs'.

They had a time slot of five minutes before the train carrying more than 200 Bewdley schoolchildren, officials from the London Olympic Games Organising Committee and John Penrose, minister for tourism and heritage at the Department of Culture, Media and Sport and MP Mark Garnier, set off again.

As an aside the railway has links to a forerunner of the modern Olympic Games. In 1850 the Wenlock Agricultural Reading Society in Much Wenlock established the Olympian Class "for the promotion of the moral, physical and intellectual improvement of the inhabitants of the town and neighbourhood of Wenlock and especially of the working classes, by the encouragement of outdoor recreation, and by the award of prizes annually at public meetings for skill in athletic exercise and proficiency in intellectual and industrial attainments".

The first meeting at Wenlock racecourse on October 22-23, 1850 comprised a mixture of athletics and traditional country sports. In 1860 the Shropshire organisation became the Wenlock Olympian Society.

The Severn Valley line carried spectators to the Wenlock Olympian Games in 1862. Baron Pierre de Coubertin visited in 1890, when the Olympian Society held a special festival in his honour. He then established the International Olympic Committee, which ran the first games under its jurisdiction in 1896.
WEST MIDLANDS SAFARI PARK

ABOVE: The Princess Royal meets Emma Harrison, the Severn Valley Railway's first female apprentice, in Kidderminster's carriage works during the royal visit on April 13, 2015, to mark the heritage line's 50th anniversary. BOB SWEET/SVR

ABOVE: Visiting from the Gloucestershire Warwickshire Railway for the 50th anniversary gala, GWR 2-8-0T No. 4270 tackles Eardington bank on March 22, 2015. BRIAN SHARPE

ABOVE: Station in bloom: visiting GWR 4-6-0 No. 4936 *Kinlet Hall* at the immaculately kept Hampton Loade in 2013. PHIL JONES

Indeed, it would take an encyclopaedia to fully document all that has been accomplished over half a century, how a succession of hurdles have been overcome to achieve what many in that pub meeting back in 1965 would have considered to be an impossible dream.

Nonetheless, it is a story everyone who played a part in establishing this marvellous heritage railway can be truly proud.

*Artist Alan Reade has produced the six art deco posters on these pages to raise money for the Severn Valley Railway Charitable Trust. With prices starting at £8 for an 8in x 6in print, £9 for an A4-sized print and £16 for a fine art print, they can be ordered direct from Smith York Fine Art Publishing Limited at Jackfield Tile Museum, telephone 01952 883461 or email: railway@syfap.co.uk

A minimum of £5 per print will be donated to the appeal fund for the restoration of SVR flagship GWR 4-6-0 No. 4930 *Hagley Hall* and the historic Bridgnorth Station buildings. ●

RIGHT: LMS Ivatt 2MT 2-6-0 No. 46521 pauses at Highley alongside Class 52 Western Region diesel hydraulic D1062 *Western Courier* on September 6, 1980. BRIAN SHARPE

BELOW: Visiting Somerset & Dorset Joint Railway 7F 2-8-0 No. 53809 from the Midland Railway-Butterley climbs towards Foley Park tunnel on October 25, 1987. BRIAN SHARPE

Chapter 1

The Severn Valley:
birthplace of the steam locomotive

This area may lack the statuesque beauty of the Lakes but it more than makes up for it with its richness of history.

The Midland plateau has its moments, but its topography can rarely be described as spectacular. The rolling green fields of Warwickshire and parts of adjacent Worcestershire contrast sharply with the workaday urban landscapes of the Birmingham conurbation and the industrial Black Country, but in terms of dramatic natural beauty, their subtle leafy lane nuances apart, they would not even try to compete with the likes of the Lake District, Snowdonia or the Scottish Highlands.

The scholar poet AE Housman was born in Bromsgrove, and as a boy often gazed to the West, dreaming of the faraway hills of Shropshire.

For him, the 'blue remembered hills' formed the basis of a fantasy kingdom, a half-made-up place; a dreamscape. Long before he had

ABOVE TOP: Cornish mining engineer, Richard Trevithick, is believed to have built the world's first railway locomotive at Coalbrookdale in 1802.
MAIN PICTURE: The modern-day working replica of Trevithick's Penydarren locomotive of 1804, seen in action at the National Railway Museum's Railfest Trevithick 200 festival at York in 2004. It has been conjectured by author, Philip Hosking, that this was the locomotive that ran at Coalbrookdale. ROBIN JONES

even set foot in the county, it inspired him to write his greatest and most popular work, his first collection of poems, A Shropshire Lad, which astounded friends and admirers when it appeared in 1896.

However, had the young future poet tried to venture forth to find those favoured hills, he would have first encountered a valley that might have exceeded his wildest boyhood imagination in terms of its beauty and stark yet homely grandeur. It was as if someone had carved a classic Welsh valley out of the Cambrian Mountains and dumped it on the doorstep of the great conurbation a few miles to the east.

THE SEVERN VALLEY

The delights of Bewdley and other Severnside settlements have not been lost to generations of daytrippers from the West Midlands. As soon as social conditions improved allowing workers to have regular weekend breaks, and later holidays, combined with access to public transport, they became a favoured haunt from Victorian times onwards. The valley was seen as the perfect and attainable place to get away from it all, even just for a day.

The River Severn is the longest river in the UK, at about 220 miles, and the second longest in the British Isles, behind the River Shannon in Ireland. It rises at an altitude of 2001ft on Plynlimon, Ceredigion near Llanidloes in the Cambrian Mountains, flowing across the border near Welshpool and into and through Shropshire, Worcestershire and Gloucestershire, with the county towns of Shrewsbury, Worcester and Gloucester on its banks. The Severn, known to the Romans as Sabrina, is also the greatest river in terms of water flow in England and Wales.

The term Severn Valley is most commonly used to refer to the section between Bridgnorth and Bewdley. To the north of Bridgnorth, the valley becomes much steeper and is known as the Ironbridge Gorge. South of Bewdley, the valley sides flatten out and disappear into an expansive flood plain. Beyond Gloucester, the river flows through the Vale of Berkeley and then the Severn Estuary.

Indeed, the Severn Valley has much in common with the glaciated Cambrian uplands, for until the last Ice Age, the river flowed into a huge lake in the middle of what is now central Shropshire, and which in turn drained into the River Trent.

Glaciers may have blocked the outlet of the lake, which measured about 35 by 25 miles, and was more akin to an inland sea. The waters rose by around 300ft, and cut through the rock barrier at Ironbridge, carving out the gorge. The deep fast-flowing channels are a marked feature of the river today.

The Romans settled in the valley, building the town of Wroxeter 10 miles below Shrewsbury. The valley came under the rule of Ceawlin of Wessex after the Battle of Deorham in 577 AD as part of the kingdom of Hwicce. In 628 AD, King Penda of Mercia's victory in the Battle of Cirencester led to his dominion of the valley.

Settlement of the valley has always been hampered by the soft sandstone banks of the river, as they proved difficult to support bridges that can bear heavy loads. The only public road bridges are at Bridgnorth and Bewdley, and there is no means for road traffic to cross the

river for 16 miles. The 'Loade' in Hampton Loade is a Saxon term for a fording place.

The Saxons built a settlement at what later became Wribbenhall, 12 miles south of Bewdley. It too was a fording place at low water, as in the Middle Ages, the Severn was tidal to this point, and on the west bank opposite, the town of Bewdley grew up, taking its name from the Norman word 'beaulieu' meaning 'beautiful place'.

The first bridge at Bridgnorth is believed to have been built at the start of the 12th century. Bewdley received its first bridge in 1336.

There is a public right of navigation between Pool Quay near Welshpool and Stourport, but this section has for a long time seen little traffic apart from canoes, small pleasure craft and tour boats in Shrewsbury, through and around which the river meanders on the bed of the ancient great lake. However, by the 14th century, the river was carrying

more traffic than any other in Britain, and Bewdley was a major inland port. Yet the navigation was fraught with dangers especially north of Bewdley, with hidden rocks and shallows providing severe obstacles. Floods saw the river race through the gorge and valley at an alarming speed.

In the first part of the 16th century, the navigation was improved by laying paths along the banks, so that vessels with a shallow draught – the 'Severn trows' – could be hauled.

The two main roads along the valley are the A442 on the east side from Bridgnorth via Alveley to Kidderminster and the B4555 on the west from Bridgnorth via Highley to Bewdley. Both of them run roughly parallel with the river north to south.

The Severn Valley is certainly not the Black Country, which prospered – and disfigured itself – on the mineral riches below ground. ▶

ABOVE: Bridgnorth Castle was founded in 1101 by Robert de Belleme, son of the French earl, Roger de Montgomery, who succeeded his father to become the Earl of Shrewsbury. Its principal feature, a square great tower, was built during the reign of Henry II. During the Civil War, Bridgnorth was one of the Midlands' main Royalist strongholds and in 1646, Oliver Cromwell's Roundheads arrived with orders to take Bridgnorth for the Parliamentarians. A three-week siege ended in victory for Cromwell who ordered that the castle be slighted. The surviving part of the great tower now leans at an angle of 15 degrees, four times the lean of the leaning tower of Pisa. PHILIP MCCAVITY

ABOVE: An Edwardian hand-coloured view of the waterfront at Bewdley. ROBIN JONES COLLECTION

However, the valley bisects the Wyre Forest coalfield, where coal had been dug since the medieval period, taken by pack horses for onwards shipment down the Severn.

At Coalbrookdale, coal mining was well underway by the 16th century. Indeed, one of the earliest wooden waggonways built to take coal from pits at Calcutts near Broseley to the river was operational in 1605; it was one of the earliest recorded railways in Britain.

On the back of coal mining, iron smelting flourished from the 15th century onwards and the Coalbrookdale Company was formed in 1709.

Coalbrookdale became one of the birthplaces of the Industrial Revolution, with Abraham Darby II starting up the first furnace at Horsehay in 1755.

Four years later, the world's first iron bridge was erected over the Severn, giving the name to the resulting town formed on its banks.

The world's first cast-iron waggonway rails were cast at Coalbrookdale in 1767. Yet a far greater feat was to come.

We often hear of County Durham described as 'the cradle of the railways' because of the desire by colliery owners in the second decade of the 18th century to exploit the recently invented steam locomotive technology to serve their mines, at a time when horses were in short supply because of the Napoleonic wars.

Then it is quickly pointed out that the steam locomotive concept in its successful form derived from Cornwall, where engineer Richard Trevithick looked at ways of carrying large loads from mines to ports without the costly use of horses and large amounts of manpower.

In those days, Cornwall was a world away from the capital, almost like a foreign country. It was best reached by sea rather

ABOVE: A sketch of 1863 depicted the world's first iron bridge. ROBIN JONES COLLECTION

than land, as the roads were either poor or all but non-existent.

In between these two rival claims, however, lies a third… from the Severn Valley itself.

Firstly, after successfully building a steam road locomotive in 1801 and demonstrating it on a trip up Camborne Hill on Christmas Eve that year, Trevithick saw that the roads of the day were nowhere near adequate to stand the weight of such machines, and so looked at running them on the horse-drawn tramways of the day.

Trevithick first visited Coalbrookdale Foundry in 1796 and it is recorded that he built his first railway locomotive in 1802, in Coalbrookdale, for use on the 3ft gauge waggonway there.

Surviving details of his Coalbrookdale engine are sketchy, and most historians believe that it never ran in public. Surviving documents indicate that Trevithick referred to it just once and then only in a passing phrase at the end of a letter written in August 1802.

Trevithick may have had very good reason in those formative years for keeping quiet about his ongoing steam experiments, for on September 8, 1803, one of his stationary boilers in London exploded killing three workmen.

In 1804, Trevithick gave the world's first public demonstration of a railway engine on the Penydarren Tramroad at Merthyr Tydfil.

Author, Philip Hosking, who has extensively researched Trevithick, believes that it was the

BELOW: The river at Bridgnorth with High Rock in the distance. NIGEL'S EUROPE & BEYOND

Coalbrookdale engine that ran at Penydarren. He claims that the popular image of the Penydarren locomotive, of which a working replica exists, is of an engine built to a Trevithick design in 1805 after he supplied drawings to Christopher Blackett, owner of Wylam Colliery near Gateshead.

Pioneer steam-locomotive engineer, John Urpeth Rastrick, built Trevithick's last locomotive, *Catch Me Who Can*, at Hazeldine Foundry in Bridgnorth. It has also been conjectured that he may have built the Coalkbrookdale locomotive at Horsehay.

Catch Me Who Can briefly ran on a circle of track in 1808 near the site of the future Euston station, and with its carriage, formed not only the world's first steam passenger train, but was also the first to collect fares from passengers. It is also Bridgnorth's first claim to steam railway fame.

Understandably as he had made little or no money from his locomotive ventures, Trevithick afterwards turned away from steam traction. The horse and cart, whether on rails, roads or on a canal or riverside towpath, still reigned supreme. Indeed, Cornwall's first public railway, the Poldice Tramway, which opened in 1809, relied on horses.

Along with many of his fellow Cornishmen, Trevithick sought his fortune in the mines of South America. He did not find it, returned home in poverty, died at the Bull Hotel in Dartford in Kent on April 22, 1833, and was buried in a now-unmarked grave in the town's churchyard. A year later, Cornwall's first steam railway, the Bodmin & Wadebridge, opened.

Regarding Bewdley's prosperity as a port, the rot set in with the opening of the Staffordshire & Worcestershire Canal in 1772, linking Stourport to the south and to the Black Country. As a counter measure, parliamentary powers were obtained the same year to create a towpath from Bewdley to Coalbrookdale and then in 1809, from Coalbrookdale to Shrewsbury.

Canals, however, became state-of-the-art transport technology as far as trade and commerce were concerned, and in 1801, moves began to build a railway from Bewdley to link with the Staffordshire & Worcestershire Canal in Kidderminster. At that time, there was no thought of using early railways as a means of transport in themselves, other than to take goods to and from the nearest canal or harbour.

The Bewdley railway scheme soon fizzled out. In the meantime, the Shropshire Canal company developed a network of canals and inclined planes, which opened in 1792, and saw a series of wharves flourish into the village of Coalport. It became so important and prosperous, shipping around 100,000 tons of coal per year at its peak, that it received its own iron bridge in 1799.

Hampton Loade also had an ironworks, and there were upper and lower forges at Eardington, which were linked to the Severn by a largely underground canal, the remains of which still exist but very much out of sight. Pig iron was shipped down the Severn from Coalbrookdale to Eardington where it was taken by barge through the tunnel to the forges.

However, the Severn iron industry went into decline in the 19th century, with the Hampton Loade ironworks closing in 1866, and the Eardington forges following in 1899. ●

ABOVE: Bishop Percy's House in Cartway, Bridgnorth, built in 1580 by wealthy shipping merchant, Richard Forster, as a home and commercial premises owing to its location near the River Severn, was one of the few properties to survive the town's great fire in April 1646 and was the birthplace of Bishop of Dromore, Thomas Percy, author and Royal Chaplain to King George III. ROBIN JONES COLLECTION

ABOVE: The sandstone bedrock of the Severn Valley provided homes to early inhabitants. The stone was so soft that it could be carved with a knife, and caves were created in Saxon times. The first inhabitant was Ethelward or Aethelard, a grandson of King Alfred, who lived in one as a hermit, hence the name, Hermitage Caves. They are located on the brow overlooking Low Town south of the Hermitage in Wolverhampton Road. In more recent centuries, the caves were converted into homes with the addition of doors and windows, including a custodian's cottage inhabited until 1939. After an accident in 2009 the caves were fenced off. ROBIN JONES COLLECTION

Chapter 2

Severn Valley Railway:
first time round

Unfulfilled expectations of a cross-country branch line.

ABOVE: A late Victorian or early Edwardian hand-coloured view of Bridgnorth station. ROBIN JONES COLLECTION

Trevithick may have thought many a time that his efforts with the railway locomotive were in vain, but he would have been aware of the opening in 1826 of the world's first public steam-operated line, the Stockton & Darlington Railway.

ABOVE: Staff at Bewdley station, possibly in late Victorian times. SVR ARCHIVES

That was followed in 1830 by the first public trains over the world's first inter-city line, the Liverpool & Manchester Railway. Yes, they were by comparison with what was to come little local affairs, but the tide had turned from equine-based and water transport to steam haulage. In 1837, the Grand Junction Railway, which linked Liverpool and Manchester to Birmingham, became the world's first trunk line. After that, steam railway landmarks came fast and furiously, leading to the notion that railway schemes were a licence to print money, and the period of the mid-1840s known as the Railway Mania. Those heady times saw the backbone of today's national network created, as speculators grabbed pencils and rulers and drew lines on maps between, it seemed, any major centres of population that took their fancy.

Clearly the Severn Valley would be an ideal route for a railway: it could take advantage of the natural contours of the land, while providing an outlet for the coal and iron from Coalbrookdale and Broseley that did not lay at the mercy of the level of the river and its shallows.

Yet where would such a line run from and to? The railway map of the West Midlands region was still in its infancy. The Grand Junction missed out Wolverhampton, while the Birmingham & Gloucester Railway avoided Bromsgrove, Droitwich and Worcester.

Frustrated Black Country industrialists drew up plans in 1845 for the broad gauge Oxford, Worcester & Wolverhampton Railway, which joined the Grand Junction north of the latter and bypassed Birmingham altogether. By 1852, it was open from Droitwich to Dudley via Hartlebury and Kidderminster,

In 1845, attention turned to the Severn Valley with the planned Oxford & Worcester Extension & Chester Junction Railway, proposed as a key link in a route connecting Liverpool to Bristol.

None other than the great Robert Stephenson surveyed the route as engineer. After different options were considered, the final choice of a main line was a route from a junction with the projected Shrewsbury & Birmingham Railway in Shrewsbury running 40 miles south to Stourport and Hartlebury, where it would join the Oxford, Worcester & Wolverhampton. There would also be a branch from Stourport to Kidderminster. Various branches would serve the industrial concerns around Coalbrookdale and Coalport, but apart from these, the route was much the same as the Severn Valley branch of the West Midlands Railway that would eventually be built.

However, the Oxford & Worcester Extension & Chester Junction Railway scheme was turned down by parliament and the company was dissolved in late 1846.

The idea of a Severn Valley line was resuscitated in 1849, surveyed by Robert Nicholson who had worked with Stephenson on the Oxford & Worcester Extension & Chester Junction Railway scheme. Nicholson proposed a line from Hartlebury to Bridgnorth and then across country to Madeley. To further these plans, the Severn Valley Railway Company was formed.

A series of public meetings was held, after which it was decided to revert to the previous scheme's route, following the river all the way to Shrewsbury.

On August 20, 1853, the Severn Valley Railway Bill received its Royal Assent. Following a series of modifications the route

TWO OWNERS IN TWO DAYS!

It was agreed that for the first five years of its life, the railway would be operated by the Oxford, Worcester & Wolverhampton Railway, and it was ambitiously scheduled to open in October 1860.

However, with echoes of what was to befall the railway in 2007, as we shall see, the route was hit by a series of landslips, the most serious of which above Highley caused the route to be diverted from its planned course.

Before it was open, the Severn Valley Railway changed hands twice in the space of two days.

The Oxford, Worcester & Wolverhampton obtained a 999-year lease on it on June 14, 1860, and then that company merged with the Newport, Abergavenny & Hereford and Worcester & Hereford railways to create the West Midlands Railway as from July 1 that year.

Nearly six decades after Trevithick's pioneering work at Coalbrookdale, a steam locomotive appeared again in the valley, drawing a substantial crowd as it ran between Bewdley and Stourport on May 5, 1861.

By then, the railway was ready apart from the stupendous Victoria Bridge, the line's own "Ironbridge".

This 200ft single-span cast-iron arch bridge over the river between Arley and Bewdley is almost identical to Albert Edward Bridge which also spans the Severn at Coalbrookdale, both having been designed by John Fowler.

Its four arch ribs each comprise nine parts bolted together. The arch elements were cast by the Coalbrookdale Company, and the bridge built by the company of Thomas Brassey, Samuel Morton Peto and Edward Betts.

Its foundation stone was laid on November 24, 1859, and it was completed on May 10, 1861, when the rest of the 40-mile railway had been built.

Following a second visit, on January 15, 1861, Colonel Yolland of the Railway Inspectorate of the Board of Trade approved the line's opening.

The most important stations on the line were Stourport, Bewdley, Arley, Highley, Hampton Loade, Bridgnorth, Coalport, Ironbridge & Broseley, Buildwas Junction, Cressage and Berrington. Apart from Bridgnorth, all were built to a basic standard design.

There were also stops at Linley, Eardington, Northwood and, opened in 1930, Burlish Halt, in 1934, Jackfield Halt and Cound Halt, and in 1935, Northwood Halt.

subsequently proposed by Nicholson, and a new Severn Valley Railway Bill was passed by parliament and received Royal Assent on July 30, 1855.

The company realised that it would have to make economies, including building only a single-track railway whereas a double-track

one had been previously approved. A final Severn Valley Railway Bill received Royal Assent on July 23, 1858.

By the time construction began in summer 1858 Nicholson had died. His replacement was John Fowler, famous for the Forth Bridge and the Metropolitan Railway.

THE LINE OPENS THROUGHOUT

A 22-coach VIP special carrying local civic dignitaries and Great Western Railway chairman, Lord Shelbourne among others, departed Worcester Shrub Hill station at 11.30am on Friday, January 21, 1862, and reached Shrewsbury at 2pm, after stopping at every station en route to be greeted by cheering crowds. Three extra coaches were added at Shrewsbury and the train returned to Bridgnorth for an assembly dinner. Fifty-three years after *Catch Me Who Can* emerged from Hazeline Foundry, steam was back in the town – and as history would show, it would stay, against the odds.

Public services in the form of three return trips a day began the next day, and on February 11, a celebratory dinner at the George Hotel in Bewdley officially launched what was the Severn Valley branch of the West Midlands Railway.

In August 1863, the West Midlands Railway was added to the growing empire of the GWR, with full amalgamation taking place on July 1, 1872.

Six years later the GWR opened a direct line from Kidderminster to Bewdley to enable trains to run through from Birmingham and the West Midlands to the Severn Valley. The 'Kidderminster Loop'

ABOVE: Busy junction: Bewdley station in late Victorian times. SVR ARCHIVES

ABOVE: The epitome of the quiet country station: Hampton Loade in the 1890s. SVR ARCHIVES

had been mooted as early as 1860, with the London & North Western Railway, joint owner of the Tenbury Railway between Woofferton Junction and the Tenbury Wells line, looked at the possibility of running into Birmingham via the Tenbury & Bewdley Railway, which was leased and then owned by the GWR.

As a junction, Bewdley sold more tickets than any other station on the Severn Valley branch.

In early 1885, a basin was opened on the Staffordshire & Worcestershire Canal to the east of Stourport station, complete with new sidings opposite the goods yard.

The basin allowed coal, iron and steel, often from South Wales, to be delivered by rail and taker by barge to Wilden Ironworks Ironworks a mile away. Coal from Highley followed the same route.

Loaded trucks came down the incline to the basin from Stourport station by gravity and were controlled by a brakeman.

There was also a short goods line serving a quarry, both belonging to Thomas Vale & Son.

ABOVE: The Severn Valley Railway and adjoining lines as they appeared on the Ordnance Survey Quarter-Inch Map Fifties Series Sheet 13 The Midlands, published in 1962 before the sweeping closures to the local rural network were implemented. The map was fully revised between 1944-56. ROBIN JONES COLLECTION

WEST MIDLAND RAILWAY.
TIME TABLE
SEVERN VALLEY BRANCH
FEBRUARY, 1862.

On and after SATURDAY, FEBRUARY 1st, 1862, the SEVERN VALLEY RAILWAY will be OPENED for Public Traffic, and Trains will run as follows:—

DURING THE MONTH OF FEBRUARY NO SUNDAY TRAINS WILL BE RUN.

A. C. SHERRIFF, General Manager.

ABOVE: A train hauled by GWR 2-4-0 No. 178 crosses Bewdley North viaduct in 1897.
SVR ARCHIVES

TO THE INHABITANTS OF THE
BOROUGH OF BRIDGNORTH
AND NEIGHBOURHOOD.

The Mayor, having received information that the

SEVERN VALLEY
RAILWAY
WILL BE OPENED FOR TRAFFIC,
ON THE 1st FEBRUARY,

Requests all persons interested in its success to attend a
PUBLIC MEETING,
ON MONDAY, THE 20th INSTANT,

AT TWELVE O'CLOCK AT NOON, AT THE TOWN HALL,
To make such arrangements as may be deemed advisable to celebrate the Opening of the Line.

Bridgnorth, January 16th, 1862.

Clement Edkins, Printer, Journal Office, Bridgnorth.

ABOVE: Woofferton station and junction in Shropshire marked the opposite end of the route from Bewdley through the Wyre Forest. It was where the the Tenbury & Bewdley Railway joined the Shrewsbury & Hereford Railway. The station opened on December 6, 1853 and closed on July 31, 1961. An unidentified GWR prairie tank is seen heading a service in British Railways days. ROBIN JONES COLLECTION

UNFULFILLED EXPECTATIONS

It had been hoped that the railway would attract traffic from the Severn barges. However, for many years before the line opened, the river traffic was in sharp decline, and all that the railway achieved was to drive the final nail into its coffin without boosting its own fortunes to any meaningful extent.

The 20th century saw the railways having increased competition from road transport, not just the motorcar but also the electric tram. On May 23, 1898, the Kidderminster & Stourport Electric Tramway opened, presenting a challenge to passenger traffic. Trams were seen as more convenient than railways, being able to offer more stops. To combat it, the GWR introduced two new local stops on the Kidderminster Loop, one at Rifle Range Halt a mile from Bewdley, and which lasted only from 1905 until 1920, and the other at Foley Park. Burlish Halt, a single platform on the far side of the 124-yard Mount Pleasant Tunnel, was opened on March 31, 1930, to serve the expanding local housing estates.

In the Twenties and Thirties, the GWR's publicity department took a leaf out of Houseman's book and promoted the valley as a tourist destination.

The previously mentioned Cound, Jackfield and Northwood halts on the main line were opened in the mid-Thirties to serve auto trains comprising a single trailer, but it was too little too late.

Midland Red bus services were slowly squeezing income from the line's passenger traffic, being able to offer more versatile routes that were not restricted to stations, which in cases, were some distance away from the villages they purported to serve, or on the wrong side of the river altogether. Yes, train travel was – and is – as a rule still faster in

BELOW: Ironbridge & Broseley station. The railway had to pass through the Ironbridge Gorge on the south side of the river, so everyone living in Ironbridge and Coalbrookdale had to pay a toll for crossing the famous iron bridge each time they wanted to access the station. Brosley, which has a population of nearly 5000 when the line opened, lay half a mile away but was reached by a very steep road, Bridge Bank. J TARRANT/ KIDDERMINSTER RAILWAY MUSEUM

STOURPORT POWER STATION

In 1918, an Act of Parliament was passed for building a coal-fired power station on the banks of the Severn at Stourport, together with a branch off the Severn Valley line to serve it.

On June 2, 1927, 1000 schoolchildren lined the streets to watch Prime Minister Stanley Baldwin perform the official opening.

The first boilerhouse was started up in 1926, the second one following 10 years later.

ABOVE: Bagnall 0-4-0ST No. 2665 of 1942 *General Wade Hayes* in the yard at Stourport Power Station along with Barclay 0-4-0ST No. 2088 of 1940 *Sir Thomas Royden* and Peckett 0-4-0ST No. 1893 of 1936 WA No. 2 on March 5, 1960. FA WYCHERLEY/KIDDERMINSTER RAILWAY MUSEUM

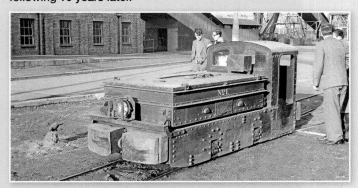

ABOVE: Dick Kerr 2ft 6in gauge four-wheel battery locomotive No. 688 of 1925 in the yard at Stourport Power Station on March 5, 1960. FA WYCHERLEY/KIDDERMINSTER RAILWAY MUSEUM

ABOVE: Linley station in 1910, looking towards Bridgnorth, with oil lighting on the only platform. This station is very similar to that at Hampton Loade. It was built as a result of a legal wrangle with landowner Thomas C Whitmore of Apley Park, an estate on the opposite side of the bank from the railway. In 1852, he delayed the railway's construction because he said it would destroy the seclusion of his mansion, and forced an agreement for three tunnels to be built. In 1855, Whitmore agreed to drop the insistence on the tunnels in exchange for £14,000 compensation and £150 per acre for any land bought by the line. The railway also had to build a station at which two regular passenger trains would call each day. D POWELL COLLECTION/KIDDERMINSTER RAILWAY MUSEUM

ABOVE: The Kidderminster & Stourport Electric Tramway, pictured in the latter's town centre, competed against the railway for passengers from 1898. ROBIN JONES COLLECTION

ABOVE: Berrington station, the first station heading south out of Shrewsbury on the Severn Valley line, pictured around 1960. J MOSS/R CARPENTER COLLECTION

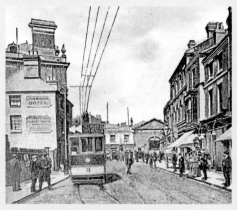

ABOVE: A tram in Oxford Street, Kidderminster, as depicted in an Edwardian hand-coloured postcard. ROBIN JONES COLLECTION

terms of A to B, but in terms of convenience for the residents of such settlements, the bus won hands down, and for those joining the rapidly growing army of car owners, there was no argument to be had. Arley, for instance, could be reached from its station only by ferry until a footbridge was built in 1872. The northern half of the line was particularly hit hard by bus competition.

The Stourport to Kidderminster tramway closed on November 30, 1928, it too falling victim to motor bus competition.

At the same time, road transport increasingly ate into rail-born freight traffic. The end of the First World War saw large numbers of Army surplus vehicles coming on to the market and bargain prices, and soldiers returning from the front grasped the opportunity to set up their own haulage businesses in competition with the main public carrier, the railway. Again, lorries and vans can go where a railway cannot, and were able to undercut railway tariffs.

A 2ft 6in gauge line was laid to carry coal from the power station's wharf to the boilerhouses and stockpiles, and motive power was provided by a pair of English Electric battery electric locomotives.

However, it was not until May 1940 that the power station was linked to the Severn Valley line with its own standard gauge sidings.

Two standard gauge 0-4-0STs were supplied to work the private siding, Barclay No. 2088 *Sir Thomas Royden* in 1940, and two years later Bagnall No. 2665 *General Wade Hayes*. In 1958, a third arrived in Peckett 0-4-0ST No. 1893, which had been delivered new to Ironbridge Power Station in 1936.

The Staffordshire Electric Power Development Company, which owned the power station, opened a siding near the future Burlish Halt in 1929. It later became used by the nearby Steatite & Porcelain Products Ltd Factory, but the siding was closed in 1966.

ABOVE: Barclay 0-4-0ST No. 2088 of 1940 *Sir Thomas Royden* at Stourport Power Station on March 27, 1970. It now runs at the Rutland Railway Museum, now trading as Rocks by Rail: The Living Ironstone Museum, at Cottesmore. F BUTLER/KIDDERMINSTER RAILWAY MUSEUM

ABOVE: Peckett 0-4-0ST No. 1893 of 1935, No.2, at Stourport-on-Severn Power Station with a rake of coal wagons. W POTTER/ KIDDERMINSTER RAILWAY MUSEUM

MINING AT HIGHLEY AND ALVELEY

The mining of the Brooch and Four Foot coal seams at Highley brought much traffic to the railway.

In the mid-1870s, the Viggars family opened a brickworks at Highley and sank a shaft in 1874 to tap into the seams.

The Highley Mining Company was formed in 1877 to mine coal and the following year a pair of 9ft diameter shafts were sunk and reached the Brooch seam at a depth of 888ft. By 1900, about 240 men and boys were employed at the coal mine, rising to 670 by 1937.

New sidings were created south of Highley station to serve the new colliery. A standard gauge incline was laid up the hillside to the colliery so main line railway trucks could be filled directly with coal. From Highley, the coal was shipped to the steam engines of the carpet factories in Kidderminster, while clay and shale from the waste tips were used to make bricks.

In 1915 the company took over Billingsley Colliery. The village of Highley quadrupled in size between 1875 and 1915, to accommodate the miners and began turning into a small town.

In 1935, a new shaft was started at Alveley for coal and man winding, with a concrete headgear and electric winder. A bridge was built over the Severn to take the coal from the mine to the railway. It was linked to

ABOVE: A train carrying coal from Alveley Colliery approaches Arley station in British Railways days. SVR ARCHIVES

the Highley workings in 1937, when Kinlet Colliery, which had proved harder to work, was closed and the men transferred to Highley Colliery, which itself closed in 1940 in favour of Alveley Colliery, a state-of-the-art concern which was fully mechanised and used electric power throughout.

It became part of the National Coal Board when the Labour government nationalised the industry in 1947. Production peaked in 1957 at more than 300,000 tons a year, at which point the mine was employing over 1000 men. The colliery was extensively reconstructed underground to allow the introduction of horizon mining to access reserves to the east of the Romsley Fault.

MISPLACED SUPPLY, ABSENT DEMAND

ABOVE: GWR 4-6-0 No. 7802 *Bradley Manor* in the train shed at Platform 4 of Shrewsbury station with an express passenger train for Aberystwyth on May 18, 1949. This locomotive is now preserved on the modern-day Severn Valley Railway. P J LYNCH/KIDDERMINSTER RAILWAY MUSEUM

The major problem with rural railways is that they were often planned by Victorian entrepreneurs to run between towns which historically had comparatively little relevance to each other, in the interests of developing new trade.

Why, for instance, would anyone want to commute from Shrewsbury to Bewdley every day? They clearly didn't. Many lines were built in the vain hope that demand would be created as new development sprang up along the new lines.

The same holds true for much shorter destinations on cross-country routes. Had the Severn Valley branch been a trunk route as part of a national network, it would probably have been a different matter, but the bulk of its passenger traffic came from local trips, mainly from villages to the nearest market town that historically served them.

Bridgnorth, historically, did not relate to Bewdley, but looked eastwards to Wolverhampton, which lay just 14 miles away and was one of the centres of the great industrial sprawl that came to be known as the Black Country.

Indeed, there were several schemes proposed to link Bridgnorth to

ABOVE: In 1936, the GWR introduced what it advertised as "camp coaches", old passenger vehicles no longer suitable for use in trains, which were converted to provide basic holiday accommodation at static locations. The Speight family is seen posing outside camp coach No. 9947 at Arley station at Easter 1938. THE SPEIGHT FAMILY//KIDDERMINSTER RAILWAY MUSEUM

ABOVE: GWR 0-6-0PT No. 6421 at Buildwas Junction station with a one-coach auto train. The running-in board behind the smokebox reads Buildwas Junction change here for Severn Valley Line. The station lay in the middle of the countryside with no passenger access apart from by train. It has a single platform for trains serving the short Much Wenlock branch which opened on February 1, 1862, the same day as the Severn Valley line. From November 1, 1864, trains also ran into Buildwas from Coalbrookdale on the lines from Madeley and Ketley Junctions. M CARRIER/KIDDERMINSTER RAILWAY MUSEUM

Wolverhampton, the first appearing in 1861. The big problem was not the terrain between the two, but Wolverhampton town centre, which stood between any proposed route and the railway on its far side. Joining a new line to the existing tracks would have been very expensive.

On July 11, 1905, the GWR obtained powers to build a line from Bridgnorth to Wolverhampton. However, the year before, the GWR bought three Clarkson steam buses and began running a public service between the two towns on November 7, at a speed of 8mph.

The buses proved cumbersome and had difficulty in winter, and so in early spring 1905 they were replaced by motor buses.

The journey took 90 minutes each way, and it was pointed out that it would be quicker to use a bicycle.

The GWR did not forget entirely about the proposed rail link, and in 1908 obtained revised powers to take the Bridgnorth line into Wombourn, where it would join the planned Wolverhampton to Kingswinford and Stourbridge Junction line.

Successive delays pushed the specified date of completion of building the Bridgnorth line back to October 1927, by which time bus travel had evolved to the point where a rail link was no longer considered viable.

So Bridgnorth was left, as far as the general public was concerned, with a "second best" in terms of rail transport, with residents having to use road transport to access their preferred neighbouring town.

During Great Western days the pattern of services remained similar, with usually four passenger trains per day in each direction over the whole of the line, and a few more on the section south of Bridgnorth.

However, the Severn Valley branch became strategically useful during the Second World War as a bypass around the West Midlands for troop and ammunition trains among others.

To the north of Stourport station, the Ministry of Food opened a substantial cold storage depot in December 1941, served by a group of sidings.

ABOVE: One of the GWR Clarkson steam buses outside Bridgnorth station in late 1904. BRIDGNORTH & DISTRICT HISTORICAL SOCIETY

LEFT: GWR railcar No. W24W is seen at Bridgnorth in 1962. MICHAEL MENSING

ABOVE: Stourport-on-Severn station.
J TARRANT/KIDDERMINSTER RAILWAY MUSEUM

RIGHT: An unidentified GWR diesel railcar stands at Cressage station. The station served a village with a population of just 350 and was built on the side of the line furthest away from it.
J TARRANT/ KIDDERMINSTER RAILWAY MUSEUM

ABOVE: GWR 43XX 2-6-0 No. 6314 at Coalport (GWR) on a freight to Coton Hill Yard in Shrewsbury on April 23, 1957. It had reversed into the Up siding for a train to pass. The station lay within sight of the LNWR counterpart at the end of its branch from Hadley Junction. The station signalbox controlled entry into a half-mile siding running south to the Exley & Sons' clay mine that was sunk in 1891, with the company opening the Coalport Tileries three years later owing to the excellent rail connections.
GES PARKER COLLECTION/KIDDERMINSTER RAILWAY MUSEUM

THE ROAD TO BEECHING

The big watershed in the history of Britain's railways in 1948 came when the national network was taken into permanent public ownership for the first time.

The nation's railways had been placed under state control during the First World War, and it was clear that the network could be run more efficiently with fewer operators. Afterwards there were calls for complete nationalisation – a move first mooted in 1850. However, the Railways Act 1921 provided a compromise with the grouping of most of the country's 120 railway companies into four main ones. These were the 'Big Four' comprising the Great Western Railway, the London, Midland & Scottish Railway, the London & North Eastern Railway and the Southern Railway.

The Second World War again saw the nation's railways acting as one company, a time when the network saw more use than at any other point in its history.

After the war, it was soon realised that the private sector could not afford to put right the damage and decay that had ensued from bombing raids, lack of maintenance and investment, and so Clement Attlee's Labour government decided to nationalise the railways under the Transport Act 1947.

It was clear from the outset that there would be closures: indeed the process of axing loss-making local lines and passenger services had begun in the Thirties.

For the record, the first official closure under British Railways was the goods-only line from

Mantle Lane East to the foot of Swannington Incline in Leicestershire, by the new London Midland Region, in February 1948. The first passenger services to be withdrawn were those from Woodford & Hinton station on the Great Central route to Byfield on the Stratford & Midland Junction Railway, on May 31,1948, also by the LMR.

Another of the very early closures was that of the 2ft 3in gauge Corris Railway, inherited from the GWR, which was axed following flood damage of August 21, 1948.

The following year, the British Transport Commission set up the Branch Lines Committee, with a remit to close the least-used branch lines.

In 1950, a total of 150 route miles were closed, rising to 275 in 1951 and 300 in 1952.

As the postwar financial situation eased, British Railways began to plan for the future in which it was now clear that unprecedented

ABOVE: A view from track level at Cressage station on July 24, 1954. Standing in the platform bunker first with the 3.50pm Shrewsbury to Kidderminster local is GWR 2-6-2T No. 5518. On the left is a Down goods headed by GWR 2-6-0 No. 6334. On the right is a lower quadrant stop signal pulled off for the train. J WOOD/KIDDERMINSTER RAILWAY MUSEUM

ABOVE: Steaming into the 559-yard Bridgnorth Tunnel that took the railway beneath the town. SVR ARCHIVES

ABOVE: GWR 2-6-2T No. 5547 at Buildwas Junction station on a train, consisting of three coaches and a van, for Shrewsbury on September 19, 1959. The track on the left, the Wellington branch, is at a higher level.
V R WEBSTER/KIDDERMINSTER RAILWAY MUSEUM

LEFT: An unidentified GWR railcar, now repainted into British Railways' green with whiskers, waits at Hartlebury station.
J TARRANT/KIDDERMINSTER RAILWAY MUSEUM

levels of competition would be presented by road transport. On December 1, 1954, the report known as Modernisation and Re-Equipment of the British Railways, or the 1955 Modernisation Plan for short, promised measures to increase speed, reliability, safety and line capacity, while making services more attractive to passengers and freight operators as well as completely phasing out steam locomotives by diesel and electric alternatives.

In 1954, Britain was one of only seven out of 17 major European countries whose railways were not 'in the red'. The following year, it recorded its first working loss.

The Modernisation Plan faltered and in many cases failed. Manufacturers rushed to bring out new types of diesel locomotives, some of which did not outlive the steam classes they replaced.

The annual working deficit in 1956 was £16.5 million: by 1962 it had reached £100 million. The promised major return on investment failed to materialise.

Historians have also blamed the declining fortunes of Britain's railways on the national rail strike of 1955.

Days after Anthony Eden's Conservative government won a General Election victory, ASLEF, the Associated Society of Locomotive Engineers and Firemen, the union representing train drivers in Britain, called a strike over a pay dispute: a rise equivalent to the price of an extra packet of cigarettes a week was demanded.

RIGHT: Bridgnorth station in 1961. SVR ARCHIVES

The strike lasted from May 28 to June 14, and brought British industry to a standstill. British Railways still managed to convey a quarter of its normal passenger traffic and a third of its freight, but the damage in the minds of the public was irreparable.

The strike led immediately to a mass switch by both passengers and freight customers from rail to road. They were forced to do so by necessity during the strike, and in a world where road transport was now far more commonplace than ever before, many customers did not return after it ended. Pick-up goods services to rural communities such as those along the Severn Valley were hit hard in the aftermath of the strike, as supplies turned to road transport and stayed there.

Meanwhile, the slow pruning of the most unprofitable fringes of the railway network had steadily continued throughout the Fifties. In 1953, 275 miles were axed, followed by around 500 miles between 1954-57, and just 150 miles in 1958. Many of these were rural routes, which served sparsely populated communities, such as the network of GWR lines serving the Wye Valley and Forest of Dean.

The early to mid-1950s saw the introduction of new diesel multiple units on many of these routes: smart, efficient and labour saving, they were welcomed by the public, but while they reduced losses on several rural routes, they could not eradicate them.

Sunday passenger services north of Bridgnorth on the Severn Valley branch were withdrawn after the Second World War. In the Fifties, many of the services using this very rural route were sparsely used or were even reported as being empty.

By the early Fifties, all clay and tile traffic on the Severn Valley line had been lost. Before the outbreak of the Second World War, the GWR had tried its hardest to persuade the tile-making firms at Jackfield to switch back from road to rail, but in vain.

THE AXEMAN ARRIVES

The October 1959 General Election saw the appointment of Ernest Marples as minister of transport. A qualified accountant, he had founded Marples-Ridgway, a construction firm that built many roads, and soon demonstrated that he preferred expenditure on motorways to investment in railways. In 1959, he gave the green light for the first inter-city British motorway, the M1.

That year, Britain's railway network suffered its biggest shock to date: the closure of a complete system, the Midland & Great Northern Joint Railway, on February 28. It was listed among the 350 route miles nationwide to be closed in 1959.

On March 15, 1961, Marples told the House of Commons that Dr Richard Beeching, a physicist and engineer from ICI, would become the first chairman of the new British Railways Board, from June 1 that year. His brief was simple: return the railways to profitability without delay.

In doing so, he would change the transport map of Britain forever, and create a new streamlined railway system out of the steam-era network.

The days of mass subsidy, with profitable services supporting the unprofitable ones, and the taxpayer footing the bill if the overall figures did not tally in the right way, would soon be over, it was intended.

ABOVE: The last British Railways' train from Bridgnorth was the 6.58pm on Sunday, September 8, 1963. Pannier tanks Nos. 9624 and 4665 were specially rostered for the service which was normally undertaken by a diesel multiple unit. SVR ARCHIVES

The Transport Act 1962, which broke up the British Transport Commission and created the British Railways Board, directed it to run the railways so that its operating profits were "not less than sufficient" for meeting running costs. From then onwards, each railway service should pay for itself or at least show that it had the possibility of doing so.

The 1962 Act also introduced new legislation for the closure of railway lines. Section 56(7) demanded that British Railways gave at least six weeks' notice of its intention to close a line and to publish the proposal in two local newspapers in the area affected in two successive weeks.

We regularly talk about the Beeching Axe, the nickname given by the press to the 148-page report published on March 27, 1963. The Reshaping of British Railways, which called for nearly a third of the rail network's 18,000 route miles to be closed and ripped up.

However, as we have seen, closures had been enacted by British Railways from the year of its formation, and had been growing at a stead pace. Divisional managers were recommending lines for closure before anyone had heard the name Beeching: indeed, those closed during his term in office between his appointment and the publication of the 1963 report were more akin to a rubber-stamping of such recommendations.

In June 1962, the Western Region announced the withdrawal of all passenger services between Shrewsbury and Bewdley. Furthermore, the services south of Bewdley to Hartlebury and Kidderminster would be cut back.

Bridgnorth Town Council objected to the closure, saying that the line should be promoted as a holiday attraction.

The local Transport Users Consultative Committee, part of a system established the under the 1962 Act to represent the railways' consumers held a public meeting at Bridgnorth on November 8 that year.

The committee then wrote to the British Transport commission objecting to the closure, saying it would cause hardship to rail users in Bridgnorth, Highley and Apley Forge and to pensioners in rural communities, as well as weekend visitors and anglers.

On the other side of the coin, the figures did not stack up. Figures for the whole of September 1962, showed that at Ironbridge, only 70 single tickets and 194 cheap-day returns to Shrewsbury were sold. If the railway was such a vital lifeline, British Railways considered, where was the patronage?

ABOVE: Bridgnorth station viewed from the footbridge looking towards Shrewsbury in September 1963, The unidentified diesel multiple unit in the foreground is on a service for Kidderminster. The southbound train has a fish van on the rear. J MARSHALL COLLECTION/KIDDERMINSTER RAILWAY MUSEUM

ABOVE: GWR Dean Goods 0-6-0 No. 2516 in GWR livery at Cleobury Mortimer station with a Stephenson Locomotive Society special on May 21, 1955. This locomotive is now preserved as a static exhibit inside STEAM – Museum of the Great Western Railway at Swindon. Then Bewdley to Tenbury Wells line lost its passenger services the year before the Severn Valley branch. A DONALDSON/KIDDERMINSTER RAILWAY MUSEUM

In August 1963, the official notice of withdrawal of services between Shrewsbury and Bewdley as from September 9 that year.

So we can say that while Beeching agreed to the closure of the Severn Valley branch, moves to axe it predated his 1963 report.

Local councils were shocked by the speed of events and wrote to protest both to Beeching and the leader of the Labour opposition, Harold Wilson, whose party officials had pledged to sack Beeching and reverse all of his cuts. (In power, Labour initially retained Beeching and then made cuts over and above those contained in his report, but that is another story).

Freight and parcels traffic continued until December 2, when all stations on the line apart from Bewdley and Stourport closed completely.

As was the case in the Beeching era, track was soon lifted, between Buildwas and Bridgnorth, the section from Buildwas to Alveley Colliery having been formally abandoned. The Wolverhampton district engineer wanted to use the track materials to enlarge Bescot yard at Walsall.

Shortly afterwards, the district engineer was replaced by Roy Hughes, who needed the permanent way dismantlers to instead work on improving the line between Smethwick and Stourport

Junction. So as soon as Bescot had enough track, he stopped the tracklifting north of Bridgnorth and moved the gangers to Stourbridge Junction.

This move had historic consequences, for it left the track in place between Bridgnorth and Alveley.

The Tenbury Wells to Bewdley line through the Wyre Forest closed to passengers on July 29, 1962, and freight on January 6, 1964, apart from the section from Bewdley to Cleobury Mortimer which, until April 19, 1965, was retained for access to the Cleobury Mortimer & Ditton Priors Light Railway which served an Admiralty depot.

The sole traffic then left on the line north of Bewdley was coal from Alveley Colliery. However, public demand for coal lessened in the Sixties, leading to a major pit closure programme. Alveley Colliery closed in 1969, after the quality of its coal deteriorated dramatically.

A sparse passenger service continued to link Bewdley with Kidderminster and Worcester via Hartlebury, until this too ceased on January 5, 1970. It had been scheduled for withdrawal on April 7, 1969, but was postponed because of local objections. The last passenger train was the 7.20pm diesel multiple unit service from Bewdley to Kidderminster on Saturday, January 7.

Coal trains still ran to Stourport Power Station, using a former siding which ran alongside the main line to the point where the Severn Valley branch turned off at Hartlebury, but the traffic ceased in March 1979 with the power station closing shortly afterwards.

In 2015, only a very small section of the original Severn Valley line remained in commercial (as opposed to heritage) use, to carry coal traffic to Ironbridge Power Station.

RIGHT: Beeching's report The Reshaping of British Railways is regarded as a watershed moment in the history of the UK network. ROBIN JONES COLLECTION

ABOVE: The introduction of diesel multiple units, such as this set seen at Arley in 1962, from the early Fifties onwards was heralded as a saviour of country branch lines. They did make savings, and were welcomed by passengers, but while they could stem some of the mounting revenue losses, they did not eradicate them, and many of the routes they served succumbed to road transport. SVR ARCHIVES

RIGHT: British Railways chairman Dr Richard Beeching unveiled his report, The Reshaping of British Railways, on March 27, 1963, but British Railway's bid to close the Severn Valley branch began the year before.

BRITISH RAILWAYS BOARD

The Reshaping of British Railways

PART 1: REPORT

The Reshaping of British Railways

REPORT AND MAPS

LONDON: HER MAJESTY'S STATIONERY OFFICE

Price £1 0s. 0d. net

LONDON

HER MAJESTY'S STATIONERY OFFICE

BRITISH SUGAR'S KIDDERMINSTER

The British Sugar Corporation's Kidderminster plant at Foley Park was built in 1926.

The corporation was created by the Sugar Industry (Reorganisation) Act to manage the entire UK sugar beet crop in 1936. In 1981, the Government sold its 36% share in the corporation which in following year became a public limited company, trading as British Sugar plc. Nine years later it was sold to Associated British Foods, which still owns it today.

Until rail traffic to the plant ended in the early Eighties, it had its own sidings linked to the Kidderminster to Bewdley line.

Three new Barclay 0-4-0 saddle tanks were supplied for use at the plant: No. 1843 of 1925 No. 1 (sold for scrap in June 1969), No. 1931 of 1927 No. 2 (moved to Wissington sugar factory in Norfolk in 1962) and No. 2248 of 1948 (moved to Wissington in June 1969)

In addition there were two Ruston Hornsby four-wheel shunters in diesel electric

No. 408866 of 1959, which arrived in February 1961, and was moved for scrap in October 1983, and diesel mechanical No. 281269 of 1950, which arrived in January 1969, and was moved to the Severn Valley Railway for preservation in September 1983.

Under strain from competition with imported sugar, the company was forced to close some of its sites. Kidderminster closed in February 2002. ●

ABOVE: Foley Park Halt in 1960. It comprised a wooden platform with minimal buildings including a GWR pagoda shelter. The sugar beet factory sidings are on the right. W POTTER/ KIDDERMINSTER RAILWAY MUSEUM

BELOW: A British Railways Standard 4MT 2-6-4T heads north of Bridgnorth with a local service in 1962, the line's last compete year of operation. MICHAEL MENSING

ABOVE: British Railways' consignment note for Foley Park siding. ROBIN JONES COLLECTION

ABOVE: GWR 0-6-2T No. 6696 enters Kidderminster Goods Yard from the south with a trainload of sugar beet for the Foley Park factory on October 30, 1960.
B MOONE/KIDDERMINSTER RAILWAY MUSEUM

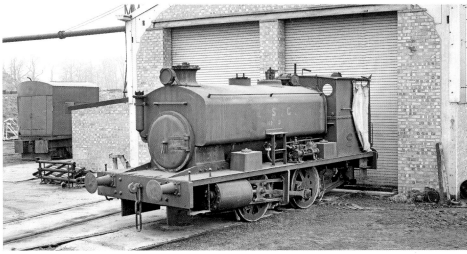

ABOVE: Barclay 0-4-0ST No. 2248 of 1948 No. 3 at the Foley Park sugar beet factory on March 2, 1968. Named *Albert* and preserved at the Nene Valley and East Kent railways, it moved to the Plym Valley Railway in 2004. LW PERKINS/ KIDDERMINSTER RAILWAY MUSEUM

ABOVE: GWR 2-6-2T No. 4144 at Bridgnorth with a sizeable mixed freight in 1962. MICHAEL MENSING

Chapter 3

The preservation principle

The Talyllyn Railway led the way for railway preservation.

Railway preservation began almost on the doorstep of the Severn Valley, and concerned a little line that ran not too far away from the headwaters of the great river.

The Talyllyn Railway was the first in the world to be taken over by volunteers and run for heritage purposes.

After having a letter published in the Birmingham Post imploring the public to help save the 2ft 3in gauge line at Tywyn, renowned transport historian Tom Rolt organised a meeting in the Imperial Hotel in Birmingham on October 11, 1950 when around 70 enthusiasts formed a committee to negotiate with the executors of the estate of the line's owner, the late Sir Henry Hayden-Jones, to take it over and save it from closure.

The newly formed Talyllyn Railway Preservation Society took over the line on February 8, 1951 and reopened its first section, between Tywyn Wharf and Rhydyronen stations on May 14, 1951.

The idea of 'ordinary people' taking over a railway was not new: the Southwold Railway in Suffolk nearly became what might have been regarded the world's first heritage line in 1929, but for the failure of efforts to save it, and in 1941, a letter in The Modern Tramway called for volunteers to restart the Welsh Highland Railway as part of the war effort. Also, there were the cases of the Fairbourne and Ravenglass & Eskdale railways, both mineral lines, which had by then long since been converted to tourist 'miniature' railways for leisure purposes, although it is highly debatable whether they could be classed as 'preservation'.

Yet were it not for the Talyllyn pioneers, the preservation movement would almost certainly have started at a later date, somewhere else, such is the extent of railway enthusiasm. Shortly afterwards, moves began to revive the Ffestiniog Railway, and a few years later, the Welshpool & Llanfair Light Railway.

The Talyllyn volunteers' exploits inspired the 1953 Ealing comedy, The Titfield Thunderbolt, about a group of villagers who saved their branch line from closure by running it themselves. Saving narrow gauge lines in the mountains of central and North Wales was a marvellous achievement, but could such principles be applied in reality as well as fiction to standard gauge lines – maybe even a redundant part of the national network?

That is what happened in the case of the Bluebell Railway in Sussex.

Sussex spinster and battleaxe Madge Bessemer, granddaughter of Henry Bessemer, inventor of the Bessemer Converter for converting pig iron into steel, sprang into action when the British Transport Commission posted notices announcing that it would close the lossmaking Lewes-East Grinstead line with effect from May 28, 1955.

Studying key documents from the line's history, she reread the small print in the Act of Parliament which had given powers for its building. It required the owners to run four trains each day. That was the loophole that she needed. Aided by local MP Tufton Beamish, she forced British Railways to reinstate the service – which it very unwillingly did in August the following year. Historians dubbed

ABOVE: Fletcher Jennings 0-4-0WT No. 2 *Dolgoch* was the Talyllyn Railway's sole operational locomotive when the volunteers staged their takeover in 1950, and was in dire need of an overhaul, leading to fears about the future of the line. It is pictured at Tywyn in February 2010. ROBIN JONES

ABOVE: The first Bluebell Railway train ran on August 7, 1960, hauled by LBSCR 'Terrier' 0-6-0T No. 55 *Stepney*. BLUEBELL ARCHIVES

ABOVE: Tom Rolt is considered to be the father of the preservation movement, having led the bid to take over the Talyllyn Railway, the world's first original line to be saved by volunteers. He is seen flagging off a train from Tywyn in June 1950. TALYLLYN ARCHIVES

ABOVE LEFT: Madge Bessemer, who all but single-handedly forced British Railways to temporarily reopen the Lewes to East Grinstead line, inadvertently providing a breathing space for the groundbreaking Bluebell Railway Preservation Society to take over part of it. BLUEBELL ARCHIVES

it the 'sulky service'. BR had to comply with the law, but blatantly did so begrudgingly. The statutory four services were mostly restricted to just a single coach, and they did not stop at Barcombe or Kingscote, because those two stations did not appear in the original Act.

Also, the restored services appeared to be deliberately timed so that they would be of little use, arriving at East Grinstead after the start of normal working hours and departing before the end of the working day.

Madge Bessemer had won a reprieve for the line until BR obtained the statutory powers for revoking the terms of the original Act.

Services were again withdrawn between Lewes and East Grinstead on March 16, 1958, but this time she could do nothing.

However, her stalwart efforts had attracted national media attention, and when the final train ran, the unduly large numbers of passengers and sightseers proved that the public at large really did care about rail closures.

On that final day, Madge Bessemer encountered Carshalton Technical College student Chris Campbell. Inspired by her efforts to save the line, Chris, then 18, wondered if it might be possible that he could take up the cudgel.

Meanwhile, Martin Eastland, a telecommunications engineering student of Haywards Heath, David Dallimore, a student at the London School of Economics, from Woodingdean, and Brighton-based Alan Sturt, also 19, who was studying at the Regent Street Polytechnic, had mooted the idea of setting up a Lewes and East Grinstead Railway Preservation Society, drawing on the example of the Welsh narrow gauge lines. They sent a letter to interested parties highlighting the Bessemer campaign and the unexpected public support that it had generated.

They initially hoped to save the entire route, reopening it stages at a time, acquiring a GWR railcar for regular use and using steam during the summer months. Incidentally, the preservation of GWR railcar W4W for Swindon Railway Museum in 1958 may be deemed to mark the start of diesel preservation.

In December 1958, Chris told a journalist on the East Grinstead Observer about the possible formation of a preservation society, leading to

ABOVE: Press coverage of the opening of the Bluebell Railway in 1960. BLUEBELL ARCHIVES

RIGHT: The end? A second closure notice for the Lewes to East Grinstead line was published in 1958. ROBIN JONES

CLOSING OF EAST GRINSTEAD-LEWES LINE

On and from MONDAY 17th MARCH, 1958, the passenger service on the line between EAST GRINSTEAD and LEWES, via SHEFFIELD PARK will be withdrawn and the following stations closed:-

WEST HOATHLY
SHEFFIELD PARK
NEWICK & CHAILEY

HORSTED KEYNES will remain open for passenger and freight traffic, and be served by trains to and from HAYWARDS HEATH.

'Bus facilities in the area are provided by Southdown Motor Services Ltd.

SOUTHERN

the headline: 'Bluebell Line Sensation – May Be Run Privately'. He travelled on a rambler's excursion from Victoria to Horsted Keynes on December 7, and met Martin for the first time. They decided to call a public meeting to officially launch the society.

The founders' meeting was held on March 15, 1959, at the Church Lads' Brigade Hall in Haywards Heath. The late Bernard Holden, a signalling assistant in the general manager's office at Liverpool Street, chaired it because the students were minors in the eyes of the then law as they were all under 21 and legally barred from holding positions. Bernard had been born in Barcombe stationhouse where his father Charles was stationmaster.

A collection raised £6 for society funds, and a meeting with the assistant general manager of the Southern Region was arranged to take place at Waterloo on April 5 that year.

The preservationists were hardly taken seriously, probably because of their age if not their lofty ambitions. A price of £55,000 for the purchase of the line between Horsted Keynes (then still in use as the eastern end of the electrified Ardingly branch) and Culver Junction was quoted, and the society was given just a month's option to purchase.

Eventually, however, an affordable £2500 per annum five-year lease on the four-mile Horsted Keynes-Sheffield Park section was agreed. With the Sheffield Park booking office rented for 2s 6d (12½p) per week, the first Bluebell train ran on August 7, 1960, hauled by LBSCR 'Terrier' 0-6-0T No. 55 *Stepney*. In the years to come, the railway continued to

build its locomotive and rolling stock fleet, at a time when steam was fast disappearing from the network.

History showed that the Bluebell was to become a market leader in the heritage railway sector in many respects, not least of all the restoration of pre-Grouping coaching bodies, some of which had spent decades in use as chicken coops. The importance of what happened at Sheffield Park all those years ago cannot be overstated.

However, the Bluebell was not the first private standard gauge railway to run trains: it was beaten by several weeks by the Middleton Railway in Leeds, an industrial concern dating from 1758, which was never under British Railways' jurisdiction. Taken over by student members of Leeds University Union Railway Society – who wanted somewhere to run their historic tramcars – it began operating public services on June 20, 1960 a few weeks earlier. The prime mover was lecturer and society president the late Dr Fred Youell.

The pair blazed trails for others to follow, but the Bluebell showed that the closure of a section of the national network did not have to mean the end of trains.

The opening of the heritage-era Bluebell Railway brought national media attention, and there were those watching from afar who wondered if their locality could have its own steam line. Maybe a Bluebell equivalent in the West Midlands…●

Chapter 4

A new spring
in the valley
The steam age begins again!

ABOVE: A scene of dereliction: closed Bridgnorth station in 1964. A running-in board is propped against a fence. C SMITH/KIDDERMINSTER RAILWAY MUSEUM

To the north of Kidderminster lies Habberley Valley, a local nature reserve, long a favoured picnic destination for West Midland families, with its heathland sandstone outcrops, and its well-known adder population.

Between there and the town lies the Habberley housing estate, which dates from the late Fifties and Sixties. At its heart stands a boarded-up public house, the Coopers Arms, which was once the focal point of social life on the estate, but which died a lingering death in the 21st century, like so many of its counterparts across the country, as social trends changed. In 2013, plans evolved to demolished the pub and replace it with flats, but as of 2015, it was still standing.

Clearly it had seen far better days, but maybe its finest hour came on July 6, 1965. A

wooden plaque commemorating the event was proudly displayed inside for many years until it disappeared without trace.

The event in question was a public meeting, which led to the immediate formation of the Severn Valley Railway Society. It was a

classic example of planting a small acorn that would later flourish into a mighty oak, or indeed a forest, for its impact on the railway preservation movement and the tourist economy of the West Midlands can never be overstated.

RIGHT: Where it all began: the Coopers Arms in Habberley as seen in February 2015. It was here that the Severn Valley Railway society was formed on July 6, 1965. Ironically, it stood derelict when the Severn Valley Railway was celebrated its 50th anniversary. ROBIN JONES

WHICH LINE COULD WE SAVE?

Back in the pre-Beeching days, the boundaries of the regions of British Railways were adjusted, broadly to simplify the network. Just as the Western Region was handed most of the Southern routes west of Exeter, and closed most of them within a few years, so Western routes in the Midlands were passed over to the London Midland Region.

One minor casualty of the boundary change was the removal of the Kidderminster portion of the 'Cathedrals Express', the premier train on the Cotswold line from Worcester to Paddington; it was last hauled by steam in 1963.

Keith Beddoes, a local maintenance fitter in his early twenties, was annoyed at the loss of the direct service from Kidderminster to the capital, and began talking to friends at work about it. The conversations expanded to the Beeching closure of lines – and whether anything could be done to save them. They looked to the example set by the Bluebell Railway – and wondered if something similar might be achieved in the West Midlands.

"I thought that if those down south could do it, why not us?" said Keith, who went on to become an accomplished railway historian.

The Bluebell revivalists had one line in their sights from the outset, but the would-be Worcestershire revivalists had a choice. They looked at the closed line from Bewdley to Tenbury Wells, and also the Cleobury Mortimer & Ditton Priors Light Railway.

The latter was built in the wake of the 1896 Light Railways Act, which empowered the building of minimalist lines to serve sparsely populated rural areas that the established railway companies did not consider economically lucrative. Stations were built on the cheap, often second-hand locomotives and rolling stock were used and as the track did not have to be up to the standard of the main line, it had maximum speed restrictions of 25mph.

Today's heritage railways run under the provisions of the 1896 Act, and indeed, the plethora of light railways that sprang up in what was the end of the age of railway building and the dawn of the motor car age have much in common with them.

The standard gauge Cleobury Mortimer & Ditton Priors Light Railway opened in 1908, running from a junction with the Wyre Forest line at Cleobury Mortimer. It ran for 12¼ miles through Cleobury Town, Stottesdon and Burwarton to Ditton Priors, accessing mineral deposits in the Clee Hills. Extensions to Bridgnorth and Coalport were among several proposed, but none were ever built.

It was taken over by the GWR at the Grouping of 1922-23. Never a good prospect for income from passenger trains, they were discontinued just before the start of the Second World War. Indeed, many of the light railways built under the Act ceased operation in the 1930s.

However, the line had a second lease of life serving the Royal Naval Armaments Depot at Ditton Priors, which opened in 1941. The railway's two Manning Wardle 0-6-0STs, which had been rebuilt by the GWR and resembled pannier tanks, were fitted with spark arrestors to avoid igniting the highly dangerous cargo. Steam was replaced by diesels in 1957.

In 1960 British Railways closed the light railway but the Royal Navy continued to use Ditton Priors until 1965. The armaments depot there, afterwards temporarily used by US forces, was finally shut in 1968.

ABOVE: Should the early revivalists have looked to go across the River Severn, from Bewdley into the Wyre Forest towards Cleobury Mortimer, rather than along it, as happened? A view from below track level of Dowles Viaduct, on the GWR line between Kidderminster and Cleobury Mortimer. Crossing the viaduct with the 3.47pm Woofferton Junction to Kidderminster on July 8, 1952, is GWR 2-6-2T No. 5110. The lattice-steel viaduct sat on the two stone pillars in the river with abutments at both ends. J WOOD/ KIDDERMINSTER RAILWAY MUSEUM

Indeed, the Cleobury Mortimer & Ditton Priors Light Railway would have made an interesting heritage line, and may well have ended up not too dissimilar from today's Kent & East Sussex Railway, widely regarded as the most complete example of a standard gauge line built under the 1896 Act.

It was, of course, never designed to be used by the heavy main line locomotives that Keith Beddoes and his revivalist friends envisaged, and what's more, there was another line, running to the east, with stupendous riverside scenery that would be a far better bet…

After a few informal meetings between friends and other interested parties, a notice was placed in the local press inviting members of the public to a meeting, at the Coopers Arms. It would be up to those in attendance to vote on which line should be saved, if possible.

A total of 50 people turned up, and chose the Severn Valley line, forming a society for the purpose of buying and reopening part of it.

The initial target would be the 4½ miles of line from Bridgnorth to Hampton Loade, to be reopened for steam trains, plus the track from Hampton Loade to Alveley Colliery sidings, from where coal trains were still being run south to Bewdley, and which would give the nascent heritage line a connection with the national network.

Decades later, Keith recalled: "We never thought at the time we would ever get back to Kidderminster. We wanted to keep the track in from Hampton Loade to Alveley, where the colliery still operated until 1969, so we thought we might acquire it in the future.

"At the time it was just a dream. The way I look back at it now was that we just wanted to play trains. It was only when businessmen and the local MP became involved that we saw we could get to Bewdley and even beyond. Four miles would have been adequate – but that little spark was there and all this has happened."

BELOW: Fitted with a spark arrestor, GWR 2021 Class 0-6-0PT No. 2144 near Cleobury Mortimer Town on the Cleobury Mortimer & Ditton Priors Light Railway with a Stephenson Locomotion Society special on May 21, 1955. Had fate played a different hand, could this interesting but featureless line have been saved instead of today's Severn Valley Railway? A DONALDSON/KIDDERMINSTER RAILWAY MUSEUM

THE TELEPHONE CALL THAT MADE TRANSPORT HISTORY

Among those in attendance at that first pivotal meeting was John Garth, who owned a family firm in Lye that manufactured items of hardware.

His presence turned out to be of paramount importance.

Having decided to try for a lease on the Bridgnorth to Hampton Loade section, the revivalists decided several days later to see the stations for themselves.

Not only was July 11 a very wet Sunday afternoon, but when they reached Bridgnorth station by road, they were greeted with initial hostility by licensee George Thorpe.

Two weeks later, on July 25, they decided to walk the line from Hampton Loade to Bridgnorth, and when they reached their destination, they were horrified to find that the track was being lifted.

An emergency committee meeting was convened for that evening, following which John Garth sent a telegram to British Railways pleading for breathing space, and promising to telephone the following day. He did so at 9am, and asked for the ripping up of the track to be suspended.

In these days of mass ownership of mobile telephones, we might take the making of such a call for granted. Yet back in 1965, how many people had time in the day to make phone calls, John, however, was his own master, and could make calls in works time, because he owned the works.

It turned out to be the most important phone call in the history of the modern-day Severn Valley Railway.

Very soon, John found a sympathetic ear, in Phil Coutanche, planning engineer at the Wolverhampton District Engineers' Department office in Wolverhampton (Low Level) station, who was in charge of the permanent way gang lifting the track.

Phil was an enthusiast himself. He lived at Linley station on the section of the Severn Valley line that had by then been lifted, and in his spare time, painted and lined out models for the former Clapham Museum. Furthermore, as a native of London, he had written books on the carriages of the South Eastern & Chatham Railway.

Fortune was smiling on John Garth, who was acting chairman of the society at the time. He might well have found a typical jobsworth of the period at the end of the telephone, but

ABOVE: Beware of the trains – what trains? Decay and dereliction are the order of the day at Eardington Halt in the mid-Sixties. SVR ARCHIVES

instead he found a sympathetic ear. Phil agreed for the contractors to leave off pending further talks, tidying up what they had done at the northern end of Bridgnorth station.

In the meantime, the railway engineers knew that the Oldbury goods branch in the Black Country needed to be lifted as a matter of urgency, as the elevated section of the M5 motorway through the Black Country was to be built across it, making the passage of demolition trains impossible. If the track

materials were to be retrieved by rail, that job had to be given priority.

The permanent way team ripping up the Severn Valley branch was diverted to Oldbury, giving the Bridgnorth line a further stay of execution. For their last two days on site at Bridgnorth, the contractors confined their activities to cutting up rails that they had already lifted instead of pulling up any more.

That was just as well, for Bridgnorth station itself was also likely to be demolished. It took two weeks in all, but the society had staved off the lifting of its preferred section of line.

FOR DETAILS OF THE SCHEME TO PURCHASE THE PICTURESQUE FIVE MILE RAILWAY LINE FROM BRIDGNORTH TO HAMPTON LOADE, IN SHROPSHIRE, AND TO RUN A SERVICE OF STEAM TRAINS AT WEEKENDS, PLEASE WRITE TO MR. A.G. CLEAVER, 10 WESTERN WAY,

SEVERN VALLEY RAILWAY SOCIETY

Hon. Sec:
D. C. BEDDOES,
18, KINVER AVENUE,
KIDDERMINSTER.

Treasurer:
COLUMB W. HOWELL,
63, UPPER STREET,
BEWDLEY.
TEL: 2279

ABOVE: The first letterhead of the Severn Valley Railway Society. SVR ARCHIVES

SEVERN VALLEY RAILWAY SOCIETY

STEAM help reopen a railway—
AT BRIDGNORTH
**FULL DETAILS FROM:- A. G. CLEAVER, 10 WESTERN WAY
KIDDERMINSTER, WORCS. Tel: 5740**

ABOVE: The first edition of the Severn Valley Railway Society's quarterly newsletter, Severn Valley Railway News, was published in November 1965. SVR ARCHIVES

A FOOT IN THE DOOR

Society officials met with British Railways, which refused a lease on the chosen section of line, requiring an outright purchase at a price to be agreed.

However, the society was permitted to occupy Bridgnorth station at a nominal rent, pending agreement on a price and payment of a 10% deposit.

Money was notoriously short, but a raffle met the society's expenses, which at that time was limited to publicity material and press releases turned out on John Garth's duplicator.

Working members, however, could do no more than weed the track and tidy up the station, which was by then as much in danger of being reclaimed by Mother Nature as the demolition team. Weeds 4ft high grew between the tracks, and a pig was grazed on the site. The society had a push-trolley, built from materials found lying around, but of course no locomotives.

On Monday, August 9, 1965, the first public meeting of the society took place in Kidderminster Town Hall at 7pm, and was attended by 70 people. The Save the Severn Valley Railway Fund was launched and £110 was raised, although three representatives of other Midland railway preservation societies voiced their disapproval of the project.

A second public meeting was held on Tuesday, August 31, in Bridgnorth's Castle Hall, and was attended by around 80 people, with fewer criticisms vocalised.

In August 1965, AG (Bert) Cleaver took over as society secretary, after his wife had suggested that he found himself a hobby. He lived in Western Way, Kidderminster, an address soon familiar to society members, and commuted each day by train to the Birmingham shipping company where he worked.

ABOVE: GWR auto tank No. 1420 and 2-6-2T No. 4555, both of which had by then been preserved, at Alveley Colliery sidings, on September 19, 1965.
ANH GLOVER/KIDDERMINSTER RAILWAY MUSEUM

THE DEAL STRUCK

At a meeting with British Railways on August 4, 1965, an estimated purchase price of £45,000 was suggested for the stretch of line.

In late 1965, society officials had the section of line valued by estate agents, and placed a £25,000 bid. In February 1966, that figure was agreed with British Railways for the freehold of land, track and buildings.

Bert recalled: "Quite a large sum to us at the time, almost laughable really, but we were optimists, we had to be.

"It was fortunate that the scheme itself was attractive, as our membership was increasing steadily. By Christmas of that first year, 1965, it had reached the 100 mark, a figure that gave us some cause for pride.

"It was apparent quite early that stock would have to be provided by other organisations, as all the money we could raise

ABOVE: In a scene which could well have been from several years in the future, on September 19, 1965, in the yards of Alveley Colliery, stands GWR 0-4-2T No. 1420. Although the Severn Valley branch north of Bewdley was by then closed to passengers, the section to Alveley was still open for coal traffic. On that day, No. 1420 and prairie No. 4555, both of which had been preserved for use on the Dart Valley Railway, headed the section of the Stephenson Locomotive Society (Midland Area)'s 'Restored Locomotives Cavalcade' from Worcester Shrub Hill, Hartlebury and Alveley, on via Bewdley and Kidderminster to Wolverhampton Low Level, and then back to Worcester. The larger trip from Birmingham Snow Hill also featured future SVR resident LNER K4 2-6-0 No. 3442 *The Great Marquess* on the beginning and end legs.
ANH GLOVER/KIDDERMINSTER RAILWAY MUSEUM

At home, Bert worked every night answering correspondence, right through to the transformation of the original society to a company in 1969. He was a lynchpin of the revivalist group. After the society ceased to exist, he and his wife moved first to the Isle of Wight and then to Scotland to run hotels.

SEVERN VALLEY STEAM

FOR DETAILS OF THE SCHEME TO PURCHASE THE PICTURESQUE FIVE MILE RAILWAY LINE FROM BRIDGNORTH TO HAMPTON LOADE IN SHROPSHIRE, AND TO RUN A SERVICE OF STEAM TRAINS AT WEEKENDS, PLEASE CONTACT MR. A. G. CLEAVER AT 10 WESTERN WAY, KIDDERMINSTER, WORCESTERSHIRE.
JOIN THE SEVERN VALLEY RLY. SOCIETY

by the methods available to us would be required to pay the 10% deposit to British Railways. Fortunately, they did not press us for the deposit immediately."

It was still very much early days in the preservation movement, and it would not be that easy to entice other organisations into the scheme. Some years before it established Didcot Railway Centre, the Great Western Society was approached, but at the time was backing the Dart Valley Railway project at Buckfastleigh in South Devon, and could not commit locomotives and stock. So the Severn Valley revivalists were left to go it alone.

During 1966, the society staged three open days, the last two of which comprised fairground-type stalls, backed up by a display of relics and photographs, but no locomotives.

Bert recalls: "I suppose that 1966 will be remembered as the most difficult year in our history. The great problem was always

to keep members' interest without being able to offer much in return. We could not really give many promises either, other than that negotiations for stock were taking place.

"We could have folded at any time with the odds against us. We had a meeting with the various parish councils, and discovered that the natives were distinctly unfriendly. However, British Railways must have thought us still a reasonable proposition, as we remained in occupation.

"Towards the end of the year, our funds improved to such an extent that we were able to pay the first instalment of the deposit. Our tenure was beginning to look a little firmer."

One of the features of the society at this time were the regular film shows held at Bridgnorth, while raffles and jumble sales were still the principal sources of vital funds.

The 10% deposit on the section of line was paid following a meeting with British Railways on February 1, 1967, and so another hurdle was crossed.

ABOVE: Society fundraising in the early days at Bridgnorth station. SVR ARCHIVES

In the meantime, the society had begun looking into the complexities of obtaining a Light Railway Order, under the provisions of the 1896 Act. Indeed, two LROs were needed, one for British Railways to downgrade the line to a light railway with the 25mph maximum speed limit, and the other to transfer operating authority for the line from British Railways to a private company. For that, a new company would have to be formed, to comply with legal requirements. It was duly incorporated on May 24, 1967, but in effect remained largely dormant for two years. ●

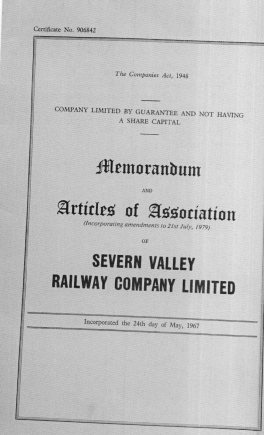

Certificate No. 906842

The Companies Act, 1948

COMPANY LIMITED BY GUARANTEE AND NOT HAVING A SHARE CAPITAL

Memorandum

AND

Articles of Association
(Incorporating amendments to 21st July, 1979)

OF

SEVERN VALLEY
RAILWAY COMPANY LIMITED

Incorporated the 24th day of May, 1967

ABOVE: The front of Bridgnorth station in January 1967. DAVID WILLIAMS

RIGHT: The articles of association of the Severn Valley Railway Company Limited, incorporated on May 27, 1967. SVR ARCHIVES

A Line Remembered

The year 1862 saw it all finished
No one thought it would be diminished.
From Kartlebury to Shrewsbury there and back
The Severn Valley Line was but single track.
In past days its patronage was great
But not it is said in days of late.
Of its scenic beauty it was often spoken
This line that was worked by single line token.
Its bridges and viaducts all built well,
Perhaps they have a tale to tell?
Of engines and men throughout the day
Toiling to make the railway pay.

In the nineteen thirties it reached its zenith,
But who could see the approaching menace?
Came the war and it did its bit
With Dukes and Manors running over it.
Troop trains it took in its stride
Perhaps it felt some silent pride.
Troop trains came – troop-trains went,
And the track it took some punishment.

When all the soldiers had gone away,
In came the men from the permanent way.
They came with the best Great Western tradition
To restore the line to A1 condition.
They did it to the best of their ability,
But then came a threat to its whole stability.
Nationalisation was its name –
The railways wouldn't be the same.
Out went Great Western – Gone With Regret,
BR schedules had to be met.

Prairies, panniers and the rest
Still worked the line and did their best.
Diesel railcars from Worcester Shed,
Did yeoman service, so 'tis said.
Class 5s and new Standards also came,
But it wasn't really quite the same.
Great Western engines – they were the best
But now they were slowly laid to rest.
Diesel sets were now in clover
The days of steam were nearly over.

From ICI came Dr Beeching,
To apply his expert business teaching.
The branch lines first came under the axe –
But it did not help our Income Tax!
The Severn Valley Line as all could see
Was now in terrible jeopardy.
But the Government had their way,
It must close – it did not pay.
To the Public it was sad news,
Nobody cared about their views.

People at Highley and Hampton Loade
Now would have to go by road.
Fishermen too would be put out
To get to the river for their trout.

All the talking was to no avail
So we near the end of the tale.
Came the day we all remember,
A gloomy day in mid-September.
They came by train, by 'bus and car
From many places both near and far.
Some little boys they came by bike
All would never see the like.

The last train on the Severn Valley Line,
Would be a memory lost in time.
The engine's whistle gave a mournful blow
When the guard waved his flag to let it go.
As all the people waved goodbye,
Even the engine seemed to sigh.
The fire in the firebox was glowing bright
As the train sped away in the evening light.

Down the line at every station,
There were people of all creation.
To see the last train was their intention –
They wouldn't have missed it for a pension.
On down the valley to its destination,
Which was, of course, Kidderminster station.
Sad they were on this last day
As from the station they went away.

Then on the line goods were still run,
But neither in quantity, nor by the ton.
And now to that last dying ember,
These too ceased in that November.
North of Bridgnorth, the track was lifted
But southwards nothing was ever shifted,
Save for the signals felled to the ground
And left for a bit lying around.

Borne by the wind were little seeds,
Which grew all round to very tall weeds.
Everything now is quiet and still,
and weeds are growing taller at will.
But does the story end here? Who can say
Perhaps there still might come a day
When the Valley once more re-echoes to steam.
What do you think – is this a dream?

A poem by Keith Beddoes, published in the
first edition of Severn Valley Railway News in
November 1965.

Chapter 5

Steam returns to Bridgnorth

The fledgling revivalist movement takes shape as the society acquires its first steam locomotives.

It was on March 25, 1967, that the revivalist project took a gargantuan leap forward in credibility with the arrival of its first steam locomotive.

GWR 0-6-0 No. 3205 arrived at Bridgnorth pulling four GWR carriages, two of which were also designed by Collett.

The locomotive was the sole-surviving member of the 2251 class, a medium-

powered freight and passenger type of which 120 were built at Swindon between 1930-48, replacing the earlier Dean goods 0-6-0s, with which they shared similarities but had more modern features such as taper boilers and full cabs. Increases in both boiler pressure and heating surface gave a useful increase in power at the expense of weight that restricted permitted

routes. Although built for use on lightly laid lines in Wales, they could be found operating on most parts of the former GWR system.

No. 3205, which was built in 1946, spent its later life at Taunton and Exeter where it had been reserved for snowplough duties during the winter. It also briefly saw service on the on Somerset & Dorset system.

When it was withdrawn from service in 1965, it was bought for preservation by the 2251 Fund, whose principal trustee was preservation pioneer, the late David Rouse. It became the second locomotive to arrive at Buckfastleigh for preservation later that year.

David looked at the society's plans, and took a leap of faith in agreeing for No. 3205 to be loaned to the Severn Valley Railway. It was hauled to Stourbridge by rail from Bristol by a Western Region Warship diesel hydraulic locomotive and then travelled under its own steam to Bridgnorth, reaching the station just after noon. As it pulled into the station carrying the headboard 'Severn Valley Special', it broke through a tape as an old-time barrel organ started up. The train was not allowed to carry passengers, as insurance could not be arranged at short notice.

The arrival of No. 3205 attracted a crowd of around 200 to Bridgnorth station, a portent of future steam galas. Many took cine films of the arrival and also made sound recordings.

Everyone now saw that the society meant business.

The line's second locomotive, LMS-designed 2-6-0 No. 46443, arrived four weeks later, coming in steam from Newton Heath near Manchester.

It was an example of a class of 128 designed by HG (George) Ivatt for work on secondary and branch line duties and rated 2MT by British Railways. ▶

No. 46443 was built at Crewe in April 1950 and was based at Derby for 11 years. In 1951, it moved to Birmingham's Saltley depot, where duties included to trip freights, shunting and passenger trains. A final move to Newton Heath in 1966 was followed by withdrawal in March 1967, when it was bought privately and moved to Bridgnorth.

Jumping a track or two, the Severn Valley bought No. 46443 in 1972, but announced in 1983 that the locomotive had been sold and would be leaving the following year. A fund was successfully launched to 'buy back' the locomotive, during which time it gained the nickname 'The People's Engine'.

No, 46443 never left the SVR and is now owned by The SVR 46443 Fund. It had covered 145,997 miles in preservation when withdrawn from service in October 2011.

The arrival of the first engines in 1967 sparked off a year of rapid expansion, with successful steam galas taking place for the first time.

Although it was not permitted to sell tickets to the general public, special trains were run for society members and day members from Bridgnorth to Hampton Loade.

Society membership soared from 500 in January to nearly 1000 in December.

In that same year Severn Valley joined the Association of Railway Preservation Societies, the forerunner of today's Heritage Railway Association.

The line's civil engineering department spent time in 1967 building a 30ft locomotive inspection pit to facilitate maintenance. A water tank was bought at Dudley and re-erected at Eardington Halt, the only source of soft water on the line.

Bridgnorth signalbox was rebuilt, rectifying the damage done by the demolition contractors, while the resignalling of the station area restarted.

STORMIER WATERS

It was shortly after the arrival of No. 3205 that the society learned about new plans for a southern bypass for Bridgnorth – one which would sever the line south of the station.

Fears about road encroachment on the length of railway earmarked for preservation were by no means new.

Back in 1965, it was feared that Shropshire County Council might object to the reopening of the Severn Valley line because it would increase the cost of building a Bridgnorth bypass. A bridge under the line would be needed, together with more extensive earthworks, should the railway be allowed to remain in place, adding £50,000 to the overall cost.

Furthermore, Highley Parish Council made much of its concern over safety on the B4555 from Bridgnorth to Highley, particularly where the line bridged the road on both sides of Eardington Halt. If the railway was closed, its formation would allow the road to be straightened at some future date. The council's objections to the railway reopening had surfaced at a meeting on September 7, 1965.

The bypass scheme would dog the revivalists for many years, and they were not

BELOW: Within two years of that landmark meeting at the Coopers Arms, GWR steam was back on the Severn Valley branch. Collett 0-6-0 No. 3205 is pictured at Bridgnorth on April 2, 1967. SVR ARCHIVES

ABOVE: Nos. 46443 and 3205 at Bridgnorth in 1967. TONY BENDING/SVR ARCHIVES

alone. The Dart Valley Railway's line from Buckfastleigh to Ashburton was taken for the building of the A38 dual carriageway. Today, it could be argued that such moves would have a detrimental effect on local tourist economies, but back in the Sixties and Seventies, motor transport was given priority when many such conflicts arose, as heritage railways were still then largely unproven.

The dispute between the revivalists and the county and parish councils led to a public enquiry into the granting of a LRO to the Severn Valley Railway Company being held at the Shire Hall in Shrewsbury, in October 1968.

British Rail backed the revivalists. Mr RC Bray, chief surveyor for British Rail had inspected the Bridgnorth-Bewdley line on a train hauled by No. 3205 on March 31, 1968, and remarked afterwards: "The company has more than demonstrated its competence to run a railway, and are not playing trains."

He provided evidence on the company's behalf.

The council's road plans were criticised as hasty and lacking in adequate evidence on road usage, while the revivalists' case was seen as better thought-out and covered all angles.

The enquiry inspector and all parties travelled from Bridgnorth to Bewdley to view the scheme for themselves.

On June 6, 1969, eight months after the inquiry ended, the inspector found in favour of the Severn Valley Railway and recommended that the LRO should be made. However, Richard Marsh MP, the Labour minister of transport did not agree and overruled him with regard to the additional costs to the public purse of the bypass, although the objections regarding potential future road improvements at Eardington were dismissed.

However, the minister requested the parties to meet again to overcome their differences. Talks led to the railway company having to agree that no extra cost should fall on public funds if the railway needed to bridge the projected bypass 300 yards south of Bridgnorth station.

The county council then withdrew its major objection to the LRO, and Marsh's successor as transport minister, Frederick Mulley, on December 4 said that the LRO would therefore be granted.

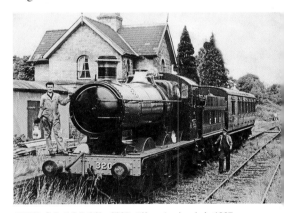

ABOVE: Collett 0-6-0 No. 3205 at Hampton Loade in 1967, driver John Hill carrying the headlamp and fireman John Denson standing on the ballast. DAVID WILLIAMS

ABOVE: LMS mogul No. 46443 hauling a brake van carrying volunteers at Bridgnorth station in 1968. J TARRANT/KIDDERMINSTER RAILWAY MUSEUM

THE STEAM FLEET GROWS

Also arriving on the line in 1967 was Manning Wardle 0-6-0ST No. 2047 of 1926.

The last locomotive to be built by Manning Wardle before the company closed because of the post First World War recession, it was assembled using standard parts from various other classes.

Delivered new to the Rugby Portland Cement Co Ltd at its New Bilton Works, it worked there until it was withdrawn in 1966.

Bought by the Warwickshire Industrial Loco Preservation Group, No. 2047 arrived at Bridgnorth in October the following year. It was steamed for the first time there on December 21, 1968, when it shunted carriages at the south end of the station.

It was named *Warwickshire* in 1970.

The same group also bought former Manchester Ship Canal Hunslet 0-6-0T No. 686 of 1898 *The Lady Armaghdale*.

On the canal system, it was numbered 14 and named *St John* after a port in Canada. Sold to ICI Dyestuffs at Blackley Manchester in 1963, the year after it was withdrawn from traffic, it was renamed *The Lady Armaghdale* after the wife of a former company chairman and attractively repainted bright red.

It operated at the company's Blackley works near Manchester until rail traffic ceased there in 1968. Sold into preservation, it arrived on the Severn Valley in July 1969.

Neither would be large enough to haul lengthy passenger trains on a regular basis: indeed, *The Lady Armaghdale* has spent much of its SVR career doubling up as Thomas the Tank Engine.

Another 1967 arrival was GWR 0-6-0ST No. 813, the sole-surviving engine from the Port Talbot Railway & Docks Company. It arrived at Bridgnorth on November 25 after purchase from the National Coal Board.

The locomotive was built in 1901 by Hudswell Clarke and became PTR No. 26. It was taken into GWR stock in 1908 but not renumbered 813 until the Grouping in 1923.

In common with many non-standard 'absorbed' locomotives rendered redundant during the depression of the Twenties and early Thirties, No. 813 was withdrawn from GWR stock in 1934 but was sold for industrial service at Backworth Colliery in Northumberland, hauling mineral trains to and from the coal staithes on the River Tyne as well as on the internal system. Subsequent restoration to Twenties/Thirties condition, and full working order, proved to be a long and drawn-out exercise. Following static exhibition at the Rail 150 Exhibition at Shildon in 1975, a return to steam in 1976, and again in 1985, both proved to be short-lived following the emergence of serious mechanical problems. Full restoration to good working order was only achieved in 2000.

At the time of writing, the GWR 813 Preservation Fund is trying to raise the final £17,000 to complete its latest overhaul.

The 3F 'Jinty' 0-6-0T was to the LMS as the pannier tank was to the GWR and used as the company's standard shunting tank locomotive.

The SVR's example was built by Vulcan Foundry at Newton-le-Willows, Lancashire and entered service in October 1926 as No. 16466 allocated to Devons Road depot, at Bow in London, but in March 1928 was transferred from the capital to Liverpool Edge Hill. It was renumbered 7383 in July 1935.

In January 1966, as No. 47383 it was transferred to Newton Heath depot in Manchester and was withdrawn along with numerous examples of the class later that year.

British Rail then found that it needed extra shunting locomotives to work the NCB siding at Williamthorpe Colliery in Chesterfield. Under an ancient agreement. No. 47383 was reinstated to fill this requirement and allocated to Westhouses depot, where it was the spare engine for four other 'Jinties'. It lasted into 1967, two weeks before the end of steam at the mine, when it was withdrawn needing new boiler tubes.

In 1966, the Manchester Rail Travel Society was formed to organise railtours to raise funds to buy a 'Jinty', and helped by large donations from several enthusiasts, No. 47383 was bought as part of an Association of Railway Preservation Society 'package deal' in November 1966.

No. 47383 was taken by lorry on May 24-25, 1967, from Blackwell 'A' Winning Colliery to Bridgnorth. It was steamed for the first time in preservation on September 4, 1973, after which it was restored to BR livery.

A popular engine that has been hired to other heritage railways, at the time of writing it is out of ticket and displayed in the Engine House museum at Highley.

In those early days, the fledgling SVR also took delivery of

ABOVE: Manning Wardle 0-6-0ST No. 2047 of 1926 was brought to the Severn Valley by the Warwickshire Industrial Locomotive Preservation Group and first steamed on December 21, 1968. SVR ARCHIVES

privately owned Peckett W6 0-4-0ST No. 1738 of 1928, which gave rides on Bridgnorth's back loop during station open days in 1968. A veteran of Hams Hall Power Station where it was No. 4 in the fleet, it later moved on to the South Devon Railway and then the private standard-gauge line at Titley Junction near Kington on the Welsh border.

Another industrial engine around that time was the Worcester Locomotive Society's ex-Corby Stewarts and Lloyds ironstone quarry Kitson 0-6-0ST No. 5474 of 1934 No. 47 *Carnarvon*. It arrived in 1969 and spent the following winter on works trains and even hauled Santa Claus himself as he rode into Bridgnorth for Christmas 1969.

Its stay was fleeting, as it moved to Bulmers Railway Centre in Hereford in 1970. During the oil crisis of 1973, *Carnarvon* shunted trains of cider apples in place of the Bulmers diesels, and appeared on national TV. It moved on to the South Devon Railway in 1993 and is now a static exhibit at Totnes (Littlehempston) station.

RIGHT: Seen in ex-National Coal Board condition shortly after arrival at Bridgnorth, No. 813 was NCB No. 11 at Backworth Colliery before being acquired by the 813 Preservation Fund in November 1967. 813 COLLECTION

BELOW: In May 1967, LMS 3F 'Jinty' 0-6-0T No. 47383 became an early arrival on the Severn Valley, but did not steam for another six years. It is pictured at Bewdley in 1975. COLOUR-RAIL

ABOVE: Kitson 0-6-0ST No. 5474 of 1934 No. 47 *Carnarvon* shunts at Bridgnorth on a frosty morning on December 20, 1969. CR JENKINS

BOUGHT OUT OF BRITISH RAILWAYS SERVICE

However, a far more useful locomotive to arrive on the embryonic heritage line was Ivatt 4MT 2-6-0 No. 43106, nicknamed the 'Flying Pig' and a veteran of the Midland & Great Northern Joint Railway system.

The sole survivor of a class of 162, No. 43106 was built at Darlington in 1951.

The design was noted for its American looks – the running plates were positioned at a high level and a gap was left ahead of the cylinders. Because of this, some thought it to be the ugliest British locomotive ever produced, hence the nickname.

No. 43106 was the final member of the class in service, and was withdrawn from Lostock Hall shed at Preston just before Easter 1968. Sold privately, it was last steamed by British Rail on August 1 that year, and departed around 3.30pm with one member of its new owning consortium, now known as the Ivatt 4 Fund, on board. There was some degree of urgency as on August 4, British

Rail would bar the use of steam locomotives apart from those involved in the 'Fifteen Guinea Special' on August 11 and *Flying Scotsman*, for which an exemption had been granted.

It steamed to the Severn Valley Railway via a route chosen as to limit the movement under the wires of the newly electrified West Coast Main Line, running via Frodsham, Chester, Shrewsbury, Wolverhampton High Level, Pleck Junction and Stourbridge Junction. On August 2, it continued to Bridgnorth.

The Stanier 8F Locomotive Society started as the 8F Preservation Society at the end of British Rail main line steam in 1968, intending to preserve a member of the class and succeeded in saving No. 48773 (LMS No. 8233).

Built in 1940 by North British in Glasgow to serve the War Department during the Second World War, it is among an elite few locomotives that worked on six railways in three continents, and defying the scrap merchants at least six times.

Originally intended to serve in France, when that country fell to the Germans, No. 8233, then WD No. 307, joined sister locomotives on the LMS, spending a year on heavy wartime traffic from Toton, Holbeck and Westhouses depots.

By December 1941, LMS No. 8233 had been requisitioned by the WD and sent to Iran. It became No. 41.109 of the Iranian State Railways and headed supply trains to the USSR.

In 1944, it was converted to oil burning, and two years later was transferred overland to the Suez Canal Zone.

Loaned for two years to the Egyptian State Railways, it returned to the WD's Suez workshops in 1948, needing a new firebox. Coming within a whisker of being scrapped, it returned to the UK in 1952 for overhaul at Derby Works. Two years later it went to the Longmoor Military Railway as WD No. 500.

In 1957, it returned to the main line in British Railways service as No. 48773, based at Polmadie depot in Glasgow. There, it was withdrawn twice and reinstated twice.

Its last shed was Rose Grove in 1968, two years after receiving a heavy intermediate repair and overhauled boiler at Crewe Works. It headed the Locomotive Club of Great Britain's 'Farewell to Steam Special' on August 4 that year, and afterwards was bought by the 8F Society for preservation, being delivered in working order to the SVR, diesel hauled via Toton and Tyseley.

At the time, it was considered by preservationists to be in the best all-round condition of the available 8Fs, with just 36,000 miles on the clock since overhaul.

THE WAITING GAME

March 31, 1968, saw a party of senior BR officers taken on a journey from Bridgnorth to Bewdley and back behind No. 3205.

Santa specials, a hugely popular feature on both the Severn Valley and virtually every other heritage line in Britain, made their appearance at Bridgnorth in December 1968, with Santa Claus by steam train on the weekend before the bank holiday.

The complete closure of Highley Colliery on November 6, 1968 and Alveley Colliery in January 1969 left the Severn Valley line between there and Bewdley devoid of coal trains after March 1969 and therefore redundant. However, it was still in place, and could be used by the revivalists for stock movements. The withdrawal of British Rail from the branch was another step towards the revivalists taking over and being able to run their own trains.

However, in early in 1969, British Rail banned operations on the Bridgnorth to Hampton Loade line. Following the last standard gauge steam train operated by British Rail, the legendary 1T57 'Fifteen Guinea Special' from Liverpool via Manchester to Carlisle and back on August 11, 1968, a ban on the use of steam locomotives apart from LNER A3 Pacific No. 4472 *Flying Scotsman* was imposed. The Severn Valley line still belonged to British Rail, and so the ban prevented the Severn Valley running any of its trains in 1969, leading to a loss of valuable income for the revivalists.

At the same time, the railway leased Bewdley goods shed to allow a rolling stock restoration team to be formed locally. The revivalists also occupied Bridgnorth goods shed after paying British Rail another £2000.

The determination to reopen the line heightened and in April 1969, society

ABOVE: Collett 0-6-0 No. 3205 leaves Knowlesands Tunnel a mile south of Bridgnorth with a stock movement on February 25, 1968, with milk brake No. 1399 immediately behind. SVR ARCHIVES

membership broke through the 1500 barrier.

Members of the society's committee felt that the time was ready for it to merge with the company. At the annual general meeting on December 6, 1969, members voted in favour of the move and the society ceased to exist.

On January 5 the following year, it was announced that the first part of the British Railways Board (Severn Valley) Light Railway Order 1970 had been granted, empowering British Rail to work the line from Bridgnorth to milepost 1441/2 near Alveley as a light

railway, although it had no intention of doing so. Two days later, the company filed for its transfer order, while this new milepost in the rebirth of the line saw SVR membership rise from 1650 on February 1 to 1899 on April 21.

Also on January 5, British Rail withdrew passenger services from Bewdley to Kidderminster and Bewdley to Stourport and Hartlebury, paving the way for a southern extension of the heritage line's planned services at a future date. ●

LEFT: The dream rapidly taking shape: Keith Beddoes, the man who called the first meeting at the Coopers Arms, at Bridgnorth, with GWR railcar No. 22 in the background. SVR ARCHIVES

SEVERN VALLEY RAILWAY

WHITSUN STEAM GALA

BRIDGNORTH

MAY 24th, 25th & 26th, 1969
(SATURDAY, SUNDAY & MONDAY)

Open II a.m. to 7 p.m.

Refreshments — Cinema Coach

OTHER ATTRACTIONS

BRING THE WHOLE FAMILY

Chapter 6

We're open!

The railway makes its first tentative steps...

Major Peter Olver, one of the Ministry of Transport's railway inspectors, visited the new Severn Valley Railway on March 14, 1970, and told his superiors that he was very impressed by what he saw.

The Severn Valley Light Railway (Transfer Order) 1970 was made on May 20.

It was less than five years since that pivotal meeting in the Coopers Arms, and while the founding society members had started with little more than raw enthusiasm, they had moved an Everest.

Once the last piece of official permission had been given, there was no stopping them. Three days later, on Saturday, May 23, the first public passenger train pulled out of Bridgnorth.

Headed by GWR 0-6-0 No. 3205 and comprising six GWR coaches, it departed Bridgnorth for Hampton Loade at 2pm.

This first train was reserved for company members who had contributed financially or practically during the efforts to re-open the railway. Guests on board included the mayor of Bridgnorth, Coun Cyril J Andrew, who was

only three days into the job, as well as other local dignitaries.

In his speech, the mayor referred to the skill and determination shown by both professionals and amateurs alike in launching the project. An hourly public service was operated thereafter.

The weekend saw trains running crammed with people at hourly intervals from Bridgnorth, and returning at 35 minutes past each hour from Hampton Loade, on Saturday from 3pm until 7pm and on Sunday and the bank holiday Monday from 11am until 6pm.

Four steam locomotives were in service – the others being Stanier 8F No. 8233 (48773), Ivatt 2MT 2-6-0 No. 43106, Ivatt 2MT 2-6-0 No. 46443 and Hunslet 0-6-0T *The Lady Armaghdale*, along with GWR diesel railcar No. 22, which figured prominently in those early years.

Built in 1940, No. 22 entered service from Newport shed on September 18 that year. Accommodation was provided for passengers in two open saloons with a total of 48 seats, with driving cabs at each end. Allocated to several different sheds in its working life, in

its later days it worked around the Worcester area and frequently ventured on to the Severn Valley branch.

It was withdrawn from service in 1962 and stored at Swindon, from where it was bought by the Midland Group of the Great Western Society for preservation in 1967. It initially worked on the Severn Valley Railway, but was moved to Didcot Railway Centre in 1978.

No. 22 is one of only three GWR railcars to survive into preservation, and is currently the only operational example. Externally it has been almost completely repaneled.

The weekend after the opening, ordinary summer weekend services commenced, on Saturdays consisting of three steam trains each way, at 2pm, 4pm and 6pm from Bridgnorth, and on Sundays at these times and additionally at noon. The local press and the public at large were jubilant as five years of hard slog had finally delivered a resounding success.

However, the jobsworths in the corridors of power were not quite defeated yet. Although the Transfer Order had been granted, HM Stationery Office had delayed printing it. As the physical copy was not ready, the services

MAIN PICTUE BELOW: Not only was GWR 0-6-0 No. 3205 the first locomotive on the Severn Valley Railway, but it also hauled its first passenger train. It is seen departing from Bridgnorth with the 2pm to Hampton Loade on May 23, 1970, hauling the inaugural train, which included GWR Ocean Saloon No. 9113 *Prince of Wales*. Ivatt 2-6-0 No. 46443 is seen in platform 2, waiting with the 3pm service. ROBIN JONES

ABOVE: The same scene was recreated on a similarly murky May 23, 2000, for the 30th anniversary of the public opening day, with No. 3205 brought back to the line for the occasion. The name of the photographer is the same, but this time round it is the author, the founding editor of *Heritage Railway* magazine, not the same Robin Jones as in 1970. ROBIN JONES

SEVERN VALLEY RAILWAY
TIMETABLE 1970
Bridgnorth—Eardington—Hampton Loade

SATURDAYS (Until October 21st)					SUNDAYS & BANK HOLIDAYS			
BRIDGNORTH dep.	1400	1600	1800	1200	1400	1600	1800	
EARDINGTON dep.	1415	1615	1815	1215	1415	1615	1815	
*HAMPTON LOADE arr.	1425	1625	1825	1225	1425	1625	1825	

*Ferry Service Available.

HAMPTON LOADE dep.	1435	1635	1835	1235	1435	1635	1835
EARDINGTON dep.	1445	1645	1845	1245	1445	1645	1845
BRIDGNORTH arr.	1455	1655	1855	1255	1455	1655	1855

RETURN FARES   ADDITIONAL TRAINS WILL OPERATE AT BUSY PERIODS.

BRIDGNORTH — HAMPTON LOADE: ADULT 6/-   CHILDREN 3/- (under 14) 2nd Class
                                          " 9/-   " 5/- 1st Class

FREE CAR PARKING   ::   REFRESHMENTS

SPECIAL PARTIES CATERED FOR—RATES ON APPLICATION.

Whilst every effort will be made to maintain the above service, the Company do not guarantee that the trains will depart or arrive at the times stated and reserve the right to cancel, alter or suspend any train without notice and accept no liability for any loss, inconvenience or delay thereby caused. The Company accept no liability for any inaccuracy in the information contained herewith. All trains are steam hauled under normal circumstances.

Published for the SEVERN VALLEY RAILWAY CO. LTD.

Severn Valley Railway	Severn Valley Railway
DAY RETURN	**DAY RETURN**
Special Party Rate	Special Party Rate
TO	FROM
BRIDGNORTH	**BRIDGNORTH**
SECOND CLASS	SECOND CLASS
FARE 5/-	**FARE 5/-**
For conditions see over	For conditions see over

Williamson, Ticket Printer, Ashton

'BLACK FIVE' RENAMED
RAF BIGGIN HILL

The next major locomotive acquisition was that of LMS 'Black Five' 4-6-0 No. 45110. Built at Vulcan Foundry, Newton-le-Willows, Lancashire, it entered service at Crewe in May 1935. A month later it was allocated to Holyhead, from where for nearly 29 years it travelled over many parts of the LMS hauling passenger and freight trains, and during the Second World War, troop and ammunition trains.

During the war, it occasionally hauled trains to London when the larger express locomotives were not available. On one journey during 1940 it was machine-gunned and its train strafed between Wolverton and Bletchley, but it came through unscathed and carried on to its destination without stopping. No. 45110 was a favourite locomotive of driver, Jack Mills, who was coshed during the Great Train Robbery in 1964 and died several years later.

The locomotive's first association with the SVR came on April 20, 1968, it when it hauled the first of Manchester Rail Travel Society and Severn Valley Railway Society joint tours of the north-west of England.

On July 29, 1968, No. 45110 worked its last regular British Rail passenger train, from Preston to Windermere and return – tender first, because the Windermere turntable had been removed the previous day. On August 1, it worked its last freight, the 7.14pm Colne-Preston parcels.

However, it then took part in the haulage of the last standard gauge steam train on British Rail, the 'Fifteen Guinea Special' from Liverpool Lime Street to Carlisle and returned on August 11, 1968. No. 45110 took the train to Manchester, and later returned it to Liverpool.

Facing imminent scrapping, professional pilot and life-long railway enthusiast, David Porter, saw the final run. Principal of the Flairavia Flying Club at Biggin Hill civil airport, he had tried unsuccessfully to save Southern Railway Bulleid Battle of Britain Pacific No. 34057 *Biggin Hill*, and wanted another locomotive to carry that name.

He felt that No. 45110 fitted the bill, and bought it days before it was due to go to a scrapyard.

David formed the Stanier Black 5 Locomotive Preservation Society to act as custodians of the locomotive, and then visited several heritage lines to find the best home for it. The SVR was chosen because of its central location and at 5.15pm on August 20, 1970, No. 45110 arrived at Bridgnorth from Bewdley under its own steam, after being delivered from storage at Ashford depot in Kent.

Among the society's members until his death was none other than Jack Mills.

On Sunday, September 12, 1971, No. 45110 was officially renamed *RAF Biggin Hill*.

LEFT: Souvenir programme for the naming ceremony for 'Black Five' No. 45110 as *RAF Biggin Hill* on September 12, 1971. SVR ARCHIVES

ABOVE: The mayor of Bridgnorth, Coun Cyril J Andrew, flags off the first train on May 23, 1970, a service for invited guests and supporters. SVR ARCHIVES

scheduled for June 13-14 and 20-21 had to be suspended, although by then, around 3000 passengers had been carried.

There was more. The ministry wrote to the railway, stating that under a clause in the Transfer Order, it became effective only when the company had acquired all of the assets.

Accordingly, the agreed £25,000 purchase was paid to British Rail on June 24, the sale including the track as far south as Alveley. The Save the SVR Fund contributed £12,000, a bank overdraft of £3000 was raised, £1200 came from trading income and two members generously agreed loans of £4300 to make up the rest.

Viscount Cobham of Hagley Hall agreed to become the line's president in late 1970.

At the end of the first season of railway operations in 1970, 63,660 passenger journeys had been recorded between Bridgnorth and Hampton Loade, despite the late arrival of the LRO and start of operations one-third of the way through the scheduled season. ●

ABOVE: LMS 'Black Five' No. 45110 climbs the 1-in-100 gradient to Eardington in October 1971. BRIAN SHARPE

ABOVE: Ivatt 4MT 2-6-0 No. 43106 heads out of Bridgnorth on the first day of public services, May 23, 1970. SVR ARCHIVES

LEFT: Open to the public with steam making its presence felt: Bridgnorth station on May 25, 1970. SVR ARCHIVES

GOING SOUTH

Buoyed by phenomenal success in such a comparatively short time, the heritage line didn't intend resting on its laurels.

After British Rail's Kiddermister to Bewdley, Stourport-on-Severn and Hartlebury passenger services ended in January, 1970, the SVR told BR that it was not interested in buying the section of line from Bewdley to Stourport. The section was to be affected by road schemes, including the elimination of Stourport level crossing and the resulting lack of access to Stourport station.

Instead, the company decided to continue with plans to extend the SVR from Alveley to Bewdley and Foley Park, maintaining connection with the national network at Foley Park's British Sugar Company sidings, 1500 yards from the main line at Kidderminster Junction.

At a meeting with British Rail's estates department on October 15, 1970, it was reported that Worcestershire and Shropshire county councils were not interested in purchasing the railway land, both legally having the first option.

The redundant railway from milepost 144½ at Alveley to a point 200 yards east of Foley Park Halt, making a total of an extra 8½ miles, was offered to the SVR for £74,000.

On February 16, 1971, this sum was agreed with British Rail. However, this time the asking price was even further out of the company's reach.

To the rescue came the Conservative MP for South Worcestershire Sir Gerald Nabarro, whose vast experience in politics and business coupled with his wealthy contacts and a passion for railways made him appear to be the ideal knight in shining armour.

ABOVE: With driver, Jack Brennan, and fireman, Don Shadwell, on the footplate, Ivatt 4MT 2-6-0 No. 43106 makes a dramatic exit from Bridgnorth on July 26, 1970. SVR ARCHIVES

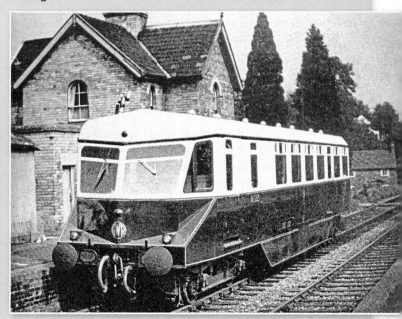

ABOVE: GWR railcar No. 22 at Hampton Loade with a morning shoppers' special to Bridgnorth in July 1970. SVR ARCHIVES

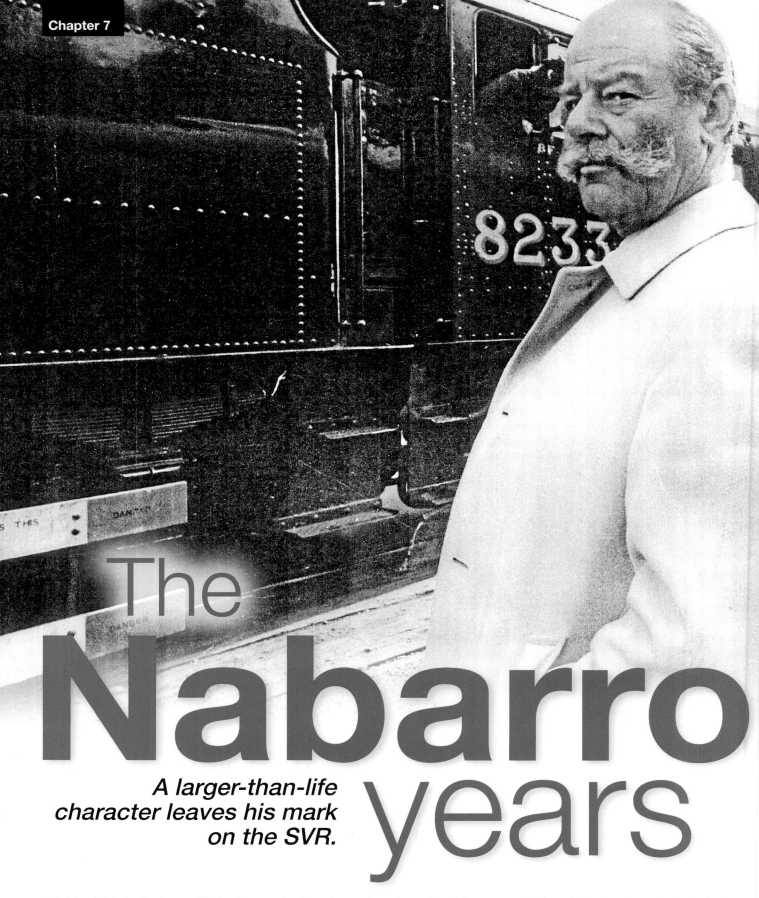

Chapter 7

The Nabarro years

A larger-than-life character leaves his mark on the SVR.

In May 1971, the flamboyant Sir Gerald Nabarro, a defining cartoon-character old-style Tory who was often parodied not only for his appearance and mannerisms but also for publicly expressed opinions that would today be considered extreme and wholly unacceptable, was elected to the Severn Valley Railway company board.

Plans were then announced for the existing company to be changed from a private company to a holdings company, which would be formed to purchase the section of line south of Alveley.

The existing company would then be wound up, with all the assets of the northern section vested in a 'members' association'. This move was agreed by the membership at an annual general meeting held at Bridgnorth that August.

However, in late 1971, it was found necessary to retain the original company, not only in order to hold the existing Light Railway Order, but also to obtain the further LRO for the planned southern extension. The LRO could not be transferred to another company.

Nabarro then formed a new company, Severn Valley Railway (Holdings) Ltd, with himself as chairman. This company became responsible for the policy and financial decisions affecting the whole railway, and specifically responsible for financing the purchase of the southern extension from Alveley to Foley Park.

LEFT: Sir Gerald Nabarro in 1973 alongside LMS Stanier 8F No. 8233. SVR ARCHIVES

ABOVE: Sir Gerald Nabarro on the footplate.

ABOVE: Sir Gerald leans out of a Severn Valley locomotive in 1971, leaving Bridgnorth station, which he would have sold off. SVR ARCHIVES

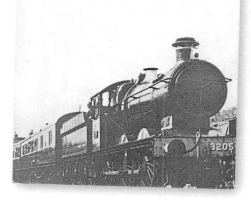

The holdings company had an authorised share capital of £150,000, and the initial share issue started on April 12, 1972.

Within 40 days, the £58,000 issue had been oversubscribed by 40%, and £24,000 had to be returned. The remaining £50,000 of the original capital was raised by a rights issue between July and December.

Lt Cdr Hugh Mossop was appointed as the first full-time general manager of the railway in July, 1971, a year in which passenger figures soared to 171,000, nearly three times that of the debut season.

During 1972-73, the railway pulled out all the stops to bring the southern extension up to passenger-carrying standard. Meanwhile, Stourport was not entirely forgotten, for the trackbed from Bewdley through Mount Pleasant Tunnel to Burlish Halt was bought for a bargain £100, just in case it might ever be needed.

The appointment of Nabarro was a big publicity boost for the railway. To the ordinary enthusiast, he was seen as a hero who was pioneering the rebuilding of the line. There is no doubt that he played a pivotal role in bringing in the vast amounts of money needed to further the extension plans.

A share issue was successfully launched to raise £110,000, including the purchase of the southern extension and much of the credit can be laid at Nabarro's door.

However, at the annual general meeting of the original company in November 1972, steps were taken to reduce the power of the holdings company following severe criticism of both it and its chairman. Matters came to a head when the line's full-time paid operating superintendent, Arthur Becker, and a large group of the line's volunteers disagreed with the actions and views of Nabarro.

Why? It had come to the attention of SVR officials that he had addressed public meetings and spoken about selling off Bridgnorth station for housing, truncating the line at Eardington Halt. That would not only free up capital but would also eliminate the need to contribute to the bypass bridge.

With some justification, Nabarro was accused of having no interest in the Shropshire side of the railway, and caring only for the length that ran through his former constituency.

The Daily Mail of March 12, 1973, carried a story headlined: 'Tyrant Nab must go say train fans'.

The report stated that 300 railway enthusiasts had called on Nabarro to quit as the railway's chairman, accusing him of arrogant and dictatorial behaviour in managing the line, and signing a petition to demand his resignation.

They also said that if he didn't go, they would resign en masse – and the SVR would not be able to start its new season on March 24.

SIR GERALD NABARRO – A BRIEF BIOGRAPHY

Born in London's Willesden Green on June 29, 1913, the son of an unsuccessful shopkeeper, he ran away to join the Merchant Navy aged 14.

Honourably discharged in 1937, he entered the timber supply industry, where he made his fortune. He also served in the Territorial Army from 1937, at the start of Second World War he was commissioned as an officer in the Royal Artillery.

You might never have suspected his humble beginnings, for he would pass in an instant as a typical Tory toff, with a Jimmy Edwards-style handlebar moustache and a Terry-Thomas accent. His personalised car numberplates NAB 1 to 8, were attached to his collection of cars, which included three Daimlers.

Two books about the heritage line, Severn Valley Steam and Steam Nostalgia, which were published under his name, were in reality ghost authored.

SVR officials recall visiting him at his home, Orchard House in Fish Hill, Broadway, and being ushered into his library. Perhaps uniquely in the preservation sector even to this day, every railway book had been bound in leather.

SVR officials recall that when he visited the railway, a policeman would arrive ahead of him to inform everyone that Sir Gerald was on his way.

Nabarro was governor of the University of Birmingham and convocation member at Aston University, president of the Road Passenger and Transport Association from 1951-55; the Merseyside area of the National Union of Manufacturers from 1956-62; the London branch of the Institute of Marketing from 1968-70; and the British Direct Mail Marketing Association during 1968-72.

At the 1945 general election, Nabarro stood as the Conservative candidate in the Labour-held West Bromwich constituency but failed to buck the national trend and win it. However, in the general election of 1950, Nabarro became MP for Kidderminster, holding the seat until 1964 when he retired on health grounds.

Given a clean bill of health, he was subsequently selected as Tory candidate for the adjacent constituency of South Worcestershire, and won the seat in the 1966 general election.

Nabarro married Joan Violet, elder daughter of Col Bernhardt Basil von Brumsey im Thuri, a British Army officer of German ancestry, on June 1, 1943.

He described himself as an old-style Tory: he opposed entry to the Common Market (now the European Union), pop music, pornography and drugs, and supported Enoch Powell during his infamous 'Rivers of Blood' anti-immigration speech made in Birmingham on April 20, 1968. Indeed, five years earlier, on April 5, 1963, he had appeared on the BBC's Any Questions? and asked: "How would you feel if your daughter wanted to marry a big buck n***** with the prospect of coffee-coloured grandchildren?" Understandably, those remarks were deleted from a repeat of the programme the following week.

Indeed, when I visited his hometown of Broadway on a family outing around 1970, I noticed that his surname was prominently daubed in graffiti on the railway bridge across Station Road, along with a swastika. Despite his early success with the SVR, clearly not everyone idolised him.

Nonetheless, Nabarro was knighted in 1963 for his public service. He claimed credit for the introduction of government health warnings on cigarette packets in 1971. Other legislation that he successfully sponsored during his career included the Clean Air

---

The volunteers said that Nabarro tried to open the new section of line against expert advice, spending £1500 on repainting Bewdley station in GWR colours even after a fairly recent British Rail repaint, and that he had sacked Arthur Becker after he defied Nabarro's order for him not to have direct contact with the Department of the Environment about railway safety.

Arthur Becker, who had since taken a new job as a lorry driver, while remaining as a voluntary SVR shedmaster, said: "I wrote to him saying I thought I should maintain this link, because I felt safety was of paramount importance. Sir Gerald saw this as a flagrant act of disobedience, and I was sacked."

The board of the original company supported the volunteers' concerns. However, at his home in Broadway, Worcestershire, Nabarro said he had dismissed Arthur with the unanimous consent of his colleagues on the holding company's board of directors.

Showing total disdain for the volunteers, he retorted: "They are volunteers and they have no standing at all.

"They can blather as long as they like about withdrawing their labour."

Events moved quickly. Nabarro was voted out as chairman at an extraordinary public meeting in May 1973, after it was found that he had broken the line's constitution by nominating two directors to the holdings company board. He resigned despite his bold assertions, and shortly afterwards quit the railway. Accordingly, the only strike ever to be threatened on the Severn Valley Railway never took place. ●

BELOW: LMS 2MT 2-6-0 No. 46443 shunts at Bewdley on January 8, 1972.
PW SOWDEN/SVR ARCHIVES

ABOVE: An official portrait of Sir Gerald Nabarro taken in 1971. SVR

Act (1956), the Thermal Insulation (Industrial Buildings) Act (1957) and the Oil Burners (Standards) Act (1960).

Outside railways, Nabarro became engulfed in controversy on the evening of May 21, 1971, when Daimler Sovereign NAB 1 was seen to swerve at speed the wrong way around a roundabout on the A36 from Southampton to Salisbury at Totton in Hampshire. Inside were Nabarro and his company secretary, Mrs Margaret Mason.

The police took him to be the driver after speaking to several witnesses – the MP was a well-known and recognisable public figure – and five months later charged him with dangerous driving, but Nabarro insisted that his secretary had been behind the wheel. She backed up his story.

A jury at Winchester Crown Court did not agree. Witness Keith Jones, an engineer from Birmingham, told the court that he recognised the driver immediately as being Sir Gerald Nabarro. "The car pulled out and overtook me, and finding difficulties with the oncoming traffic, pulled in sharply and braked, causing me to swerve and brake," he said. "There was a heavy lorry coming in the other direction," he added. "The car was tight into the roundabout and the lorry swerved to avoid it."

The jury found him guilty, and he was fined £250 by Mr Justice Bridge who described the incident as "a deliberate and outrageous piece of driving".

Accompanied by his private secretary Christine Holman, better known today as the media personality and author Christine Hamilton, he stood on the court steps and immediately announced his appeal, saying that his political career would continue "unabated and undiminished" despite the conviction.

On June 12, 1972, the Court of Appeal in London granted him leave to appeal against his conviction.

However, on the day he was due to appear in court his counsel revealed he was seriously ill in hospital and unlikely to be fit enough to attend his retrial for some time. Nabarro had suffered two strokes since the first trial and his health was said to be rapidly deteriorating. Three months later, the second trial began and four new witnesses appeared, claiming that they had seen a woman driving the car on the A36.

This time, he was found not guilty, leading to commentators of the day believing that the jury had delivered a verdict to spare him a perjury trial.

Outside on the court steps, Nabarro told the waiting media: "It underlines the simple point I made, that if a man can afford to pay he will secure justice. The man who cannot afford to pay will rarely secure it."

He vowed to return to Parliament despite being under intense stress because of the trials, but later decided to retire on the grounds of ill health. Three months after his acquittal, he died at his home, in Broadway on November 18, 1973.

As far as "his" railway was concerned, love him or hate him, the charismatic MP had a way of getting things done, and there is no doubt that his early efforts contributed greatly to the line we have today. However, had he not been reined in, the railway would have been left with a northern terminus of Hampton Loade and probably fewer volunteers. So 11 out of 10 to Sir Gerald for spearheading the extension of the line to Bewdley and Foley Park, but minus several million for planning to leave Bridgnorth bereft of steam and the Severn Valley a line from somewhere to nowhere.

Sir Gerald told: Quit as chairman or railway line will close

Birmingham Post Reporter

The Severn Valley Railway, which operated nearly 200,000 tourist trips last summer, will come to a halt before the new season begins unless Sir Gerald Nabarro, chairman of its two companies, resigns.

Volunteer workers, incensed at his attitude, sent an ultimatum to directors of Severn Valley Railway (Holdings) Ltd. last night calling for Sir Gerald's resignation.

If he does not relinquish the chair, the volunteers will withdraw their labour and the railway will not open for its summer season on March 24.

Sir Gerald, M P for South Worcestershire, said last night: "They are volunteers and they have no standing at all. They can blather as long as they like about withdrawing their labour."

The volunteers, who keep the railway running as the Severn Valley Railway Company, have been angered by the dismissal of Mr Arthur Becker as full-time superintendent of the line and have demanded his reinstatement.

'Respected'

Mr David Williams, a director of the Severn Valley Railway Company, the guarantee company, said last night: "Mr. Becker was highly respected as a very good man for the job."

Directors of the guarantee company board told fellow

'Tyrant' Nab must go say train fans

By KEITH COLLING

THREE HUNDRED amateur steam-train fans yesterday called on Sir Gerald Nabarro to resign as chairman of a tiny railway company.

They accused him of arrogant and dictatorial behaviour in bossing the Severn Valley Railway.

Strike

The enthusiasts, who turn out at weekends to run the railway, said that if he refused to resign they would go 'on strike.'

And that would mean that the four-engine, four-mile line near Bridgnorth, Shropshire, would not be ready for the new tourist season on March 24.

Sir Gerald, Tory MP for South Worcestershire, was invited to a meeting yesterday of the guarantee company

which organises to weekend railwaymen But he did not turn up.

The MP is chairman of both the guarantee company and the holding company which has raised more than £100,000 to run the railway.

The weekend volunteers say Sir Gerald:

Tried to open a new section of line against expert advice;

Spent £1,500 on repainting a station in the colours of the old Great Western Railway; and

UPSET members with his 'arrogant attitude.'

Last straw was when he sacked Mr Arthur Becker, £2,500-a-year full-time operations manager.

Mr Becker, of Ventnor Avenue, Hodge Hill, Birmingham, said he was sacked because he defied an order by Sir Gerald not to have direct contact with the Department

of Environment about railway safety.

'I wrote to him saying I thought I should maintain this link, because I felt safety was of paramount importance. Sir Gerald saw this as a flagrant act of disobedience, and I was sacked.'

'I suppose that of the 4,000 members of our society, about 400 are volunteers, who actively work on the line. More than 300 have signed the petition calling on Sir Gerald to resign.'

Consent

The resign call was supported yesterday by the board of the guarantee company.

At his home in Broadway, Worcestershire, Sir Gerald said he dismissed Mr Becker with the unanimous consent of the holding company's board of directors.

Mr Becker is now a lorry driver. But yesterday he was still working as a voluntary engine-shed master for the railway.

ABOVE: Sir Gerald Nabarro with his trademark NAB 1 numberplate. SVR ARCHIVES

ABOVE MIDDLE: Ever the English gentleman, or a caricature thereof: Sir Gerald Nabarro. SVR ARCHIVES

NAB in the cab

LEFT: Press coverage of the volunteers' rebellion that led to the ousting of Sir Gerald Nabarro from the railway.

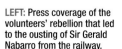

Chapter 8

Reopening to
Bewdley

By the end of the Seventies, the SVR was on track to become one of the best-supported heritage lines in the world.

Sir Gerald was gone, but another threat to Bridgnorth remained. At an extraordinary general meeting on May 18, 1973, members and shareholders voted overwhelmingly in favour of assuring the future of Bridgnorth by building a bypass bridge if necessary, and a fund was opened for the purpose.

Nabarro's fundraising prowess had made the extension of the line beyond Hampton

Loade a possibility if not a certainty, and that should never be taken away from him. However, during 1973, it became increasingly evident that the Light Railway Order for the extension would not be granted in time for services to commence that year, and also that engineering work could not meet the target.

Nevertheless, the restoration of Arley and Highley stations began, while Northwood

Halt was renovated by a group of children from Harry Cheshire High School as a project. At Bewdley, work on a new building and siding for a carriage paint shed began, along with a building for administrative and catering needs on the site of the cattle dock.

Two water tanks of GWR and LNWR design from Wednesbury and Wellington were erected at the planned new terminus, along with a loco inspection and maintenance pit.

BELOW: A great British achievement: Ivatt 2-6-0 No. 43106 heads the re-opening train from Bridgnorth to Bewdley through Arley on May 18, 1974. SVR ARCHIVES

In November 1973, the engineering firm of Rubery Owen offered the railway a loan of £150,000, to be converted to shares.

The railway was inspected by the Department of Environment in June 1973, and the Light Railway Orders for the southern section were finally granted on March 29, 1974.

The first public passenger train to Highley left Bridgnorth on Good Friday, 1974, hauled by WD 2-10-0 No. 600 *Gordon*.

Three trains ran at 45-minute intervals, crossing at Hampton Loade.

Yet the railway was still not ready. It was discovered in early 1974 that the deck of the rail-over road bridge at the south end of Highley needed complete replacement; Rubery Owen designed and built a much stronger deck within a few weeks.

Also, a major programme of scrub clearance south of Highley was needed in a hurry, and a professional team was employed. Major Olver revisited the line on May 16 and recommended to the Department of the Environment that the line should be opened to Bewdley.

Just two days later it happened.

A well-patronised diesel shoppers' service using railcar No. 22 formed the first train of the day at 9am from Bridgnorth to Bewdley and back. The shoppers' specials, offering half fare, had already proved a great attraction

for passengers travelling from Hampton Loade to Bridgnorth in the line's early years and were now extended to Bewdley.

Union flags bedecked the platform canopies, music for the occasion was provided by the Cleobury Mortimer Silver Band and in the distance a special peal of bells echoed from St Peter's Church.

Among the locals in the crowds at the station was 75-year-old Albert Jones who worked for 31 years as a relaying ganger on the Severn Valley branch. He recalled the days when the line from Arley to Highley won awards for the best-kept section of line in the district.

The first steam train left Bewdley behind GWR pannier No. 5764.

Over the loudspeaker came the announcement: "The train now standing

ABOVE: The first public train into Bewdley on May 18, 1974, comprised GWR railcar No. 22 running the 9am from Bridgnorth. D BEECH/SVR ARCHIVES

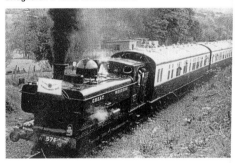

ABOVE: The first Severn Valley public steam train from Bewdley to Bridgnorth was headed by GWR 0-6-0 pannier No. 5764, carrying a 'Cheltenham Flyer' headboard, proclaiming that it as the world's fastest train! D BEECH/SVR ARCHIVES

on platform 2 is the 11.45 to Bridgnorth calling at Northwood Halt, Arley, Highley, Hampton Loade, Eardington Halt and Bridgnorth." The driver was Alan Garbett of Wolverhampton who, during the week, worked as a British Rail driver on the West Coast Main Line.

Travelling on that first train was Cheshire teacher, David Marchant, who had led the Northwood restoration parties. "The line up to Highley over the Victoria Bridge is by far the most scenic part of the route," he said.

After a short stop at Northwood, more than 80 villagers greeted the train's arrival at Arley, the first advertised-steam-hauled passenger train to call since the station first closed in 1963. The first public steam train from Bridgnorth to Bewdley was headed by No. 43106. ▶

BELOW: The Light Railway Order of 1974 empowered the Severn Valley Railway to run passenger trains to Bewdley. SVR ARCHIVES

STATUTORY INSTRUMENTS

1974 No. 643

TRANSPORT

The British Railways Board (Severn Valley) Light Railway (Transfer) Order 1974

Made - - - - 28th March 1974
Coming into Operation 29th March 1974

The Secretary of State for the Environment on the application of Severn Valley Railway (Holdings) Limited and in exercise of powers conferred by section 24 of the Light Railways Act 1896(a) as amended by the Light Railways Act 1912(b) and Part V of the Railways Act 1921(c) and now vested in him (d) and of all other powers enabling him in that behalf hereby makes the following Order:—

Citation and commencement

1. This Order shall come into operation on 29th March 1974 and may be cited as the British Railways Board (Severn Valley) Light Railway (Transfer) Order 1974.

Interpretation

2.—(1) In this Order unless the context otherwise requires the following expressions have the meanings hereby respectively assigned to them (that is to say):—

"the Board" means the British Railways Board;
"the Company" means Severn Valley Railway Company Limited;
"the Holdings Company" means Severn Valley Railway (Holdings) Limited;
"the principal Act" means the Light Railways Acts 1896 and 1912 as amended by the Railways Act 1921;
"the principal Order" means the British Railways Board (Severn Valley) Light Railway Order 1973(e);
"the railways" means the railways authorised by the principal Order to be worked as light railways under the principal Act.

(2) The Interpretation Act 1889(f) shall apply for the interpretation of this Order as it applies for the interpretation of an Act of Parliament.

(a) 1896 c. 48.   (b) 1912 c. 19.
(c) 1921 c. 55.   (d) S.I. 1970/1681 (1970 III, p. 5551).
(e) S.I. 1973/357.   (f) 1889 c. 63.

[DOE 17693]

ABOVE: A station just waiting for a train: Bewdley station was disused between 1970-74. COLOUR-RAIL

ABOVE: Highley station before its refurbishment by volunteers. COLOUR-RAIL

ABOVE: Arley station being renovated in 1973 ahead of the opening to Bewdley. SVR ARCHIVES

By 3pm, more than 160 people had bought tickets at Bewdley station and receipts were well in excess of £100.

The following week saw the start of a timetable featuring five trains between Bewdley and Bridgnorth on Saturday and Sunday and four every day during bank holiday week. Additional shuttle services were run between Bridgnorth and Hampton Loade, because the re-laying of the passing loop at Arley prevented the immediate introduction of a more intensive timetable. The loop was completed in 1976.

SANTA SPECIALS BEGIN

Today, Santa specials create a huge slice of the SVR's income, with seats for the November and December trips booked well in advance. Indeed, for many West Midlands families who are not 'ordinary' railway enthusiasts, a visit to Santa's grotto behind a steam train is part and parcel of the Christmas calendar.

The SVR did not invent Santa specials: they had their origin just before the dawn of the preservation movement, when the Fairbourne Railway near Barmouth began running a Christmas train for pupils at the village school in 1949.

The bodyshell of Lister locomotive *Gwril* would be removed and turned into a reindeer, while a moth-eaten stag's head from the Fairbourne Hotel was fixed to the front of the grille, and a bearskin rug used to cover the engine. Father Christmas rode on a flat truck suitably decorated for the occasion.

The Fairbourne's last Christmas special ran on the line in 1967, just before the school closed. However, its success had shown nascent heritage railways that vital money could be made outside the summer season; today they are big business.

Previously Santa Claus had appeared at Bridgnorth, and later, Hampton Loade, in the waiting room shelter. Now the line from Bewdley was open, a sackful of new opportunities arose. From December 1975 onwards, he has waited at Arley station while shuttles from Bewdley packed with happy families come to his grotto.

ABOVE: GWR 4-6-0 No. 7819 *Hinton Manor* passes Northwood Lane with a Santa special in December 1989. Today, Santa specials are a core part of the railway's business and a must-visit for families all over the West Midlands and beyond, with more than 30,000 passengers carried in the run-up to the festive season each year. COLOUR-RAIL

LOOKING BEYOND BEWDLEY

ABOVE: LMS 'Black Five' No. 45110 in adorned in patriotic colours for the Queen's Silver Jubilee celebrations on June 6, 1977. It is seen passing the West Midlands Safari Park en route to Foley Park. COLOUR-RAIL

Bridgnorth to Bewdley made for a magnificent journey, but the SVR was already looking beyond.

As stated earlier, the SVR had bought the trackbed of the northern part of the line to Stourport-on-Seven, even though it had no aspirations to run into the town.

However, in September 1975, track was relaid on this line in September to within 300 yards of Mount Pleasant Tunnel for the purposes of filming the The Seven Per Cent Solution, with a pastiche of a Sherlock Holmes story. The aim was to depict trains converging on two lines. Sadly, the track was lifted again shortly afterwards.

Kidderminster, however, was another story. The railway had bought the line from Bewdley to Foley Park, and on March 25, 1977, Major Olver gave the go-ahead for SVR trains to run there. They had to be in top-and-tail mode, with a locomotive at each end, as there was no run-round loop at Foley Park. Such trains were run at gala weekends and special events only.

At the same time, the railway became the starting point for main line steam specials, using its GWR set of coaches. In 1976, GWR 4-6-0 No. 6000 *King George V* and LMS Pacific No. 6201 *Princess Elizabeth* hauled this train. Destinations covered from Bridgnorth were Paddington, Plymouth, Kingswear, Chester and Pwllheli.

On May 5, 1979, the Monmouthshire Railway Society ran a special from Cardiff: it was the first through train from British Rail on to the heritage line.

Furthermore, on four Saturdays that August, British Rail ran an experimental DMU service between Birmingham New Street, Kidderminster and Bewdley. It proved so popular that it was repeated for the next four years, but residents' hopes that it would lead to a more permanent service, like the one that was withdrawn in 1970, were not to be realised.

In 1979 the railway received a prestigious award from the Association of Railway Preservation Societies for the most outstanding contribution to railway preservation.

By June, 1980, just past the 10th anniversary of the reopening, members of the railway had passed the 10,000 mark, making it one of the best-supported heritage lines anywhere in the world.

That anniversary was marked by a visit by the then chairman of British Rail, Sir Peter Parker.

In 1982, Highley was named Britain's best-preserved station.

BELOW: Flyer advertising the return of British Rail services to Bewdley. SVR ARCHIVES.

TRAVEL BY TRAIN TO THE SVR

Saturdays 11th July, 8th August, 12th September, also Bank Holiday Monday 31st August

THROUGH BR TRAINS TO BEWDLEY (SVR):-

From		dep.		
Birmingham New St.		10.00	11.00	12.00
Stourbridge Junc.		10.25	11.25	12.00
Kidderminster		10.50	11.50	12.50
Bewdley	Return	19.00	17.30	18.30

WHEN THROUGH TRAINS ARE NOT RUNNING, TRAVEL AS FOLLOWS:-
TO BRIDGNORTH — TRAVEL BY TRAIN TO WOLVERHAMPTON, THEN MIDLAND RED BUS No. 890 TO BRIDGNORTH (Wolverhampton Bus Station is adjacent to Wolverhampton BR Station).
TO BEWDLEY — TRAVEL BY TRAIN TO KIDDERMINSTER, THEN MIDLAND RED BUS No. X92 or X2 TO BEWDLEY. (Kidderminster Bus Departure Point is in Corporation St., 10 minutes walk from Kidderminster BR Station).

SEVERN VALLEY RAILWAY CO. LTD.

The Severn Valley Railway is pleased to announce the first ever special excursion train of Severn Valley Railway coaches on a

THROUGH TRAIN FROM

BRIDGNORTH

TO

PADDINGTON

ON

SATURDAY NOVEMBER 13th 1976

This is your opportunity to travel on the first Severn Valley Railway Passenger train into Kidderminster.

ABOVE: One of British Rail's DMU services from Birmingham New Street to Bewdley seen in 1981. COLOUR-RAIL

Chapter 9

The locomotive fleet expands

Bridgnorth shed sees a 'Big Bang' of steam locomotives in the Seventies.

The Severn Valley revivalists had made an excellent start on building up their locomotive fleet before the heritage line opened in 1970. While like so many other 'starter' outfits both then and now there was a fair collection of industrial types, yet from the outset there was a strong presence of main line types.

The Seventies marked the 'Big Bang' where the modest steam fleet rapidly expanded into the size it is today, for a variety of reasons. The Severn Valley was not the first standard gauge heritage line, but was still very much ahead of the game, and as the years passed since the end of steam on the national network, the supply of locomotives would inevitably dwindle rapidly.

This chapter looks at the many locomotives that arrived in that decade, most of them going on to enjoy an illustrious future either on the SVR or elsewhere.

RUSTING HULKS RESTORED

The first ex-main line locomotives to arrive on the Severn Valley had come straight out of British Railways' service. However, with the demise of steam in 1968, the availability of such locomotives would be rapidly curtailed by circumstance.

The standard fate of locomotives withdrawn from the national network was that they would be scrapped either at a railway works or privately, after being sold for their scrap value. There were many scrapyards around Britain that were eager to buy redundant locomotives and within days cut them up and make a substantial profit.

Among the scrapyards that bought engines from British Rail was Woodham Brothers of Barry Island in South Wales. It acquired its first redundant engines in 1959. At first, the scrapyard broke up locomotives within a few days of their arrival, but in 1965 proprietor Dai Woodham made a business decision, unique among the scrap dealers, to concentrate on the easier and more profitable task of scrapping redundant railway wagons, leaving his stock of locomotives for later.

This decision may have seemed like small beer at the time, but it had a profound and far-reaching impact on both the railway preservation movement and in turn, Britain's transport heritage.

When no more locomotives were available out of British Railways service, preservationists looked instead to the vast fleet of rusting hulks at Barry Island.

The first to be bought was Midland Railway 0-6-0 No. 43924, for the Keighley & Worth Valley Railway, in September 1968. It was followed by 212 steam locomotives bought for preservation purposes. The geographical position of Barry Island meant that the majority of its saved locomotives were of Great Western or Southern origin, or other types that had served in the areas they covered: this has led to an imbalance in the representation of the 'Big Four' companies in the heritage sector's steam fleet today, but underlines the importance of that decision made by Dai Woodham half a century ago, the same year as the SVR founders met in the Coopers Arms. In short, without Dai Woodham, today's preservation sector would be very different and much the poorer.

Many ex-Barry engines were to run on the SVR in the years that followed.

ABOVE: Rows of condemned rusting British Railways' locomotives stand in lines at Dai Woodham's scrapyard at Barry, and many of them would be given a second life in preservation. The Severn Valley was a significant beneficiary. FOTORUS

PRAIRIE TANKS BACK ON THE BRANCH

ABOVE: GWR prairie No. 5164 is thrown into silhouette as the sun dips down over Shropshire on December 10, 2011. SVR

Prairie tanks were part and parcel of the GWR rural scene for six decades, and ran on the Severn Valley branch from the 1920s until 1961.

Small prairie No. 4566 emerged from Swindon Works in October 1924 and was first allocated to Newton Abbot. Indeed, after service at several other sheds, No. 4566 was the last steam locomotive to be repaired at Newton Abbot 'factory', being ceremonially driven out of the repair shop by the local council chairman, himself a Western Region driver, on July 15, 1960.

Withdrawn from Plymouth Laira depot in September 1961, it was officially withdrawn the following April, having run 967,914 miles, and ending up at Barry in July 1962.

Looking for a 2-6-2T to preserve, in 1969, members of the future 4566 Group examined all small Prairies at Barry and No. 4566 was found to be in generally good condition. Bought by the group, it was moved from Barry to Bewdley by freight train on August 24-25 1970. Restored to operating condition at Bewdley shortly afterwards, No. 4566 steamed again in July 1975, just in time for the line's 10th anniversary. It is a regular and popular performer and has also visited other heritage lines.

Large prairie No. 5164 was built at Swindon in October 1930 and was first allocated to Tyseley. It remained in the Wolverhampton motive power district until August 1956 and was subsequently allocated at various times to Stafford Road, Wellington, Stratford-upon-Avon, Leamington Spa and Birkenhead. It was a regular on Birmingham Snow Hill local services.

No. 5164 was then based at Newton Abbot, and performing banking duties over Dainton and Rattery banks, as well as local passenger duties to Paignton, Kingswear and Exeter. It was condemned at Pontypool Road in April 1963, having clocked up 811,367 miles, and sold to Barry scrapyard in October 1963.

A scheme under the banner of the 5164 Group was set up to buy it in 1971, and carried out much preparatory work in Woodhams scrapyard before the purchase price was raised in mid-1972.

It arrived at Bewdley on January 6, 1973, along with *Hagley Hall*, *Hinton Manor* and large prairie No. 4141 (the restoration of which on the SVR had stalled by 1988 when it was sold on. It ran on the Llangollen Railway for many years before being bought by the Epping Ongar Railway).

No. 5164's overhaul included replacement of missing fittings and was carried out at Bewdley. It made its debut on the Santa services in December 1979. For years a regular performer, it is now waiting its turn in the restoration queue.

ABOVE: Restored GWR small prairie No. 4566 at Kidderminster Town on November 6, 2011. TONY HISGETT*

ABOVE: Large prairie No. 5164 catches the last of the evening light as it heads into Bewdley station on March 5, 2010. DUNCAN HARRIS*

ABOVE: BR Standard Pacific No. 70000 *Britannia* departs from Bewdley with the Bulmers' cider train Pullmans on September 10, 1978. BRIAN SHARPE

STANDARDS JOIN THE SEVERN VALLEY

Bereft of finance, postwar Britain did not follow the lead taken by countries such as the USA in eradicating steam in favour of diesel and electric. Such a step was inevitable, but British Railways played it safe in 1951, and Robert Riddles, Member of the Railway Executive for Mechanical and Electrical Engineering, oversaw the design and production of 12 new Standard classes, which would in the meantime replace types that had passed their sell-by dates.

The first of 999 Standard-class locomotives was built at Crewe in January 1951, Class 7 Pacific No. 70000 *Britannia*. At first allocated to the Eastern Region's Stratford depot, it made regular runs from Liverpool Street to Norwich including the Parkeston Quay boat trains attaining constant speeds of 90mph. In February 1952 its cab roof was painted white when it hauled King George VI's funeral train from Norfolk to London. In March 1963 *Britannia* was transferred to the London Midland Region working between Manchester, Carlisle, Glasgow and Perth, and was withdrawn in May 1966.

Britannia was earmarked for the National Collection of steam locomotives because of its historical significance, but owing to its prototype design and construction differences, sister No. 70013 *Oliver Cromwell* made the final list instead.

No. 70000 was bought by the Britannia Locomotive Company Ltd in 1969 and after a series of moves was relocated to the SVR

on April 11, 1971 for restoration for working order.

It was returned to steam in 1980, and rededicated by Riddles himself who was joined by five hostesses from Britannia Airways in a ceremony witnessed by more than 300 people.

Britannia entered SVR traffic, but owing to its axle weight of 20 tons, it was too heavy for the line at that time, and was transferred to the Nene Valley Railway in 1981. It worked there for several years, eventually being withdrawn from traffic with a defective firebox and tubes.

With the aid of a financial backer No. 70000 was moved to the former Steamtown museum at Carnforth, now the headquarters of West Coast Railways, to be fully overhauled to main line condition. That was completed in August 1991, and destinations visited by *Britannia* over the next six-and-a-half years included Carlisle, Liverpool, Holyhead, Swansea, Bristol, Exeter, Penzance, Eastleigh, Dover, Cambridge and Norwich. It was then withdrawn from service with its firebox, roof stays and some boiler platework down to minimum permissible thickness.

It was sold to Pete Waterman's Waterman Heritage Trust in 2000 and then to Jeremy Hosking's Royal Scot Locomotive and General Trust in 2006. It returned to steam in 2011, and is now a regular performer on the main line once more. In March 2015, it was back on the SVR as a star guest for the spring steam gala.

CHURCHWARD HEAVY FREIGHT

ABOVE: GWR 2-8-0 No. 2857 heads a GWR goods train towards Foley Park tunnel on May 22, 1988. BRIAN SHARPE

Built at Swindon in May 1918, Churchward heavy freight 2-8-0 No. 2857 was first allocated to Salisbury shed, but was soon transferred to Pontypool Road and Aberdare, before moving to Old Oak Common and then Newton Abbot.

Further moves were back to Aberdare and Pontypool Road, and stints at Cardiff and Plymouth. It spent most of the Fifties in the West Midlands, mainly at Banbury, hauling the heavy ironstone trains to South Wales, but was also based at Stourbridge, and is therefore a local engine to the SVR.

It returned to Pontypool Road for a third time in June 1958 and was withdrawn from Neath shed in April 1963.

It reached Barry in September 1963, and was to spend 12 years rusting in the salty Severnside air before leaving for the SVR in August 1975. It was bought by the 28XX Fund, now the 2857 Society, which had been launched by a group of Severn Valley Railway members in late 1971, when the price of a 28XX was £500. No. 2857 was selected as being in the best all-round condition out of the 14 class members still at Barry.

It was first steamed in preservation on September 9, 1979, minus cladding, and was one of five engines returned to steam that year on the SVR, earning the railway the 1979 award from the Association of Railway Preservation Societies.

Elsewhere, a very popular performer both on the SVR and the main line in preservation was BR Standard 4MT 2-6-4T No. 80079, built at Brighton Works in March 1954.

A veteran of the London Tilbury & Southend line, when that route was electrified it was transferred to Croes Newydd depot, Wrexham, and worked over the Cambrian system from Oswestry to Welshpool, Machynlleth, Aberystwyth and Pwllheli.

Withdrawn in July 1965, it went to Barry scrapyard, and in early 1971 a group of SVR members raised the money to buy it after finding it to be the best of the 14 class members there.

It was moved from Barry to Bridgnorth by rail behind Class 35 Hymek diesels on May 15, 1971. No. 80079 entered Severn Valley traffic on April 16, 1977, after a major overhaul by members of then owning group the Passenger Tank Fund.

It gained a main line certificate and participated in the Rocket 150 celebrations at Rainhill, before working several railtours and heralded the return of steam to the Central Wales line with a trip from Shrewsbury to Carmarthen on May 16, 1993.

Having extensively toured on the main line, its boiler ticket expired on May 12, 2002, after which it was cosmetically restored for static display, including a spell at the National Railway Museum's Locomotion outpost in Shildon from March 2005 to October 2006, and at the Warley Model Railway Exhibition at the NEC near Birmingham from December 2-3, 2006.

At the time of writing No. 80079 is on display in the Engine House museum at Highley, pending overhaul.

Swindon-built British Railways Standard 4MT 4-6-0 No. 75069, one of the last batch of the type to be built, was completed in September 1955 and fitted with a large-capacity tender, it was allocated to the Southern Region, where water troughs were not available.

Withdrawn from Eastleigh in September 1966, after just 11 years of service, it ended up in Barry scrapyard the following year.

In 1971, SVR members formed the 75069 Fund to buy it, and it was hauled by a diesel from Barry to Bewdley on March 31, 1973. Its rebuild at Bridgnorth began in July 1977, and was completed in August 1984. Having proved its worth in SVR traffic, it returned to the main line heading the 'Red Dragon' from Newport to Swindon on March 2, 1985.

At the time of writing, it was undergoing its latest overhaul at Bridgnorth.

RIGHT: BR Standard 4MT 2-6-4T No. 80079 and Pacific No. 70000 *Britannia* on the back road at Bridgnorth, awaiting restoration. Both arrived in 1971. SVR ARCHIVES

BELOW LEFT: BR Standard 4MT 4-6-0 No. 75069 passes Northwood with a Santa special. BRIAN SHARPE

BELOW: BR Standard 4MT 2-6-4T No. 80079 on shed at Bridgnorth.

Shortly afterwards No. 2857 worked its first passenger train on the line, but was later withdrawn with a cracked cylinder block. It re-entered traffic in 1985, and had the very rare honour of hauling a demonstration freight train on the main line through Newport that September as part of the GWR 150 celebrations.

It returned to steam following its latest overhaul in July 2011.

BELOW: GWR 2-8-0 No. 2857 works a goods train past East Usk yard at Newport during the GWR 150 celebrations on September 10, 1985. BRIAN SHARPE

CHARLES NEWTON'S MOGULS

Now based at the Great Central Railway, LMS 2-6-0 No. 46521, a member of the same class as No. 46443, emerged from Swindon Works in February 1953 and was first allocated to Oswestry. Spending most of its working life in Wales, it was withdrawn in October 1966.

Despatched to Barry early the following year, it was inspected by SVR member, Charles Newton, in early 1969 and found to be in good condition. He bought it, and it arrived at Bridgnorth on March 20, 1971.

It returned to traffic in July 1974 in the BR Brunswick green livery in which it ended its service first time round.

Returned to steam, it worked on the SVR as well as other heritage lines and the national network. In winter of 1994 it worked Kensington Olympia circular trains, and Paddington shuttles.

In 1995, No. 46521 was named *The National Trust* in honour of that organisation's centenary, and the following year starred in the BBC1 TV comedy series Oh! Doctor Beeching. It was then renamed *Blossom*, the name it carried in the series, at Kidderminster on February 17, 1997.

It steamed on the SVR until 2000. However, Charles Newton, who did not want to see the locomotive take several years to reach the head of the restoration queue again, agreed with the Loughborough Standard Locomotive Group to move it to the GCR.

There, No. 46521 moved under its own power for the first time again shortly before Christmas, 2011.

Another locomotive, which was first preserved by Charles Newton at the SVR but moved to the GCR, was BR Standard 2MT 2-6-0 No. 78019, representing an evolution of the design of the LMS 2-6-0. The type appeared in 1952, and was so similar to their Ivatt predecessors that the question was often asked whether it was worth the time and trouble in improving the design.

Built at Darlington in March, 1954, it was first allocated to Kirkby Stephen and worked on local and banking duties through the Lake District. Withdrawn from Crewe South in November 1966 and also bought by Charles Newton, it left Barry for the SVR in March 1973, and a start was made on restoration in 1980, but it never ran on the line.

Eventually, Charles made a deal with the Loughborough Standard Locomotive Group on the same lines as the later one involving No. 46521, which involved joint ownership.

In 1998, it moved to Loughborough for restoration to begin, and made its public debut in steam at the GCR summer gala in 2004.

BELOW: The Severn Valley is a line for all seasons, as seen in this quintessential snow scene at Northwood Lane, with Ivatt 2MT 2-6-0 No. 46521 passing through on December 12, 1981. COLOUR-RAIL

ROYAL TRAIN LOCOMOTIVE

GWR 4-6-0 No. 7819 *Hinton Manor* emerged from Swindon Works in 1939 as the last in the first series of this superbly versatile class, and was immediately allocated to Carmarthen. Its finest moment came when it hauled the Royal Train carrying the Queen to Pwllheli on August 10, 1963.

It was withdrawn from service in November 1965 and arrived at Barry scrapyard in early 1966, but was rescued by the Hinton Manor Fund, which was backed by the SVR company and arrived on the railway in 1973.

It entered traffic in late summer 1977. And during the GWR 150 celebrations in 1985, ran special trains on the main line. During summer 1987, it visited Aberystwyth and Pwllheli, working the 'Cardigan Bay Express' special service.

Since the mid-Nineties it has been in storage awaiting major repairs. It is currently on display at the McArthur Glen Swindon Designer Outlet, having replaced No. 4930 *Hagley Hall*.

ABOVE: GWR 4-6-0 No. 7819 *Hinton Manor* departs from Bridgnorth with a Great Western Society railtour of GWR stock on September 15, 1979. BRIAN SHARPE

LEFT: In GWR green livery, GWR 4-6-0 No. 7819 *Hinton Manor* crosses Bewdley South Viaduct on April 16, 1978. BRIAN SHARPE

SEVERN VALLEY PANNIERS

Not all ex-main line steam locomotives came either from main line service or Barry scrapyard. Some found their way to the Severn Valley after a second life in industry.

The Great Western Railway pannier tank needs little introduction. The basic 0-6-0 with distinctive oblong side tanks hung either side of the boiler like donkey panniers emerged from Swindon in several different versions over five decades as the design evolved from converted Victorian saddle tanks.

However, by far the biggest class was Charles Collett's 5700 class, of which a total of 863 examples were built between 1929-50, making it the largest class of tank engines and the second-biggest steam locomotive class in British railway history, apart from the LNWR DX Goods 0-6-0 tender locomotives of which 943 were built at Crewe between 1858-72.

Panniers were found right across the GWR system, hauling empty coaching stock in and out of Paddington, heading rural branch line services and marshalling coal trains in the South Wales coalfield. After Nationalisation, several found their way to other regions of British Railways, giving sterling service until the inevitable happened and they were ousted by diesels.

A SECOND LIFE IN THE VALLEYS

Some 57XXs lasted in National Coal Board ownership for several years after the end of British Railways steam.

No. 7714, which was built by Kerr Stuart of Stoke-on-Trent, entered service in April 1930 at Tyseley shed.

In January 1959, it was withdrawn a month later sold to the NCB for use at Penallta Colliery near Rhymney.

The Severn Valley Railway Association's Kidderminster branch decided to buy another pannier, in view of the popularity of No. 5764, and No. 7714 was moved by lorry to Bridgnorth on March 29, 1973.

Following an extensive and long-running rebuild, No. 7714 first steamed at Kidderminster on July 28, 1992.

RIGHT: GWR 57XX No. 7714 with a demonstration goods train stands at Bewdley. ROBIN JONES

ABOVE: Full circle: GWR 0-6-0PT No. 5786, which began its heritage-era career at the Severn Valley Railway, made a return visit to celebrate the line's 50th anniversary by starring in the March 20-22, 2015 spring steam gala. Back in London Transport livery as No. L92, it is seen rounding the curve by the West Midlands Safari Park towards Foley Park tunnel. ALAN WEAVER

LAST STEAM ON THE UNDERGROUND

Several panniers were sold off privately into industry, and 13 were bought by London Transport, to haul engineering trains on London Underground. Carrying maroon London Transport livery, these panniers outlived steam on British Rail by several years, the last Underground pannier coming out of service on June 6, 1971.

Built at Swindon in June 1929, No. 5764 was shedded at Old Oak Common throughout its main line career, until it was sold to London Transport in May 1960 and became L95. Used on night-time engineering trains on the Underground, it headed the system's 'rubbish train' to and from the refuse tip at Watford.

It continued in traffic until the last day of Underground steam haulage, when it was sold directly out of service to the Severn

Valley Railway after the line's Kidderminster branch set up a fund to acquire one of the three panniers still working for London Transport.

L95 was steamed on June 19, 1971, the day it arrived at Bridgnorth, being lit up before it had been removed from the low-loader on which it was delivered.

It was used in London Transport maroon livery during its first season on the Severn Valley, but was restored to GWR Brunswick green in 1972. It appeared several times in the 1976 BBC TV adaptation of Charles Dickens' short ghost story The Signalman.

At the time of writing, it is out of ticket awaiting overhaul. It currently carries the boiler from No. 3612 and sits on that locomotive's wheels.

So where then, is No. 3612? It is a rare example of a preserved locomotive that effectively ceased to exist.

Built at Swindon and outshopped in March 1939, it worked from various sheds in South Wales until withdrawn in October 1964 and ended up at Barry scrapyard the following March.

It stayed there until December 1978, when it was bought by the Severn Valley Railway. There was never any intention to restore it to running order: it was seen as a source of spares for the line's two other 57XX pannier tanks, Nos. 5764 and 7714.

No longer permanently on the SVR – but which returned to the line for its March 2015 spring 50th anniversary gala, was 1929-built No. 5786, another Valleys veteran. It was sold to London Transport on April 20, 1958 and became L92. Withdrawn from traffic on October 3, 1969 it was sold for £1100 in full working order to the Worcester Locomotive Society.

No. 5786 was taken by lorry to the SVR on October 4 that year, and was subsequently restored to GWR livery.

LEFT: London Transport pannier L92 (5786) arrived at the Severn Valley on October 4, 1969. SVR ARCHIVES

BELOW: GWR pannier No. 5764 departs from Bewdley with a three-coach service train en route to Kidderminster. BRIAN SHARPE

ABOVE: GWR 57XX No. 5764 picks up speed at Eardington on the Severn Valley Railway on September 25, 2009. RAY O'HARA

During May 1970 the locomotive travelled in steam to Tyseley for a festival of transport. While it returned to Bridgnorth, it never worked on the Severn Valley again.

Instead, it was moved by road to the former Bulmer Railway Centre at Hereford, a heritage railway venue set up by cidermaker HP Bulmer, and used for short passenger trips and for brake van rides.

The centre was closed in 1993 to make way for more space at the cider plant, and the owning group moved No. 5786 to the South

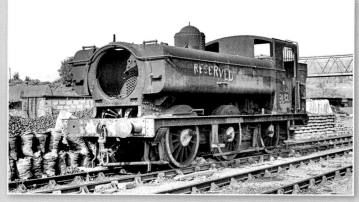

ABOVE: The Severn Valley's preserved pannier that wasn't – at least in its own right. GWR 57XX No. 3612 stands next to the coaling point in Barry scrapyard in 1978, the reserved tag on the tank suggesting it has a bright future in preservation. However, the SVR broke it up for spares to keep other panniers in service. JOHN WILTSHIRE

Devon Railway, where it has been based ever since.

It returned from its latest overhaul in March 2013, wearing London Transport maroon livery as L92 once again, to mark 150th anniversary of the opening of the first section of London Underground in 1863.

THE THREE PANNIERS THAT MADE ONE

The final manifestation of the Swindon pannier design was Frederick Hawksworth's 1500 series, of which only 10 were built, the first appearing in 1949.

No. 1501 was outshopped from Swindon on July 31 that year and was sent to Old Oak Common shed. It was used on carriage pilot duties.

It was withdrawn from Southall shed on January 31, 1961, and along with sisters No. 1502 and No. 1509, was sold to the National Coal Board. Repainted maroon, the three arrived at Coventry Colliery at Keresley in late 1961, for use both on the colliery internal system and its two-mile steeply graded connecting branch with the main line at Three Spires Junction.

Replaced by diesels, No. 1501 was the last in steam at Keresley, being taken out of traffic in September 1969.

All three were sold in 1970 to a group of SVR members who wanted to preserve an example of the class. Sadly, the purchase price was too big an ask. They had to buy all three just to get one, and the purchase was made possible only by keeping the best of the trio and selling the other two on to a scrapyard.

Today, the situation would be unthinkable. No UK preservationist would dream of scrapping a main line steam locomotive, no matter how bad its condition. However, back then, the vast majority of locomotives yet to be saved from Barry scrapyard were still there, and few thought that they might one day all be sold into preservation.

Nos. 1502 and 1509 were used as sources of spares for the restoration of No. 1501, which arrived at Bridgnorth on November 7, 1970, moved there by rail via Tyseley. Some of the parts

found their way to Didcot Railway Centre, where, because of Churchward's policy of interchangeable components, they were used in the restoration of GWR 4-6-0 No. 5900 *Hinderton Hall*. The remains of No. 1502 and 1509 were scrapped at the Cashmore yard in Great Bridge in October 1970.

No. 1501 resteamed on May 29, 1997, following a rebuild that lasted nearly three decades. Its most recent overhaul was completed in 2012.

ABOVE: WR 0-6-0PT No. 1501 in lined British Railways' black livery in action on March 23, 2013. TONY HISGETT*

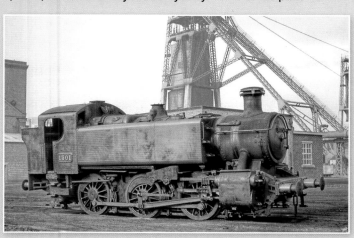

ABOVE: Carrying red National Coal Board livery during its days at Coventry Colliery is 15XX pannier No. 1501, photographed on March 5 1967. JOHN WILTSHIRE

ABOVE: Seen at Coventry Colliery is No. 1509, one of three 15XX panniers bought by Severn Valley Railway revivalists, who back in the early Seventies had to sell two, including this one, on for scrap to finance the purchase. That would be unthinkable today. DAVID WILLIAMS

ABOVE: WD Austerity 2-10-0 No. 600 *Gordon* crosses the Victoria Bridge over the River Severn. BRIAN SHARPE

GORDON ARRIVES

A popular arrival on the line was North British-built War Department Austerity 2-10-0 No. 600 *Gordon*.

Only the second engine to emerge from a class that eventually numbered 150 engines, a distinctive feature of the class is that the middle driving wheels have no flange, to ease turning on tighter tracks.

Named in honour of the Royal Engineers' most famous general, Charles Gordon (Gordon of Khartoum), after the war it was used on the LMR, which itself provided a Sixties bolthole for preservationists.

The last steam locomotive owned by the British Army, it featured in public steam events at Longmoor, the last being on July 5, 1969. It also hauled at least one enthusiast tour, along the main line from Woking to Longmoor.

However, when a bid to preserve part of the LMR failed, the Transport Trust was asked by the Army to find it a suitable home. It duly arrived on the Severn Valley Railway in 1972 and entered traffic from July 29 that year. At the time, it was the biggest locomotive to have run on the heritage line.

Fully restored at Bridgnorth Works, in May 1980 it took part in the Locomotive Parade at Rocket 150, the 150th anniversary of the opening of the Liverpool and Manchester Railway at Rainhill. On the SVR, *Gordon* has also served as Gordon the Big Engine during the SVR's Days Out With Thomas events.

On July 25, 2008, *Gordon* was formally handed over by the Army to the SVR, which had been looking after it in a caretaker capacity. At the time of writing, it is awaiting overhaul, and displayed in the Engine House museum at Highley.

ABOVE: Walsall station in January 1972, with Ivatt 2-6-0 No. 43106 and WD 2-10-0 No. 600 *Gordon* on their way to the Severn Valley Railway. SVR ARCHIVES

CONTINENTAL STEAM'S BRIEF SHROPSHIRE FLING

Arguably the most unusual steam locomotive to ever run on the Severn Valley Railway was a German 2-6-2 tank engine.

The Class 64s were built from 1928-40 and were used on branch lines and light suburban passenger work all over Germany. After the war, the Class 64s were spread out across Europe with examples serving in Austria, Poland, Czechoslovakia and the Soviet Union.

ABOVE: Krupps Class 64 2-6-2T No. 064 305-6 at Bridgnorth. COLOUR-RAIL

In May 1974, the German 064 Klasse Fund, set up to buy such a locomotive for use on the SVR, bought No. 064 305-6, built by Krupps in 1934, from Weiden depot, 30 miles from the Czechoslovakian border.

However, it then found itself shortly of money to pay for it to be delivered to Bridgnorth, so it was stored at Stolberg depot near Aachen, where the shed staff kindly remetalled the motion parts and replaced all worn or damaged fittings before repainting it.

Eventually, the money was raised for the journey to Britain. It arrived at Bridgnorth on July 17, having cost £29,800 to buy and £3900 to transport.

Why a locomotive that was built to the larger Berne loading gauge was ever considered for the Severn Valley is beyond me. It made one run out of Bridgnorth, to Eardington Halt, where it was stopped halfway along the platform, after it was realised that clearances were getting a little too close for comfort. Otherwise, it spent most of its time in steam shunting at Bridgnorth.

While it could not run on the SVR, the Nene Valley Railway at Peterborough was an entirely different matter, as locomotives and stock built to the wider continental loading gauge can run there.

It 1977 it was purchased by Richard Hurlock and taken to the Nene Valley that August. Sold to the Nene Valley in 1985, it was taken out of traffic two years later. While in storage, its air pump was loaned to LNER A3 Pacific No. 4472 *Flying Scotsman* in preparation for working air-braked stock during its tour of Australia in 1989-90. That is the locomotive's finest contribution to preservation to date.

No. 064 305-6 is still in storage at Wansford awaiting a major overhaul.

HAGLEY HALL – THE FLAGSHIP

ABOVE: GWR 4-6-0 No. 4930 *Hagley Hall* heads the 'Severn Valley Limited' towards Foley Park tunnel.

ABOVE: Four locomotives from Barry scrapyard arrived at Bewdley on January 6, 1973. They were GWR 4-6-0 No. 4930 *Hagley Hall*, prairies Nos. 5164 and 4141 and 4-6-0 No. 7819 *Hinton Manor*. SVR ARCHIVES

Considered by many to be a flagship locomotive for the SVR, GWR 4-6-0 No. 4930 *Hagley Hall* emerged from Swindon in May 1929 and first allocated to Wolverhampton Stafford Road shed.

During its career it was allocated to Oxley, Chester, Bristol St Philip's Marsh, Stafford Rd, Weymouth, Chester, Tyseley, Leamington, Tyseley, Bristol Bath Road, Westbury, Taunton, Exeter, Old Oak Common and Swindon.

Withdrawn from service in December 1963, having run 1,295,236 miles, it arrived at Barry scrapyard in April 1964. Bought by the SVR holdings company in June 1972, it was brought by rail to Bewdley dead on January 6, 1973.

Its restoration began at Bewdley and was stepped up at Bridgnorth after it moved there in 1978.

Hagley Hall made its passenger debut on September 22, 1979, when it double-headed LMS 'Black Five' No. 5000 on the main line with an enthusiast special. The following day, it entered SVR traffic on a regular basis as well as making occasional forays on the national network, including events in 1985 to mark the 150th anniversary of the GWR.

It was withdrawn from SVR traffic in 1986 and stored pending overhaul. In 1999 it was loaned to the Macarthur Glen shopping centre, which had been set up in part of the former Swindon Works, and became a static exhibit. In June 2007 it was returned to the SVR; where its overhaul is, at the time of writing, at an advanced stage.

TO THE MANORS BORN

GWR 4-6-0 No. 7802 *Bradley Manor* was built at Swindon Works in January 1938 and first allocated to Old Oak Common. In August 1964, Shrewsbury became its last depot.

It was a regular performer on the 'Cambrian Coast Express' and headed the Stephenson Locomotive Society's farewell train over the Welshpool to Whitchurch line on January 17, 1965.

Withdrawn in November 1965, it arrived at Barry scrapyard in July 1966.

The Erlestoke Manor Fund bought No. 7802 initally as a source of spare parts, and in November 1979 it was towed from Barry to Bewdley. However, offers of spare parts were forthcoming, and it was eventually decided to return No. 7802 in its own right.

It steamed again on April 5, 1993, and it has since worked both on the SVR and the main line. At the time of writing it is undergoing an overhaul at Tyseley Locomotive Works.

GWR 4-6-0 No. 7812 *Erlestoke Manor* itself emerged from Swindon Works in January 1939 and was first shedded at Bristol Bath Road depot. It served at several West Country sheds until the Western Region's early dieselisation saw it transferred to the Cambrian section in 1960. Withdrawn from Shrewsbury in November 1965, it arrived at Barry scrapyard the following June.

A group of Gloucestershire enthusiasts under the banner of the Erlestoke Manor Fund bought the engine in June 1973 and took it to the now-closed preservation centre at Ashchurch near Tewkesbury in May 1974. It was moved to Bewdley on April 23, 1976. There, it was restored to working order, and steamed again in September 1979. It headed several main line tours in the North West in 1984, bowing out of traffic for overhaul in 1985.

It returned to Swindon Works in 1990. Part of Brunel's great works was then occupied by the Swindon Heritage Trust which undertook some repair work. However, fund members decided to complete the overhaul on the SVR and brought it back in 1998.

Eventually, the overhaul was completed in 2008. On March 20, No. 7812 made its comeback by hauling a VIP special, over the full length of line from Bridgnorth to Kidderminster; the first train since the railway was badly affected by the freak flooding in the summer of 2007.

ABOVE: GWR 4-6-0 No. 7802 *Bradley Manor* crosses Victoria Bridge. MIGHTY SHREW

ABOVE: GWR 4-6-0 Nos. 7812 *Erlestoke Manor* and No. 7802 Bradley Manor double-head a special train on September 25, 2009. SVR

DOCKYARD BARCLAY

Another industrial locomotive in the form of Barclay 0-4-0ST No. 2220 of 1946 *Invicta* spent three years on the SVR in the early Seventies.

Supplied new to Chatham Dockyard, it became No. 417 in its fleet. Withdrawn from service, it was sold to the Invicta Locomotive Preservation Society in 1972.

On June 30 that year, it arrived at Bridgnorth. Steamed on arrival, it recorded four miles in use during 1972, but no further mileage was recorded before the locomotive left in spring 1975 for the Chasewater Railway.

It then went into storage at the MoD Royal Engineers depot at Long Marston. In late 2009, the locomotive returned to Chatham Dockyard for restoration to working order.

ABOVE: Hunslet Austerity WD No. 193 at Bridgnorth in 1977. COLOUR-RAIL

HUNSLET AUSTERITY WD NO.193

A locomotive with a Shropshire pedigree arrived on the SVR in 1971 in the form of Hunslet Austerity 0-6-0ST No. 3793 of 1953, supplied new to the War Department where it became No. 193.

By 1955 it was based on the Shropshire & Montgomeryshire Light Railway based at Kinnerley.

On March 20, 1960, it hauled a Stephenson Locomotive Society train over the line.

In the Sixties, it was kept in store at the MoD Royal Engineers' depot at Long Marston, and was then bought by the SVR, arriving on August 7. It was named *Shropshire* in 1977 and repainted in crimson lake livery.

It went on loan to the Bulmers Railway Centre at Hereford on January 30, 1981, and was then sold privately, first being taken to the former Peak Rail base at Buxton. It then visited several heritage lines including the now-closed Steamport Museum at Southport where it ran shuttles, and is now part of the Ribble Steam Railway collection at Preston Docks.

ABOVE: Barclay 0-4-0ST *Invicta*, which barely steamed on the SVR, and BR Standard 2MT 2-6-0 No. 78019 that never steamed there at all, on the back road at Bridgnorth. AMANDA HAMBIDGE

'BLACK FIVE' FROM THE NATIONAL COLLECTION

In 1977, the SVR took delivery of LMS Stanier 'Black Five' No. 5000 on loan from the National Railway Museum.

Built at Crewe in 1935, it was numerically the first of its class. However, it was not the first 'Black Five' to be built: Vulcan Foundry had turned out the first of its order, No. 5020, the year before. No. 5000 also ceased to be the first numerically when No. 4800 was built in 1944: the LMS had run out of available numbers after No. 5499 was built.

Withdrawn from Lostock Hall shed near Preston in 1967, No. 45000, its post-Nationalisation number, was chosen to represent the 842-strong class as part of the National Collection, because it had a domeless boiler and was broadly in as-built condition. It was repainted in its original LMS lined black livery, despite modifications that had been made during its years in traffic.

Returned to steam on the SVR, it also ran on the main line once more. One trip, on September 2, 1979, saw it double-head with *Hagley Hall* from Hereford to Chester, in what was No. 4930's comeback to the national network following restoration.

It left the SVR in 1988, and is now a static exhibit in the Locomotion museum at Shildon.

BELOW: LMS 'Black Five' 4-6-0 No. 5000 arrives at Arley on April 12, 1987 and passes LMS Jubilee 4-6-0 No. 5690 *Leander*. BRIAN SHARPE

A MODIFIED HALL BACK ON THE MAIN LINE

Designed to fulfil the wartime need for extra mixed-traffic locomotives, GWR chief mechanical engineer Frederick Hawksworth's Modified Halls were exactly that, a modification of his predecessor Charles Collett's Hall class 4-6-0s.

Built at Swindon in March 1944, because of the wartime restrictions on the use of brass, No. 6960 did not carry the name *Raveningham Hall* until June 1947 when plates could be made again. First shedded at Old Oak Common, it worked a variety of trains to most parts of the Swindon empire system, including the Paddington to Weymouth Channel Islands boat trains. By 1953 it was based at Reading where, in addition to taking the semi-fast and stopping commuter trains up to London, it often ran as far north as Chester with the Margate to Birkenhead through services and even appeared on the 'Torbay Express' in summer 1954.

In August 1963, *Raveningham Hall* was transferred to Oxford where its duties included the services to Paddington, Wolverhampton and Gloucester, as well as taking over the York to Bournemouth through train at Oxford.

Withdrawn in June 1964, it reached Barry the following month.

In late 1972, it was bought by the directors of the Steamtown museum at Carnforth and following a complete overhaul was one of the few GWR representatives in the 1975 Rail 150 cavalcade held at Shildon.

Restored in 1975, by then it was based at the SVR where it ran with *Hagley Hall's* tender while its own went behind No. 4930.

Extensively having worked on the SVR, it also made regular main line outings including the GWR 150 specials between Swansea and Carmarthen in the late summer of 1985.

It left the SVR in 1996. Bought by multi-millionaire enthusiast Jeremy Hosking in 2008 in was taken to Bill Parker's Flour Mill workshops at Bream in the Forest of Dean for a complete overhaul. It is now running on the West Somerset Railway.

ABOVE: WR Modified Hall 4-6-0 No. 6960 *Raveningham Hall* crosses Victoria Bridge. BRIAN SHARPE

ANOTHER TREVITHICK PRODUCT IN BRIDGNORTH!

Towed to Bewdley by a Class 47 diesel, LNWR 2-2-2 No. 3020 *Cornwall* arrived on loan from the National Railway Museum on August 16, 1979 with the intention of being restored to working order.

There was an historic connection with Bridgnorth: *Cornwall* was designed by Francis Trevithick, whose father Richard built his *Catch Me Who Can*, the world's first passenger-carrying railway locomotive, at Bridgnorth's Hazeline Foundry in 1808 to *Cornwall*, was named after the family's home county.

In its day, *Cornwall* was cutting-edge technology as far as fast passenger travel was concerned.

However, the boiler barrel was found to be too thin for it to be steamed – the boiler inspector's hammer went straight through the bottom – and it returned unrestored to York on September 6, 1982, only three years into a five-year loan period. It is now on static display at the Locomotion museum in Shildon but thought unlikely to ever be steamed again.

ABOVE: LNWR 2-2-2 No. 3020 *Cornwall* AT Bridgnorth on September 10, 1981. COLOUR-RAIL

Chapter 10

Into the Eighties

Bypass bridge built and Kidderminster Town opens.

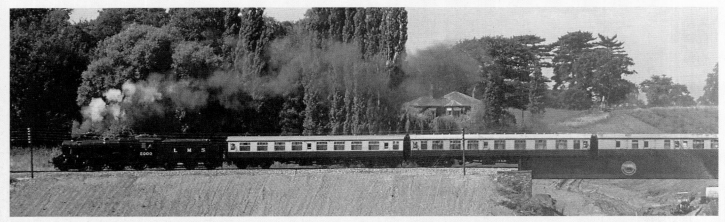

ABOVE: LMS 'Black Five' No. 5000 heads a passenger train across the Bridgnorth bypass bridge before the road was opened. SVR ARCHIVES

The Bridgnorth bypass scheme reared its ugly head again in the summer of 1980. However, by now the scheme had been revised, with the width of the road halved, resulting in a 50% reduction in the cost of the bridge.

The railway could therefore cover its contribution from the holdings company's overdraft facility, but times had changed over the past decade. The SVR was now established as a major tourist attraction, and the county council could not exert the same sort of pressure as it did in 1969.

Under a fresh agreement with the local authority made in January 1982, the railway ended up contributing only 30% of the cost.

On October 31 that year, SVR volunteers lifted the track in readiness for contractor EE Jeavons to begin work. During the wettest October for 20 years, around 2000 cu m of earth was shifted.

Two girders weighing 18 tons each were lifted into position by the railway's 30-ton steam cranes.

The railway bridge, which involved around 40 tons of steelwork, was completed on March 5, 1983 at a cost of £104,981.

A nightmare that had dogged the railway for 15 years was now over. It could breathe again.

However, all was not as it seemed. On April 30, Southern Railway N15 King Arthur 4-6-0 No. 777 *Sir Lamiel*, which was briefly on loan

from the National Collection, had just made a return trip from Bridgnorth to Bewdley when the embankment south of the bridge collapsed.

Bob Massey was driving *Gordon* at the time and reported sensing that it wobbled as it approached the bridge.

Officials set out to inspect the embankment, and to their horror found it falling down, leaving the rails suspended in mid-air.

The problem was that the Highley road below the railway had been lowered so it could pass beneath the bypass, and the embankment on the Severn side was left unsupported. Left sodden by the autumn rain, it gave way.

The county council immediately effected repairs, and because the slippage was down

BELOW: GWR 4-6-0 No. 4930 Hagley Hall prepares to haul the 'Kidderminster Venturer' out of the basic platforms of the incomplete Kidderminster Town station on July 30, 1984. DAVID WILLIAMS

ABOVE: The Bridgnorth bypass bridge under construction. SVR ARCHIVES

ABOVE: The construction of the Bewdley bypass in 1986-87. SVR ARCHIVES

ABOVE: BR Standard 9F 2-10-0 No. 92220 *Evening Star* threads its way through Eymore Wood just south of Victoria Bridge with a Bewdley to Hampton Loade service on May 13, 1983, while Bridgnorth was cut off from the rest of the line by the bypass bridge embankment slippage. HUGH BALLANTYNE

to the road works, the railway was not held to be liable for the bill. Trains north of Hampton Loade were suspended during the repair work, but resumed on May 18. The first train over it was the last steam locomotive built by British Railways, Standard 9F 2-10-10 No. 92220 *Evening Star*, which was also visiting on loan from the National Collection.

So, the railway had a narrow escape; the consequences of the slippage could have been far worse. Nonetheless, heavy rain and a landslip would return one day to haunt the SVR.

The bypass was eventually opened in 1985. A bridge was also required south of Bewdley when the proposed A456 bypass for that town was built in 1987. However,

in this instance the fact that the railway was operating meant that the local authority had to foot the bill.

LEANDER ARRIVES – TWICE

The Severn Valley once owned one of the most popular steam locomotives currently on the main line.

LMS Jubilee class 4-6-0 No. 45690 (5690) *Leander* was resident on the line between 1980-81 and 1983-94.

Leander was built in 1936 at Crewe and was shedded at Crewe North depot until 1947, when it was transferred to Bristol (Barrow Road). It was withdrawn in March 1964 having recorded 1,589,826 miles in service.

In July, it was sent to Barry scrapyard, where it remained until July 1972 when it was bought by Brian Oliver and restored by the Leander Locomotive Society at Derby later becoming a resident at the now-closed Dinting Railway Museum in Glossop.

It arrived at the SVR August 1980 for a boiler repair and overhaul to main line standard, and left in late 1981. During its first stay on the line, good relationships were established between the owning group and SVR staff, so much so that when the engine was offered for sale in November 1983, it was bought by the SVR holdings company.

That purchase also included sister engine No. 45699 *Galatea*, another Barry wreck that had been bought as a source of spares for *Leander*, with Ivatt 2MT No. 46443 originally offered in part exchange.

When the sale went through, *Leander* was busy on main line duties, and returned to the SVR on February 20, 1984 working there until the winter of 1989, when it was withdrawn for a major overhaul.

Five years later, the SVR holdings board announced that it had been sold to the late Morecambe GP and locomotive saviour Dr Peter Beet, because funds were not available for a general repair. The decision prompted an angry reaction from some SVR members.

Leander was restored to running order on the East Lancashire Railway and painted in LMS crimson lake livery. It returned to the SVR for the line's 40th anniversary autumn steam gala in 2010. Owned by Dr Beet's son, Chris, it is still very much active on the main line, as is *Galatea*, which was rebuilt in its own right by West Coast Railways at Carnforth.

ABOVE: LMS Jubilee 4-6-0 No. 5690 *Leander* crosses the Victoria Bridge over the River Severn on June 12, 1988. BRIAN SHARPE

ABOVE: LMS Jubilee 4-6-0 No. 5690 *Leander* departs from Bridgnorth on October 7, 1984 and crosses the new bridge over the town's bypass which was then under construction. BRIAN SHARPE

STEAMING BACK INTO KIDDERMINSTER

When the British Sugar Corporation sidings at Foley Park fell into disuse on January 22, 1982 the one-and-a-half mile section of line through to Kidderminster Junction became available.

The railway then successfully launched a £500,000 share issue to purchase the route, which runs from Kidderminster footbridge to Bewdley.

In 1983-84 more than £370,000 was raised by share issue; £80,000 of which was used to fund the purchase of line between Foley Park and Kidderminster Junction. Another £60,000 came from the Heart of England Tourist Board.

Three acres of land, which formed the southern half of Kidderminster freight yard in Comberton Hill, were then leased from British Rail.

Public SVR trains began running from Bridgnorth to Kidderminster on Monday, July 30, 1984.

Accompanied by a brass band, GWR 4-6-0 No. 4930 *Hagley Hall* was adorned with the 'Kidderminster Venturer' for the VIP run out of Kidderminster at 11.23am.

The first public train was hauled by LMS Jubilee 4-6-0 No. 5960 *Leander* at 1pm.

The company's then managing director, Michael Draper, said: "This is the end of the beginning.

"We knew there would one day be an extension in Kidderminster but we could not have done it without the dedicated support, drive and enthusiasm of the volunteers who worked on the project."

The guest speaker at the opening was Dr John Prideaux, director of the British Railways Board policy unit. A noted railway historian and enthusiast, he is now chairman of the Ffestiniog & Welsh Highland Railways.

ABOVE: WR Modified Hall 4-6-0 No. 6960 *Raveningham Hall* passes the remains of the sugar beet factory sidings at Foley Park on March 31, 1985. BRIAN SHARPE

ABOVE: LMS Jubilee 4-6-0 No. 5960 *Leander* sets off railway detonators as it arrives at Kidderminster on the official opening day of July 30, 1984. **BELOW:** *Hagley Hall* pulls away with the 'Kidderminster Venturer' from Kidderminster on July 30, 1984. SVR ARCHIVES

SEVERN VALLEY RAILWAY

THE KIDDERMINSTER VENTURER

The first Severn Valley train from Kidderminster to Bridgnorth

MONDAY 30th JULY 1984

Bridgnorth Station
Shropshire WV16 5DT
Telephone Number 4361

Bewdley Station
Worcestershire DY12 1BG
Telephone Number 403816

ABOVE: Malcolm Broadbent proudly displays the 1987 Ian Allan Railway Heritage Award presented the following year to the Severn Valley Railway for its construction of the terminus.

ABOVE: A rare example of a member of the SVR locomotive fleet with direct historical connections with the line; Ruston and Hornsby 0-4-0 diesel mechanical shunter No. 281269 of 1957 previously worked at the BSC factory at Foley Park. After it closed, the engine was bought by the SVR in September 1983. It was driven to Kidderminster Junction shortly after the section of track east of Foley Park was bought, and was repainted into British Railways' colours as No. D2960. Now the carriage works shunter at Kidderminster, it has kept the Silver Spoon nameplates from its BSC days. SVR

On display at Bridgnorth station was the National Railway Museum's GWR 4-4-0 No. 3442 *City of Truro*, which in 1904, became the first steam engine to have been unofficially recorded as breaking the 100mph barrier.

For the event, BR laid on a special £4.50 return rail journey to Kidderminster from within an area banded by Wellington, Walsall, Lichfield, Coventry, Leamington, Stratford-upon-Avon and Worcester.

The share issue left enough funds available for a new showpiece station to be built on the leased land, and the SVR looked to replicate a traditional GWR design.

The new station, named Kidderminster Town, was based on the GWR station at Ross-on-Wye as it was at turn of the century.

The name Kidderminster Town was chosen because the GWR custom was where there were two stations in a town, to give the Town designation to the closer one to the town centre. The Severn Valley station just about manages to beat its Network Rail counterpart by around 150ft in this respect.

When the station building was constructed, insufficient funds meant only two wings of the basic building could be completed.

Since then a number of these missing features have been constructed and erected by volunteers including a cantilevered canopy in the 1880s porte-cochere style at the front of the building and the replica ornamental crestings adorning the two towers.

A canopy covered the station concourse. The design of the steelwork for this canopy was closely based on the former GWR Wolverhampton Low Level station.

In July 1986, the GWR Kidderminster goods shed and its site was purchased for £75,000.

ABOVE: The GWR black-and-white mock Tudor Kidderminster main line station building viewed from the footpath from Comberton Hill. It is reputed that the station was originally intended to be erected at Stratford-Upon-Avon but was redirected to Kidderminster when the original station was destroyed by fire. Sadly, it was demolished in 1969 and replaced by a small functional modern brick building. DAN RATCLIFFE/KIDDERMINSTER RAILWAY MUSEUM

ABOVE: The original Kidderminster Town terminus was a run-round loop with basic platforms. TONY BENDING/SVR ARCHIVES

ABOVE: The concourse of Kidderminster Town station today. ROBIN JONES

ABOVE: The front of Kidderminster Town station is based on the GWR station at Ross-on-Wye. SVR ARCHIVES.

ABOVE: The replica WHSmith bookstall, once a typical feature of railway stations, on the concourse at Kidderminster Town. ROBIN JONES

CITY OF TRURO AND GWR 150

Steam icon GWR 4-4-0 No. 3440 *City of Truro*, which set an unofficial world steam speed record of 102.3mph on Wellington bank in Somerset on May 9, 1904, was brought from Swindon's GWR museum in July 1984 to the SVR for restoration in time for the following year's GWR 150 celebrations.

The overhaul included the lifting and repair of the boiler and the remetalling of the running gear. It was completely repainted at Bewdley into its elaborate early livery, with fine-lined panels on tender and vermillion frames.

While there, a spoof was undertaken whereby one side of it was painted as a joke in the black livery it would have carried during its years as No. 3717.

It hauled several railtours during GWR 150 and was based at the SVR until June 1986, afterwards moving to the National Railway Museum from where it was occasionally used on main line outings. It made a return

ABOVE: GWR 4-4-0 No. 3440 *City of Truro* arrives back at Kidderminster from its main line test run to Gloucester on September 3, 1985. BRIAN SHARPE

visit to the SVR in September 1991.

City of Truro was again restored to full working order in 2004 to mark the 100th anniversary of the record-breaking run, but

was withdrawn from traffic at the Bodmin & Wenford Railway in early September 2011 with serious tube leaks, and is now a static exhibit at the NRM.

ABOVE: GWR 4-6-0 No. 4930 *Hagley Hall* stands alongside Tyseley's No. 7029 *Clun Castle* during the GWR 150 celebrations on July 6, 1985. Kidderminster station is under construction in the background. BRIAN SHARPE

ABOVE: *City of Truro* on arrival at Bridgnorth for overhaul, in later GW livery as No. 3717, alongside BR Standard 4MT 4-6-0 No. 75069. BRIAN SHARPE

BELOW: Newly restored GWR 4-4-0 No. 3440 *City of Truro* climbs towards Foley Park tunnel on October 13, 1985. BRIAN SHARPE

ANOTHER LMS MOGUL STEAMS

In 1971, the Stanier Mogul Fund was formed to preserve LMS 2-6-0 No. 42968 in running order and it was bought from Barry scrapyard 1973.

Built at Crewe in January 1934 and first allocated to Willesden as No. 13268, it was renumbered 2968 in September 1935 and 42968 at Nationalisation in 1948. It was withdrawn in December 1966 and towed from Springs Branch shed at Wigan to Barry behind a diesel loco during spring 1967.

It was moved by rail to Bewdley on December 14, 1973, and on to Bridgnorth in July the following year.

It returned to steam at Bridgnorth on November 12, 1990, and entered passenger service on April 4, 1991. In addition to being a regular SVR performer, it has also travelled widely over the national network with charters, and also took part in the Steam on the Met event on London Underground in the 1990s.

At the time of writing, it is out of traffic awaiting overhaul.

ABOVE: LMS Stanier mogul No. 2968, newly restored in LMS livery, passes Hay Bridge on April 12, 1992. BRIAN SHARPE

AT LAST: A GWR MOGUL

ABOVE: GWR Collett 2-6-0 No. 7325 passes Northwood Lane on January 10, 1999. PAUL CHANCELLOR

In May 1974, the GWR (Severn Valley Railway) Association bought Churchward 4300 2-6-0 No. 9303 from Barry scrapyard.

Built at Swindon in February 1932, it was first allocated to Penzance. The front bufferbeam steel slab was removed in June 1958, and the engine was renumbered 7325. It was withdrawn from Pontypool Road in April 1964 with a recorded 993,765 miles on the clock.

It first steamed on the SVR on June 25, 1992.

It subsequently hauled specials both on the national network and London Underground, making two spectacular climbs of the Lickey incline near Bromsgrove in late 1997 and early 1998. Out of ticket at the time of writing, it is displayed in the Engine House museum at Highley.

ABOVE: As it was: No. 7325 (ex-No.9303) with Churchward 3500-gallon tender at Dai Woodham's scrapyard in Barry in May, 1967. HUGH LLEWELLYN*

THE VISCOUNT AND *THE GREAT MARQUESS*

ABOVE: Soon after completion of its restoration, LNER K4 2-6-0 No. 3442 *The Great Marquess* heads towards Foley Park tunnel with the 'Severn Valley Limited' dining train on October 14, 1990. BRIAN SHARPE

LNER K4 2-6-0 No. 3442 *The Great Marquess* is the sole survivor of a class of six Gresley locomotives designed for the West Highland line from Glasgow to Fort William and Mallaig and was introduced in 1937.

No. 3442 spent its pre-preservation working from Eastfield depot, Glasgow, until transferred to Thornton Junction, Fife, early in December 1959. As No. 61994, it was withdrawn on December 30, 1961.

In March 1963, the K4 was bought by Lord Lindsay (then David, Viscount Garnock), and sent to Cowlairs Works, Glasgow, for repair and restoration to original LNER livery. It moved from there to Leeds in April 1963, and, based at Neville Hill shed, working several railtours, between May 1963 and April 1967.

After the British Rail steam ban was imposed in 1968, the owner decided not to carry out boiler repairs. The K4 was taken to the SVR in September 1972, and boiler work was carried out at Bridgnorth.

Extensive boiler and mechanical work was carried out between 1981-89, and No. 3442 was returned to working order only a few days before British Rail chairman, Sir Robert Reid, officially recommissioned it at Kidderminster Town on April 18, 1989.

By then, Lord Lindsay had become SVR president after earlier serving as its chairman. The K4 briefly returned to the West Highland Line, and Lord Lindsay travelled on the footplate from Fort William to Banavie a few days before his death on August 1, 1989.

The K4 became a regular performer on the SVR, hauling the line's rake of teak coaches, in addition to main line railtours and visits to other heritage lines.

For the line's 1997 autumn gala, it was repainted in BR black as No. 61994. However, that October, it suffered a wheelslip that required major repair work.

Following Lord Lindsay's passing, No. 3442 was bought by John Cameron and the locomotive left the SVR for overhaul at Crewe in 2005. It has since moved back to Scotland where it now hauls specials on the national network.

FROM THE SUNNY SOUTH

It was in August 1985 that the Severn Valley took delivery of partially restored Bulleid West Country light Pacific No. 34027 *Taw Valley*.

The locomotive was built in 1946 at Brighton Works and originally allocated to Ramsgate where it entered service as No. 21C127, becoming No. 34027 at Nationalisation.

In 1947 *Taw Valley* moved to Exmouth Junction, working mainly in Devon and Cornwall. Here the locomotive would have hauled named trains such as the 'Atlantic Coast Express' and 'Devon Belle'. In 1957, after being rebuilt, with its air-smoothed casing removed, *Taw Valley* worked commuter services from Bricklayers Arms depot in London Brighton and then Brighton. Following transfer to Salisbury in 1963, *Taw Valley* was withdrawn by British Railways in August 1964 and in December moved to Barry scrapyard.

In April 1980, No. 34027 became the 112th locomotive to leave Barry first being taken to the North Yorkshire Moors Railway and then, in November 1982, to the East Lancashire Railway. Its restoration under then owner the late Bert Hitchen was completed in the autumn of 1987.

In 2000, *Taw Valley* was painted in distinctive non-authentic red livery, becoming the first locomotive to masquerade as the fictional Hogwarts Castle from JK Rowling's Harry Potter books. That July, it hauled a nationwide tour train for the promotion of the fourth book, Harry Potter and the Goblet of Fire, with author herself on board signing books and giving interviews.

However, it was not used for Warner Bros Harry Potter films because director, Chris Columbus, decided it was too 'modern' in appearance and wanted a more classic British steam locomotive. He chose West Coast Railways' GWR 4-6-0 No. 5972 *Olton Hall*, which in the years that followed became the most famous steam locomotive in the world as far as a new generation was concerned.

Later, *Taw Valley* assumed the guise of long-since scrapped sister engine No. 34045 *Ottery St Mary*, a favourite of No. 34027's majority shareholder Phil Swallow. It became a regular performer on Venice-Simplon-Orient-Express excursions.

Its main line career ended in June 2005, when after completing a 'Cathedrals Express' run to Weymouth, the left-hand cylinder was found to be cracked.

No. 34027 returned light engine from the Mid Hants Railway to Bridgnorth patched up by John Robinson's engineering team, and starred in the SVR's September 24-25 autumn gala that year, under the identity of another scrapped class member, No. 34036 *Westward Ho!* After being given a three-month extension to its boiler ticket, No. 34027 was withdrawn in January 2006 for a heavy overhaul.

That was completed in spring 2015, when *Taw Valley* resumed its place in the SVR's operating fleet.

BELOW: Newly restored SR West Country Pacific No. 34027 *Taw Valley* emerges from Foley Park tunnel with a Santa special on November 26, 1988. BRIAN SHARPE

NO MORE BOILERS OUTDOORS IN BRIDGNORTH!

As the Severn Valley Railway grew in stature, so its locomotive fleet expanded, probably way beyond what the original pioneers had envisaged.

Of course, if you want to run a substantial number of locomotives, then you need the facilities to service and overhaul them.

From the outset, heavy engineering on the locomotive fleet, including boiler overhauls has been exclusively based at Bridgnorth.

To cope with the high pressures that boilers are subjected to, and to allow for necessary expansion and contraction, hundreds of rivets are needed.

For the early SVR revivalists, boiler riveting was a noisy outdoor task, hated by neighbours, so much so that complaints to the local council led to a court order being obtained in March 1986 banning outdoor riveting.

The only solution was to take the job indoors, and so a share issue to raise the estimated £300,000 for the desperately needed new boiler shop at Bridgnorth was launched.

The result: a soundproofed building 100ft long and 45ft wide that was equipped with an electric travelling overhead crane with a lifting capacity of 30 tons and a single-storey compressor house.

There was some degree of urgency for completing this vital project, for unless a start on the workshop was made by November 1, 1988, then the railway would be banned from undertaking any further boiler repairs on the existing open-air site, placing in jeopardy the future of steam on the line.

Not only that, but the existing boiler repair facility in an open-air area of ground next to the locomotive maintenance facilities and depot allowed for a maximum of five boilers to be worked on at any one time. Good weather was always a prerequisite for work to be undertaken.

By that time, the SVR was not only undertaking its own boiler repairs, but tackling work for other locomotive owning groups, bringing in extra revenue to the railway. Despite the handicaps of the open-air site,

ABOVE: Not satisfactory: in the early days, boiler repairs were undertaken in the open at Bridgnorth. SVR ARCHIVES

the SVR had by then received considerable national acclaim for its boiler work.

The share issue was successful and completed in 1989. It was named in memory of George Knight the deputy chief boiler inspector of the London Midland Region, who had passed down techniques to the early SVR boilersmiths.

In 1990, *Hinton Manor* became a royal engine once again, conveying the Duke of Gloucester from Kidderminster to Bridgnorth for the official opening of the boiler repair shop. The Duke, a first cousin of the Queen and a keen enthusiast himself, drove No. 7819 for part of the journey.

In 1997, the duke agreed to become patron of the railway, and has visited it on several occasions since. ●

ABOVE: The new boiler shed being erected. SVR ARCHIVES

ABOVE: The finishing touches are made to the boiler shop in 1989. DAVID WILLIAMS

ABOVE: The boiler of GWR 4-6-0 No. 7802 *Bradley Manor* being worked on in April 2015. PAUL APPLETON

Chapter 11

The Nineties and beyond

Established as a firm favourite in the West Midlands' tourist economy, the railway continued to both consolidate and grow.

ABOVE: Visiting LNER A3 Pacific No. 4472 *Flying Scotsman*, the world's most famous steam locomotive, emerges from Foley Park tunnel on October 14, 1990. BRIAN SHARPE

The railway faced one last battle to secure complete ownership of its present route in 1994. Early that year, British Rail, anxious to realise the value of a prime asset, announced that the former Kidderminster goods yard, by then occupied by the new Kidderminster Town station, was on the market. The asking price was a whopping £450,000.

In February that year, bridging finance was agreed with the company's bankers before the successful launch of a share offer. By then, the railway had grown in support and stature to the extent that not only was the asking price raised but the share issue meant that there was money to spare.

Chairman, Michael York, commented in the final paragraph of his letter to prospective shareholders: "It is vital to secure outright ownership of the entire railway from bufferstop to bufferstop."

The purchase complete, the SVR now owned every inch of its running line from Bridgnorth station to Kidderminster.

Had it not been for that share offer, a supermarket would now occupy the site. Who knows where the SVR trains would have terminated.

In September that same year, the turntable from Fort William was inaugurated, as a prelude to plans launched in 1997 to develop much of the rest of the Kidderminster former freight yard for a carriage shed and other facilities.

The biggest SVR station had been saved, and two years later, the smallest was opened. A new request halt, Country Park, opened between Highley and Hampton Loade on April 4, 1996.

In 2003, with financial assistance from the Heritage Lottery Fund, a carriage storage and maintenance building was erected at Kidderminster with a carriage washing plant added shortly after. Kidderminster Town station was completed in 2006 with the addition of a glazed concourse canopy and a purpose-built refreshment room and hospitality facility.

RIGHT: In 1990, Severn Valley founder members met up again at the Coopers Arms in Habberley, celebrating 25 years since the meeting that launched the revival of the branch. SVR ARCHIVES

THE BIGGEST CARRIAGE SHED OF THEM ALL!

ABOVE: Kidderminster's carriage shed is more than a fifth of a mile long. This aerial view was taken by Terry Fitzsimmons, who at the time worked in the locomotive department at Bewdley and was also a flying instructor at Coventry Airport. SVR

The second edition of *Heritage Railway* carried the story that the SVR had been awarded £1,757,000 by the Heritage Lottery Fund to build a carriage shed more than a fifth of a mile long at its Kidderminster terminus.

The £2.3-million four-road steel-fabricated shed covers 67,000sq ft and is longer than the *Titanic* making it the largest carriage shed on any heritage railway in Britain.

The decision, announced on May 12, 1999, ended a nail-biting two years for SVR officials following the exhaustive preparation of the Lottery bid.

The shed, built on a curve to follow the constraints of the site alongside the running line to Bewdley, includes an eight-coach inspection pit. The grant also covered the restoration of 10 carriages.

Indeed, by then, the SVR boasted Britain's finest fleet of pre-Nationalisation carriages, with two complete GWR trains, a complete LMS train and a full set of LNER coaches. The oldest SVR coach, GWR Toplight No. 9055, dates back to 1912.

The shed was designed to provide covered accommodation for all of them, safe from the ravages of wind and rain and the threat of vandalism.

In order to qualify for the Lottery award, the railway had to change the constitution of its company. Two major changes meant that shareholders could no longer receive dividends, and in the event of the operation being wound up, they would not be entitled to share the surplus from assets – which would have to be transferred to another charity.

David Morgan, then chairman of the Heritage Railway Association and a SVR vice-chairman, said: "I regard coaches as the Cinderella of the heritage railway movement, and it is high time that they were given a much-greater status and protection. Coaches are important because they are our shop window to the public."

SVR traffic manager, Dewi Jones, said: "The shed will protect our coaching stock from the elements. Some members of our carriage and wagon department have been there for 20 years and do not want to see their lifetime's work fall apart because of a lack of covered accommodation. The carriage shed will be saving

ABOVE: The front of the carriage shed just after completion. SVR

a significant part of the nation's transport heritage for future generations."

The original design for the shed, which involved a brick building with traditional 'loco shed' appearance, was discarded after it became obvious that it would be too expensive.

Under the terms of the grant, the SVR had to find more than £500,000 as its contribution to the shed project, but by the time the grant announcement was made, much of that sum had been raised.

The Lottery award came after a bumper year in which the railway attained a record turnover of £3.25 million.

Planning permission was obtained from Wyre Forest District Council; building contractor Carillion began work and handed the keys to the completed shed to SVR directors on time on April 20, 2000, when the first carriages were moved inside as a 'trial' but it was a nonetheless symbolic movement.

The railway's volunteers completed the shed by laying the four roads inside. The first, which runs over the inspection pit, was also ready by April 20 and the second came on line on May 5.

The construction of this storage facility complements the purchase back in 1985 of the large goods shed at Kidderminster, once used by Pickfords, the removals and storage company. This building, now known as just Pickfords, houses the team that carries out heavy engineering on the carriage fleet.

LANDMARK LOCO BACK FOR 30TH ANNIVERSARY

ABOVE: Back on the Severn Valley Railway to mark the line's 30th anniversary of the first public train, GWR Collett 0-6-0 No. 3205 is seen double-heading with GWR 2-6-0 No. 7325 during a re-run of the 'Cambrian Coast Express' during a Bob Branch 26D Rail Recreations charter on May 8, 2000. GEOFF LEE

ABOVE LEFT AND RIGHT: There was much debate at the time about when the new millennium began. The Tony Blair government wanted to instil the "feel good factor" throughout the nation and said it was 2000, but historians argued that a new century begins with the year one. Before dawn at Bewdley on January 1, 2000, LMS 'Black Five' No. 45110 is prepared for the first services of what may or may not be the first services of the new millennium/century, depending on your point of view. ROBIN JONES

In 2000, a famous old SVR campaigner returned to the line, GWR Collett 0-6-0 No. 3205 hauled the railway's first public train on May 23, 1970, over the modest four miles from Bridgnorth to Hampton Loade, and had also been the first locomotive to arrive on the line three years earlier.

By then based at Buckfastleigh on the South Devon Railway, it returned for a replay of that first train, on May 23, 2000.

It hauled a six-coach VIP special, which included the only passenger coach from the original train of 1970 still on the railway, GWR brake composite No. 6562, and carried 94 guests from Kidderminster on the 16-mile journey to Bridgnorth and return.

It was a great day for renewing old friendships, with founding and early members meeting up again, some for the first time in many years – Christopher George, Ken Durnell, Jeremy Colborn, Roger Hobson, Tony Brookes, Adrian Turley, John Dew, Keith Harris, David Howley and Jack Bond. Driver John Hill who drove that first train, and retired as the line's operating superintendent only two years before, again took charge of the locomotive for part of the return journey.

The guests included Coun Mrs Judy Lea, the new mayor of Bridgnorth, and the town's Conservative MP Christopher Gill, whose presence reflected somewhat the help given to the fledgling line by the late Sir Gerald Nabarro.

At Bridgnorth, volunteer engineman, Rev Mike Kneed, conducted a short but poignant service of remembrance for all the SVR members who had passed away during the society's 35 years in existence.

Once again, lineside photographers occupied much the same positions to the south of Bridgnorth station as they had done in 1970.

MALLARD'S SISTER ON THE VALLEY

One of six surviving LNER A4 streamlined Pacifics, No. 60009 *Union of South Africa* has been based on the Severn Valley Railway.

A sister of world record holder No. 4468 *Mallard, Union of South Africa* was given the name *Osprey* during construction. It was outshopped by Doncaster Works in June 1937 as No. 4488, and became simply No. 9 in the 1946 renumbering and No. 60009 at Nationalisation in 1948.

One of the last six A4s in service, it was bought upon withdrawal in June 1966 by Scottish farmer and enthusiast, John Cameron, who used it as the flagship locomotive on his now-defunct Lochty Private Railway in Fife.

In 1978, No. 60009, returned to the main line to work railtours, and SVR engineers undertook specialist work at Markinch, and Thornton Junction in Fife and later at Bridgnorth.

International public disgust at the

RIGHT: On its first passenger run after overhaul at Bridgnorth, LNER A4 Pacific No. 60009 *Union of South Africa* approaches Arley on February 16, 1990. BRIAN SHARPE

continuation of apartheid in South Africa during the Eighties and early Nineties meant that No. 60009 carried *Osprey* nameplates during this time.

John then decided that the SVR would be an ideal base for main line exploits as well as running in traffic on the heritage line, and so in May 1994 it left Markinch for the last time, on a low loader bound for Bridgnorth. Its route took it over the Forth Road Bridge and in doing so it became the

only steam locomotive to cross both the Forth Bridge and the adjacent Forth Road Bridge.

On October 29, 1994, it hauled the first steam train from King's Cross for 30 years on a railtour to Peterborough, under the banner of the 'Elizabethan'.

Its last overhaul, which cost nearly £1 million, was at Pete Waterman's LNWR Workshops in Crewe. Not based at Bridgnorth since 2006, it is a regular performer on the main line.

ABOVE: LNER K4 2-6-0 No. 3442 *The Great Marquess* departs from Hampton Loade with LNER coaching stock in September 1997. BRIAN SHARPE

HAGLEY HALL VISITS HAGLEY HALL!

SVR ARCHIVES

In 1999, agreement was reached between the Severn Valley Railway and McArthur Glen for the loan of flagship GWR 4-6-0 No. 4930 *Hagley Hall* as an appropriate exhibit for display inside the Designer Outlet shopping mall site of the former GWR Swindon Works. It was cosmetically restored before the move, and was tended by a group of volunteers from the nearby STEAM – Museum of the Great Western Railway during its seven-year stay in Swindon.

On June 7-8 2007, No. 4930 returned from Swindon to the SVR by road. En route, No. 4930 made a detour to nearby Hagley Hall, the stately home after which it was named. This diversion, allowed by Lord and Lady Cobham, was believed to be unique in the history of GWR named locomotives.

SVR ARCHIVES

SVR ARCHIVES

ABOVE: Over the years, the Severn Valley Railway has not only grown into one of the world's leading heritage lines, but it is a splendid venue for all sorts of shows and festivals. tThe first-ever Vauxhall Victor from 1957 was proudly displayed by its owner at this vintage transport show in 2007. SVR ARCHIVES

Chapter 12

Double tsunami destruction

During the unprecented freak flooding of 2007, disaster struck the SVR not once, but twice…

Think of any railway's worst nightmare – and then go another mile…

The struggle to get the Light Railway Order; the Bridgnorth bypass campaign; the end of the Nabarro era – all of them pale into insignificance when compared with the events of two days in 2007.

During violent thunderstorms on the night of June 19 and with heavy rain coincidentally exactly a month later on July 19, the railway sustained more damage than in its entire history. Rain descended on already saturated ground causing major damage to the line in 45 separate locations. At 10 of these locations the damage was so serious that major engineering solutions had to be found before reconstruction could commence.

The disaster began when two weeks' rain fell in just 45 minutes after 9.30pm on June 19. Successive bands of rain and thunderstorms had been triggered by a mixture of warmth and damp, the situation being exacerbated by warm air coming in off the continent.

Two-thirds of the 16-mile line was hit by embankment slippages, landslides and flash floods.

BELOW: The worst of the damage on June 19, 2007 was this washout at Fisherman's Crossing south of Highley, where the running line was left 30ft in the air. Pictured the morning afterwards. SVR

ABOVE: The approach to the new Engine Shed museum and visitor centre at Highley, with the track undermined by floods.
SHROPSHIRE STAR

ABOVE: The washout on the south side of Victoria Bridge exposed the abutments for the first time since 1862.
BOB SWEET

ABOVE: The formation undermined by a raging torrent at Oldbury Viaduct. SVR

ABOVE: The washout beneath the track at Highley station left daylight showing between the sleepers and rails. BOB SWEET

The sudden build-up of rainwater on already saturated ground created nine major blockages between Bridgnorth and Northwood Lane, where flood damage to the line was reported.

At Fisherman's Crossing half a mile south of Highley, one stretch of embankment was washed away completely, leaving the rails suspended 30ft in mid-air. Highley's Up starter signal was washed away down the embankment.

Another slippage undermined the track in Highley station. The landslip shifted three holiday chalets towards the River Severn.

At Victoria Bridge, one of the abutments, which had not been seen since the great structure across the river was built in 1862, was left exposed by a 70ft-long slippage beneath the running line on the southern approach.

A landslip, which had occurred at Knowle Sands in 2003, slipped again in two places, rendering the track impassable, with debris 4ft deep lying on top of the line. Water gushing down the sodden hillside washed part of the track away.

There were further serious washaways at Oldbury Viaduct, with both sides affected, and the outer home signal for Bridgnorth was left in place only by its concrete anchor, which was left fully exposed.

A landslip occurred at Eardington station, but it did not affect the track. North of Hampton Loade, however, part of the

formation was washed into a caravan site.

At Hampton Loade the village served by the railway was cut off after its main road was swept away leaving more than 50 people trapped in their homes. The absence of a roadway hampered the railway's efforts to rectify the damage here.

Between milepost 139 1/2 and 139, the bank moved, leaving bungalows under threat. Elsewhere, there were several smaller washouts, including two at Country Park halt near Alveley, while cuttings along the line became blocked with fallen trees and debris, while gulleys, drains and culverts were blocked up en masse.

Ironically, the point on the line considered to be at the greatest risk from flood erosion, Sterns near Bridgnorth, remained totally unaffected. The river regularly floods fields close to the railway and so in 1996 3000 tons of rock were deposited to shore up the embankment.

A 5mph speed restriction at Sterns, which had remained in place up till then was recently raised to 15mph.

Up to two inches of rain fell over the region in two hours, leaving the Wyre Forest area being described as a 'mini Boscastle' by Kidderminster fire station watch manager, Mel

Turbutt, recalling the freak flash floods that affected the Cornish harbour in August 2004 in similar weather conditions.

Fire crews in the region were stretched to breaking point with hundreds of calls for help. Off-duty crews volunteered to help out with 300 call-outs in the space of six hours in Worcestershire alone. At least 10 homes were flooded in the Bewdley area.

SVR directors were left stunned by the extent of the damage when daylight broke the next morning and early estimates indicated a repair bill of at least £500,000. There was no alternative but to introduce an emergency timetable and restrict services to the southernmost stretch between Bewdley and Kidderminster.

Activities at the line's big money-spinning 1940s wartime weekends of June 23-24 and June 30-July 1 were restricted to Bewdley and Kidderminster stations. Passenger loadings were said to have held up well in the circumstances, especially on the Saturday when the rain held off. "In the great British wartime tradition, everyone decided to carry on," said the late SVR marketing manager, John Leach.

However, a further slippage occurred on the line on June 25, during further heavy rain. ▶

ABOVE: That sinking feeling: the undermined track at Borle on June 22, 2007. SVR

The water around Borle Viaduct near Arley became sufficiently deep to wash away fill from around the supports.

The first big casualty of the storm was the opening of the £4.5 million Engine House museum and visitor centre at Highley, which had been planned for August 1, and had to be cancelled. Furthermore, while an emergency

timetable allowed trains to run between Bewdley and Kidderminster, much of the locomotive fleet and stock was marooned at the northern end of the line, with it being impossible to take anything bigger than a pannier tank out of Bridgnorth yard by road. There were just three steam locomotives at Bewdley – LMS mogul No. 46443, 'Black

Five' No 45110 and GWR prairie No. 4566. Cut off from Bridgnorth Works, the three had just 20 to 30 days before being due for boiler washouts.

Within 48 hours of the full extent of the storm damage becoming apparent, railway officials drew up plans for a national fighting fund appeal for funds to help reopen the line.

BELOW: The landslip near Highley as viewed from a helicopter. The River Severn is beyond the top of the photograph, and the washout is running down from the railway line to a lake that formed in the field beyond. This image appeared on the front of the SVR's flood appeal leaflet. SVR

ABOVE: Rebuilding work on the south end of Victoria Bridge. DAVID SYMONDS ASSOCIATES

A flyer was being hastily prepared for handing out at shops, buffets and in the railway's quarterly members' magazine. Before the appeal was officially launched on June 25, a total of £3500 had been received at the SVR's Bewdley office.

Two Kidderminster schoolgirls turned up at Bewdley station and donated their pocket money of £20.

One of the first offers of physical help came from the Mid Hants Railway and further offers of help were received from the West Somerset, Bluebell, Great Central, Dean Forest and Gloucestershire Warwickshire railways.

Severn Valley directors arranged to meet local MPs at the House of Commons in a bid to enlist their help in reopening the line throughout.

IT GETS WORSE

With the repair bill having soared to more than £2 million, within weeks an emergency appeal from supporters had raised nearly £250,000, however, a second deluge on July 21 saw a month's rainfall descend on Shropshire and much of the rest of the UK in a day.

The previous month's scenes of flooding and devastation returned, with reports of 10 people rescued from houses in nearby Tenbury Wells, crews from the RNLI called in to make inland rescues in Worcestershire and main line railways and motorways blocked by floodwater throughout southern England. Ten thousand drivers spent the night in their cars on the M5 after being marooned by floodwater.

Again rain that fell on the hillsides overlooking the SVR ran down already-sodden ground straight towards the line, creating further landslips and blocked culverts, while exacerbating the extensive existing damage.

At Knowle Sands outside Bridgnorth, where the running line had already been lifted to facilitate repairs, more of the embankment collapsed. South of Knowle Sands Tunnel, floodwater brought more debris off the fields on to the track.

Several locations between Eardington and Highley, including Country Park Halt, were again affected by debris blocking up culverts.

Near Hampton Loade, an 8ft square piece of embankment near to the track disappeared.

At Highley, the scene of the worst devastation in the first floods, there were further washouts. At Fisherman's Crossing,

ABOVE: A further landslip appeared above New Stanley Cutting between Bewdley and Arley. The slippage started in the garden shed top left in the picture. Before the flood, the shed would not have been visible from this point, but mature trees have slipped down the slope towards the railway. People claimed that they had stood at this point and heard trees moving. SVR

where the running line had been left 30ft in the air, more material was washed by the rain into the adjacent field.

At Folly Point, contractors working on repairs to the railway were withdrawn after

the heavy rain and the danger from already unstable ground.

Operations manager, Dewi Jones, said: "You can't even stand on the ground in places without sinking."

ABOVE: Repair work in progress at Knowle Sands Trading Estate near Bridgnorth. DAVID SYMONDS ASSOCIATES

ABOVE: Gabions, or rock-filled cages, being placed in position at Folly Point. SVR

ABOVE: The major landslip at Highley. Three holiday chalets were moved by the washout that occurred on June 19. SVR

A £1.25-million emergency grant aid package was announced, with the European Regional Development Fund giving £750,000 towards the flood repair bill. However, initial hopes of having the whole 16-mile length between Kidderminster and Bridgnorth reopened by November that year vaporised.

The sudden heavy rain on July 21 also caused flooding in several places along the Gloucestershire Warwickshire Railway, with water reaching the top of platforms at Winchcombe and the trackbed at Woodmancote becoming a river. One of the worst-hit areas in Britain was Tewkesbury, which was all but completely cut off and needed to be supplied by helicopters. With all roads impassable, the only route in and out was via the old embankment, which carried the long-since-lifted Midland Railway line from Ashchurch.

THE DUNKIRK SPIRIT

GWR pannier No. 7714, which the railway was able to take out from Bridgnorth shed by low loader, went on loan to the Swanage Railway for two months, in exchange for the services of Class 20 D8188, which was then used on works trains.

Pat McFadden, Labour MP for Wolverhampton South East and Minister of State at the Department for Business, Enterprise and Regulatory Reform, visited the line on September 3 to see for himself the full extent of the damage. He spoke to local

ABOVE: As part of the clearance of the Highley site, this gatepost was temporarily removed to allow access for large vehicles. Remarkably, it appears to have been carved from a tree trunk and is in one piece. SVR

business leaders who were dismayed at the loss of income from tourism because of the closure of the line. If anything, their words underlined the fact that much of the local economy now depended on the successful operation of the railway.

Thousands of people turned up to attend two Thomas the Tank Engine weekends in September despite the annual event being restricted to the Bewdley to Kidderminster section.

Despite the closure of the uppermost 13 miles of the line, the September 21-23 steam gala went ahead, again with more than a little help from friends.

Thanks to the generosity of the owners of two Tyseley-based GWR 4-6-0s, No. 4936 *Kinlet Hall* and No. 4953 *Pitchford Hall*, two services on each of the weekend days were extended eastwards – over Network Rail metals into Birmingham Snow Hill station. The owners of the 4-6-0s generously agreed to donate their steaming and hire fees to the flood disaster appeal, Sadly, a third Hall, Tyseley's own No. 4965 *Rood Ashton Hall*, pulled out the day before, with superheater flue problems. It had been due to take its turn on the Snow Hill shuttles, the roster for which had to be reshuffled.

As a result, on-loan D8188 was pressed into service to handle some of the timetabled Kidderminster-Bewdley services instead of steam.

The other big draw was the National Railway Museum's LNER V2 2-6-2 No. 4771 *Green Arrow*, nearing the end of its current operating career. It performed faultlessly with the line's rake of matching Gresley teak coaches and took its turn on some other services as well, as the line ran one of the most intensive timetables in its history.

Despite the fact that the gala was severely pruned, and it was held over the same weekend as the Mid Hants Railway's autumn gala more than 2500 visitors turned up. Hundreds of West Midland families were determined that the weather damage would not deter them from visiting 'their' heritage line. The October diesel gala that year also went ahead, but again, it was severely pruned back out of necessity.

All was not quiet on the closed section of the line beyond Bewdley, however. At

Bridgnorth, LMS mogul No. 42968 was in steam, giving demonstrations within the station confines.

Extra beer was ordered for the Railwayman's Arms pub, a 7¼in gauge live steam railway offered rides, an OO gauge model layout was in operation and a special blacksmiths demonstration was held in Bridgnorth locomotive shed's boiler shop. Indeed, over the August bank holiday period and subsequent weekends, trains ran from Bridgnorth station as far south as the town bypass, using LMS Stanier 8F No. 48773 and two LMS coaches.

Santa services that year were rescheduled to run between Kiddeminster and Bewdley, not Arley as usual.

HELP FROM THE NORTH

Britain's most popular heritage line in terms of passenger numbers, the North Yorkshire Moors Railway, held a Valley Aid gala as a mixed traction event over the first weekend in November to raise money for the flood disaster appeal. The special event included Severn Valley-based Class 50 No 50049 *Defiance* as special guest, becoming the first member of the class to run on Network Rail's Esk Valley branch.

Some members of NYMR staff donated their weekend's wages to the appeal. In addition, many of the owners of the locomotives working over the weekend provided engines free of hire charges.

NYMR general manager, Philip Benham, said: "Like everyone in the heritage movement, we were horrified to see the damage caused to the Severn Valley."

On the Saturday, the NYMR was signalled throughout by Severn Valley signalmen. SVR volunteers also assisted with a major resignalling project at Grosmont – and in return, the NYMR's permanent way department loaned its track gopher – a machine that digs contaminated ballast from under the sleepers without needing to lift the track – to the Severn Valley. It was used to clean ballast contaminated by floodwater south of Bridgnorth.

An edition of the NYMR's in-house magazine, Moors Line, included a copy of the leaflet for the SVR Flood Appeal. The NYMR's Valley Aid gala raised around £15,000 for the Severn Valley.

Meanwhile, among the bigger donations to the SVR flood disaster appeal was a £10,000 cheque from a man living in Harpenden, who was neither a member nor shareholder of the railway and said very little in his accompanying letter as to why he had chosen to make such a large contribution.

Local independent MP, Dr Richard Taylor, a Severn Valley member and shareholder, donated a railway relic that he dug up in his back garden – a Great Eastern Railway wagon axlebox cover, which had traces of BR rail blue paint on it, for a fundraising auction. It was speculated that it had come from a parcels van that survived in main line use until the 1970s.

TURNING THE CLOCK BACK

When the Severn Valley Railway opened to the public in 1970, it ran services over the section between Bridgnorth and Hampton Loade.

ABOVE: Owner, David Hurd, agreed the loan of Class 73/1 No. 73101 for use on works trains. It arrived in Kidderminster on July 18 from the Avon Valley Railway. SVR

ABOVE: Crisis – what crisis? LMS 8F No 48773 prepared to depart from Bridgnorth with an August bank holiday service – but it could run only as far as the bridge that carries the town bypass over the line. COLIN HARSLEY
RIGHT: The flood disaster appeal poster. SVR

That is just what happened again 38 years later during the February half-term week in 2008, when officials were able re-open the same stretch, to an ecstatic public response.

Over the weekend of February 9-10, a total of 570 passengers travelled between the two stations. Between Kidderminster and Bewdley, 310 travelled. Around 4000 passengers travelled over the line during February, against a budgeted figure of 1625.

THE SUN SHINES AGAIN

Good Friday fell on March 21 in 2008. However, for the Severn Valley Railway, it was more like Christmas rather than Easter had come early – not only with the whole line being re-opened following repairs costing more than £3 million, but with the Engine House museum and visitor centre opening their doors for the first time.

Lured by unprecedented media publicity in the days beforehand, and maybe the sight of TV gardener, Charlie Dimmock, breaking a bottle of bubbly over the bufferbeam of newly overhauled GWR 4-6-0 No. 7812 *Erlestoke Manor*, around 8000 people rode on the rebuilt railway over the bank holiday weekend, despite wintry weather keeping many families at home. On the Friday, crowds started to form at Bridgnorth station two hours before departure and by midday the platform was inundated.

The first movement over the full length of the rebuilt line had come on March 10, when Class 73 electro-diesel E6006 ran from Bridgnorth to Bewdley without encountering any problems.

The day before the public reopening on Good Friday, a VIP special with about 150 people on board including civic dignitaries and Charlie Dimmock travelled the full route from Kidderminster to Bridgnorth. The special was Severn Valley general manager, Nick Ralls', first-ever ride on the line since he had taken charge of the railway a week after the flood devastation nine months earlier.

Mick York, chairman of Severn Valley Railway Holdings, who delivered a speech ▶

ABOVE: GWR small prairie No 4566 is seen on Eardington bank on the first weekend of Bridgnorth-Hampton Loade running. PAUL STRATFORD

ABOVE: GWR 4-6-0 No 7812 *Erlestoke Manor* departs from Highley across the reinstated formation and trackwork, and passes the Engine House. FRED KERR

The public appeal had by the time of reopening raised £575,000, but without the help of the European Regional Development Fund, and regional development agency, Advantage West Midlands, which together contributed £1.25 million, as well as the Heritage Lottery Fund giving £250,000, the railway could not have been rebuilt within the nine-month timescale, officials said.

Nick Ralls said: "There was no way the SVR could have ever resourced such major reconstruction work from its own reserves, so the contributions we have received from these, our main funding partners, have been absolutely vital in helping us restore the railway as one of central England's major tourist attractions."

The reopening special – which carried the same headboard as Collett 0-6-0 No. 3205 when it hauled the opening train in 1970 – was the first passenger working in 23 years for *Erlestoke Manor*.

Last operated on the railway in 1985, *Erlestoke Manor*, had begun its major overhaul in 1990. Before the relaunch, the locomotive undertook several running-in turns with empty coaches, on part of the newly rebuilt SVR.

Erlestoke Manor also hauled the first public train from Bridgnorth over the full length of the line since the flooding devastation at 11.05am on the Good Friday after 'Black Five' No. 45110 hauled the first departure, from Kidderminster, the same day at 9.55am. Among the first locomotives to operate along the whole length that Easter was also Somerset & Dorset Joint Railway 7F 2-8-0 No. 88, on loan from the West Somerset Railway.

The nightmare was over. ●

at Kidderminster Town station before the departure of the special, said: "This was a bigger job than anyone ever expected."

Advantage West Midlands chief executive, Mick Laverty, said: "The Severn Valley Railway is unique in terms of the impact it has on the rural economy in the west of our region.

"It provides a gateway to the counties of both Shropshire and Worcestershire,

bringing in more than 250,000 visitors each year upon whom many of the guest houses, pubs, restaurants and attractions along the route depend.

"Back when the floods happened, we recognised the need to make our investment in the repairs in order to start the ball rolling and the way volunteers and railway members have worked to get the trains moving again has been nothing short of phenomenal."

LEFT: TV gardener, Charlie Dimmock, gets ready to crack a bottle of champagne over the bufferbeam of GWR 4-6-0 No. 7812 *Erlestoke Manor* on March 20, 2008. ROBIN JONES

BELOW: Visiting Somerset & Dorset Joint Railway 7F 2-8-0 No. 88 crosses Victoria Bridge on the approach to Arley. MAURICE BURNS

Chapter 13

The Engine House

One of the jewels in the crown of today's Severn Valley Railway is the Engine House museum and visitor centre at Highley station.

Described as Shropshire's own version of the National Railway Museum, it allows out-of-ticket locomotives and priceless items of historic rolling stock to become visitor attractions in themselves as static exhibits, rather than be allowed to rust away under a tarpaulin in a station siding while waiting many years for their time in the restoration queue to come again.

Cosmetically restored and placed safely under cover, future bills to rectify further deterioration of locomotives from the elements are eradicated, while providing an added incentive for visitors to stay longer on the railway. There are even steam simulation machines under the front bogies.

The Engine House also includes audio-visual displays, such as a special feature on carriage restoration, with 'before and after' scenes of coach seats, and the story of the railway itself.

From the first-floor exterior balcony outside a splendid, spacious restaurant, visitors have a grandstand view of the running line and are able to watch every arrival and departure from Highley. Indeed, it is a 21st-century version of the Fifties schoolboy trainspotters' paradise location of a favoured viewpoint alongside the main line, and a state-of-the-art attraction for the discerning modern visitor. Other amenities include a gift shop and picnic area.

The Engine House has been built on the former Highley Mining Company sidings opposite the station that dates back to the 1880s. In later years of the local mining industry, the 10-acre site was a landsale yard for coal from Alveley Colliery.

The sidings themselves were connected to Highley Colliery by a rope-worked incline. Full wagons of coal descended to the sidings, and hence the railway, pulling empties back up to the colliery. The route of the incline is now the footpath linking the Country Park car park with the station and a section of old track can be seen by its side, together with some lengths of wire rope.

The green light for the £4.5 million Engine House project, on which former Severn Valley general manager, Alun Rees, worked extensively, was given by the Heritage Lottery Fund. The Lottery provides £3.3 million of funding, with the balance of £1.2 million being met by the European Regional Development Fund.

It was opened to the public on Good Friday 2008, the same date as the rebuilt 13 miles of line north of Bewdley, which had been extensively damaged by the floods. It has since become a popular and versatile attraction and added yet another string to the railway's bow. ●

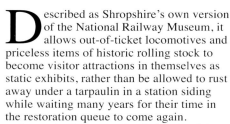

LEFT: Two of the locomotives displayed safely under cover in the Engine House are Stanier 8F No. 48773 and Austerity 2-10-0 No. WD600 *Gordon*, which also worked on the Longmoor Military Railway. In October 2011, the 1940-built 8F, which was ordered from the North British Locomotive Company of Glasgow by the War Department, became the focal point of a service in the Engine House honouring nine people killed during the Battle of Britain when a German bomber attacked the Melbourne Military Railway near Castle Donington in Derbyshire. SVR

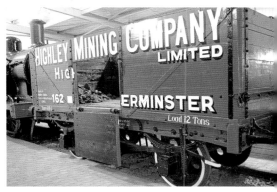

LEFT: These 21st-century trainspotters have a grandstand view of locomotives inside the Engine House from the viewing galley, including LMS 'Black Five' No. 45110, Manchester Ship Canal Hunslet 0-6-0T No. 686 *The Lady Armaghdale* and, in the middle, Hughes 0-4-2ST No. 3 *Sir Haydn*, which joined the revived Talyllyn Railway from neighbour the Corris Railway in 1951. It visited the SVR in 2013.

ABOVE: One of the first exhibits to arrive at the Engine House museum was the National Railway Museum's Midland compound 4-4-0 No. 1000, pictured arriving at the line in the summer of 2007. However, it had to wait several months to get access to the new showpiece building because of the flood devastation at Highley. DAVID MEE/SVR

ABOVE: The original Highley Mining Company wagon No. 425 was built by the Gloucester Railway Carriage & Wagon Company Limited, but this replica was derived from a similar vehicle donated to the SVR by the British Sugar Corporation. ROBIN JONES

LEFT: The Highley Colliery brass band, positioned next to GWR 4-6-0 No. 4930 Hagley Hall, performed at the official opening of the Engine House on March 20, 2008. ROBIN JONES

BELOW: The superb view of the line from the balcony at the Engine House: GWR 4-6-0 No. 7812 *Erlestoke* Manor returns to Bewdley on March 20, 2008. ROBIN JONES

Chapter 14

Building for the next
50 years

As the SVR celebrates 50 years it's put in place schemes to ensure the success of the railway continues.

AT THE CUTTING EDGE OF THE MODERN STEAM ERA

Faces from the early years of the preservation movement were again reunited when the Severn Valley Railway celebrated its 40th anniversary with a special train.

The train, hauled by Ivatt 2-6-0 No, 43106, left Bridgnorth at 2pm on May 23, 2010 – 40 years to the day that Collett 0-6-0 No. 3205, hauled the line's first public train.

Bridgnorth's mayor, Coun Val Gill, praised the success of the railway before waving it off from the station. "It brings so many visitors and it's a credit to the town," she said. "All the people put so many hours of work in to keep it going."

Among the guests on board were several founders of the Severn Valley Railway Society from that meeting at the Coopers Arms in 1965.

Those early pioneers reminisced about the days when Green Shield stamps donated by members and supporters were used to buy a Black & Decker power drill, a 200ft reel of hosepipe, hammers and other tools for the small working parties patching up derelict Bridgnorth station on Sunday afternoons.

Back then, newspapers were saved and bundled by the mountainload to be sold for pulping to raise cash. There were jumble sales, prize draws and bingo nights in Bridgnorth station. Among endless appeals for donations and working materials published in the quarterly, Severn Valley Railway News, were pleas for paintbrushes, shovels, forks, pickaxes and wheelbarrows, and even weedkiller.

John Hill, 71, a former SVR traffic manager, who drove that first public train in 1970, and who retired from the line in 1998, stepped up on to the footplate for the journey to Kidderminster. He said: "We have come from having absolutely nothing to a railway with 30 engines, 60 coaches and a variety of wagons."

The railway had by then grown from carrying 32,000 passengers between May and December 1970 to 250,000 a year, with an annual turnover of more than £6 million.

No. 3205 was not available to take its place at the head of the anniversary train, as it did 10 years previously, as it was in the final stages of its overhaul at the South Devon Railway's Buckfastleigh workshops.

ABOVE: Founder members of the Severn Valley Railway gather alongside the anniversary VIP special from Bridgnorth. ROBIN JONES

RIGHT: Bridgnorth mayor, Val Gill, and SVR founder member, Don Wilcox, with No. 43106 which had just hauled the 40th anniversary VIP special from Bridgnorth into Kidderminster on May 23, 2010. ROBIN JONES

ABOVE: Retired driver, John Hill, who drove the first Severn Valley public train on May 23, 1970. ROBIN JONES

THE 2010 SHARE ISSUE

The year 2012 was the 150th anniversary of the first public train to travel along the line of the Severn Valley Railway. Officials began thinking – how should the heritage line mark the 50th anniversary of the line's founding society?

Feedback from shareholders, supporters and volunteers indicated that the time was right for the board to embark on a major investment programme to prepare the railway for the next 50 years.

A share issue was duly launched, and raised more than £2 million through the sale of shares at £1 each.

Among the projects to benefit was the completion of the overhaul of the line's flagship locomotive, GWR 4-6-0 No. 4930 *Hagley Hall* and the associated GWR carriage set.

Much of the money raised has been earmarked for improved visitor facilities at Bridgnorth station, planning for which was still underway at the time of writing in preparation for the planning application to Shropshire County Council.

A new station gateway building, spectator gallery overlooking the motive power department, and a new visitor centre were among the projects being considered for development over a 10-year period.

SVR general manager, Nick Ralls, said: "The development projects present a design challenge, in order to meet our ambition to present the new Bridgnorth in an agreeable style, and also to meet the requirements of Shropshire County Council's planning and conservation officers.

"In so far as the Severn Valley Railway preservation plan was started at Bridgnorth in the 1960s, the natural focus of the line's development until now has been away from the town, southwards to Kidderminster, and to a large extent it's true that Bridgnorth station hasn't kept pace with the remarkable growth of the SVR within the leisure and tourism industry.

"Now we've set out our stall to realise the station's enormous potential as an outstanding general visitor and enthusiast destination."

The proceeds will also support improved motive power department facilities, necessary to provide more efficient overhaul, preparation and maintenance of locomotives, as a centre of excellence for the overhaul of the fleet, plus the upgrading of other infrastructure throughout the line.

MAIN PICTURE ABOVE: Making what was, in reality, a rather pedestrian climb on Eardington bank during the March 23-25 spring steam gala, visiting LNER A4 Pacific No. 4464 *Bittern* gives a clear impression of speed. On December 5, 2013, *Bittern* set a new heritage-era steam speed record by hitting 93pm between Doncaster and York. ROBERT FALCONER

BELOW: All-night running has become an increasingly popular feature of the Severn Valley Railway's autumn galas. On September 23, 2011, GWR 4-6-0 No. 6024 *King Edward I* waits at Bewdley's platform 2 to depart with its last train of the day, to Kidderminster. ALAN CORFIELD

ABOVE: Caledonian Railway 0-6-0 No. 828 from the Strathspey Railway pilots LMS 3F 'Jinty' 0-6-0T No. 47406 from the Great Central Railway on March 23 during the 2012 spring steam gala. HUGH BALLANTYNE

BY ROYAL APPROVAL

In another major national accolade for the line, Severn Valley Railway volunteers were presented with the prestigious Queen's Award for Voluntary Service during a ceremony on October 21, 2013.

As part of the celebrations to mark the 60th anniversary of the Queen's coronation that year, the SVR's volunteers were selected by the Queen to receive the award, while the railway was presented with a commemorative piece of crystal and a certificate signed by the Queen.

The Queen's Award for Voluntary Service rewards excellence and outstanding achievement by groups of volunteers who regularly devote their time to helping others in the community and providing an outstanding service.

The presentations were made by Lt Col Patrick Holcroft LVO OBE, Lord-Lieutenant for Worcestershire, and Algernon Heber-Percy, Lord-Lieutenant for Shropshire.

SVR general manager, Nick Ralls, said: "The passion, commitment and enthusiasm of our volunteers is really what makes the Severn Valley Railway the huge success that it is today. We are a very largely volunteer-run organisation, and to put it bluntly, without the dedication of our volunteers, we could not continue to operate."

In celebration of the achievement, four longstanding SVR volunteers, Hugh McQuade, Columb Howell, Gary Williams and Martin White were invited to sample royal hospitality at a garden party at Buckingham Palace.

LEFT: Severn Valley company deputy chairman, Alan Longdon, holds the prestigious Queen's Award for Voluntary Service on October 21, 2013.*SVR*

LADIES FIRST

ABOVE: Making history: Emma Harrison, the railway's first female apprentice. *SVR*

Among the first to join was 17-year-old Emma Harrison, the railway's first female apprentice. Emma's love of all things heritage and steam was instilled in her by her father and late grandfather, and family holidays regularly included trips to various heritage railways, such as the Talyllyn Railway, were Emma had volunteered since 2011, joining the locomotive crew on their early-morning starts to clean the engines and see them out of the shed for their day's running.

Emma, from Wolverhampton, said: "A great saying in our family is 'a holiday is never a holiday without a railway in it', which developed my love for railways and steam engines, and got me involved in heritage engineering."

In joining the scheme, Emma was fulfilling a family legacy, as her late grandfather was a member of the Gloucestershire Warwickshire Railway, as well as a financial supporter of the SVR, along with Emma's grandmother.

She said: "It's a daunting thought that I'm the first female apprentice with the SVR, but it's a learning curve for both me and the railway."

The academy is now looking to recruit five new trainees each year, Shelagh Paterson, fundraising manager for the SVR Charitable Trust, said: "Thanks to the incredible generosity of individuals and grants, the charitable trust is delighted to be able to financially support the academy and invest in the future of the Severn Valley Railway."

50MPH STEAM ON THE VALLEY!

Today's heritage lines operate under the provisions of the 1896 Light Railways Act, which sets a maximum speed limit of 25mph.

That rule is, for all normal intents and purposes, set in stone. However, it is possible to obtain dispensation from the statutory body, the Office of Rail & Road (formerly the Office of Rail Regulation), for locomotives and trains to be run at speeds higher than 25mph in special circumstances, such as test runs. In such cases, an engineering possession of the line has to be made, which rules it off limits to the public for the duration of such runs, and prohibits the operation of other trains.

World headlines and heritage railway history was made on Sundays January 13 and 20, 2013, when Metropolitan Railway 0-4-4T No. 1 hauled a series of public passenger trains comprising vintage coaches and a teak milk van as a secondary water carrier through the tunnels of London Underground's District and Circle lines.

Who would have thought that running a Victorian train of wooden-bodied coaches and a steam locomotive dating from 1898 in-between modern electric tube trains would have been possible?

Yet it happened, in a joint venture between the Underground and London Transport Museum to mark the 150th anniversary of the Metropolitan Railway, the world's first subway line, with the locomotive being loaned long-term from the Buckinghamshire Railway Centre and most of the coaching stock borrowed from the Bluebell Railway.

A series of stringent tests had to be carried out before the authorities would permit such an operation.

One such test involved running No. 1 at 50mph – backwards

from Bewdley to Kidderminster on the Severn Valley Railway, complete with a three-coach train, and all officially sanctioned.

The £250,000 overhaul, for which a nationwide public appeal had been successfully launched by the Covent Garden museum, was completed at Bill Parker's Flour Mill workshops at Bream in the Forest of Dean, a specialist in the restoration of Victorian steam engines, on November 21, 2012. That day, it steamed outside the workshops in unlined red livery.

Two days later, again amidst secrecy, it arrived for three days of running in on the Avon Valley Railway, where teething problems were picked up.

After that, it moved to the Severn Valley, were more test runs were undertaken on November 28-29, with No. 1 hauling three Mk.1 coaches. Advantage was taken of the SVR's load weight apparatus to ensure that the wheels were properly balanced, and it was found that a slight adjustment had to be made.

Finally, on Friday, November 30, the history-making high-speed runs took place. These trials were necessary because of the risks involved in running steam trains on the Underground between regular service trains carrying up to 1200 people. Organisers of the Metropolitan Railway 150 event had to be assured that the locomotive would cope.

Firstly, a run took place at 25mph, between Bewdley and Kidderminster, bunker first. The run was repeated at 35mph, then 40mph.

Finally, the moment of truth came, when No. 1 repeated the trip at 50mph – and passed all the tests with flying colours. The high-speed runs were made on the eastbound leg of the journey, with the returns, chimney first, all at 25mph.

PRESERVING THE SKILLS OF THE STEAM ERA

We have seen how the Severn Valley expanded from 4¼ miles in length to 16 miles, and then embarked on a horizontal programme of expansion, adding groundbreaking facilities such as the Bridgnorth boiler shop and Kidderminster carriage shed, keeping the line at the forefront of the heritage railway sector.

Yet would magnificent facilities alone be enough for the future? What use would they be if there was nobody around with the skills to use them?

Steam on British railways ended in August 1968, and by then much of the expertise required to keep steam locomotives running on the main line had disappeared.

Many former BR workers gave their time and experience freely to help the early heritage lines, but as the steam era passes further into the realms of history, and the old hands are no longer around, a new generation must replace them.

Hence the Severn Valley's Heritage Skills Training Academy, a major project of national significance, which was funded by the proceeds of the share issue. The aim is to arrest the decline of heritage engineering skills and hence ensure this piece of local living history continues well into the future.

The academy is designed to train young apprentices in the traditional methods of working and to instruct them in the essential skills of locomotive fitting, boiler making, carriage joinery, maintenance and restoration as well as the restoration of heritage buildings. Such skills can be applied not only on the SVR but in many other railway and engineering settings.

A pilot scheme involving three apprentices began in September 2013.

The academy was officially opened in September 2014, with five more apprentices joining up for four-year courses geared towards a Level 3 NVQ in engineering. For the first two years, students spend three days a week studying at Telford College of Arts and

LEFT: Young apprentices are 'shadowed' by an experienced member of the workshop staff. SVR

Technology and two days doing paid work at the railway, learning about all aspects of its operation.

In the third and fourth year, typically one day a week is spent at college, while the other four days are spent in the SVR's workshops.

Throughout the course, all college fees and daily transport expenses from key points along the SVR will be covered for trainees.

Trainee, Max Green, 17, said: "It's great because there's so much variety to the scheme. Every day is different; you're never doing the same job."

At the autumn 2014 steam gala, the academy received a delivery of £8000 worth of tools from B&Q. Each apprentice was presented with their own tool set to keep.

ABOVE: Metropolitan Railway 0-4-4T No. 1 heads back towards Bewdley from Kidderminster at 25mph on November 30, 2012. PAUL CHANCELLOR

The following Tuesday, December 4, No. 1 was back on home territory, having been taken by low loader to the museum's Acton depot.

No. 1 then undertook a series of private night-time test runs from London Underground's Lillie Bridge depot to Earls Court and Baker Street early on December 16.

I was a guest on board those runs. I will never forget the look of shock and amazement on the crack-of-dawn commuters' faces as we passed through Earls Court on the final run back to Lillie

Bridge, as several of them scrambled for their mobile telephone cameras to back up the story that none of their friends would ever believe, that they had seen a steam train on the Underground and had not been out drinking the night before.

The exploits of No. 1 throughout the Met 150 celebrations that year won the Underground and the museum the Heritage Railway Association's top award, the 2013 Peter Manisty Award for Excellence.

And the Severn Valley Railway played its part.

The Valley at the movies

From small TV productions to big movies the Severn Valley Railway has had a starring role in them all.

One big spin-off for the heritage railway sector is the ability to hire out lines and stations for location filming work for TV drama series or big-screen movies.

With the demise of steam on the national network, the wholesale closures of country branch lines and the eradication of much classic railway architecture in the name of modernisation, filmmakers who need to capture transport scenes of yesteryear are left with few alternatives.

The Severn Valley has much to offer film directors, with its varying landscape and classic railway structures.

Over 35 days in 1975, portions of The Seven Per Cent Solution were not only filmed on the railway, but part of the lifted Stourport branch was relaid specially for the occasion.

This Hollywood film, which starred Laurence Olivier, Vanessa Redgrave, Robert Duvall, Samantha Eggar, Jill Townsend and Nicole Williamson was based on the 1974 Sherlock Holmes pastiche by American writer Nicholas Meyer. Published as a 'lost manuscript' of the late Dr Watson, the book recounts Holmes' recovery from cocaine addiction and his subsequent prevention of a European war through the unravelling of a sinister kidnapping plot – with a train chase thrown in for good measure.

The Stourport branch was relaid to within 200 yards of Mount Pleasant Tunnel because a sequence in the film required two converging tracks and it was the only suitable location on the railway. Track was lifted from Alveley sidings in 60ft lengths using the steam crane and concrete sleepers that had been stored at Arley. More rail was purchased from Windsor Street gasworks in Birmingham, and a quantity of BR reinforced concrete sleepers were bought from a store at Cambridge and brought in by rail. Some of the rails used were from the Tenbury Wells branch. It was not the intention to leave the track down permanently as the rails were needed to relay the SVR running line.

Hunslet Austerity 0-6-ST No. WD193 and four coaches were used to test the relaid track

ABOVE: Three quarters of a mile of the Stourport line from Bewdley South Junction was relaid in late summer 1975 for the filming of The Seven Per Cent Solution. Hunslet Austerity 0-6-0ST No. WD193 is seen testing the relaid section near Mount Pleasant on September 28. R AMIES/SVR ARCHIVES

up to 25pmh just before it was declared safe in time for filming to start on September 29.

The filmmakers needed to have the same locomotive running in different directions, but at the time the SVR did not have a turntable. So, the two LMS moguls, Nos, 46443 and 46521, which faced the opposite direction, were repainted in red to appear as a foreign locomotive, 'No 60016'. Similarly, 'Black Five' No. 45110 and Stanier 8F No. 48773 doubled up as the same engine, but this time in black.

The 1976 BBC television adaptation of Charles Dickens' short story The Signalman was filmed around the cutting on the Kidderminster side of Foley Park tunnel. A replica signalbox was constructed in the cutting, while interior scenes were filmed in the real one at Highley.

That year, scenes for Walt Disney's film Candleshoe starring David Niven and Jodie Foster were filmed between Bewdley and Hampton Loade. The film was released in 1977 the same year as the screening of the British and Canadian TV version of Arthur Conan Doyle's Silver Blaze, which starred Christopher

Plummer and was also filmed on the railway.

The 1978 film remake of The Thirty Nine Steps was partly filmed on the SVR. In one scene, Hannay, played by Robert Powell hangs from Victoria Bridge. The scene is supposed to be set in Scotland, and the landscape is very out of place for that area.

The BBC TV children's series God's Wonderful Railway, screened in 1980, was filmed on the line, while the following year, Bridgnorth station was used a sketch for the TV comedy Not the Nine O'Clock News, in which Mel Smith's character observes a steam train passing by without stopping and refers to it as an "old chuffer". Also in 1981, the railway popped up in Game for a Laugh presented by Joe Brown and Matthew Kelly.

Joanna Lumley and Michael York appeared in the 1984 TV movie The Weather in the Streets, while The Fasting Girl starring Iain Cuthbertson also included SVR scenes.

In 1984, scenes for the BBC TV series The District Nurse were filmed at Bewdley station. Also that year, Arley station was used for the BBC adaptation of John Masefield's children's ▶

ABOVE: Laurence Oliver with LMS 2-6-0 No. 46443. SVR ARCHIVES

RIGHT: The Seven Per Cent Solution film crew in action. SVR ARCHIVES

LEFT: One of the line's two LMS moguls was repainted red for The Seven Per Cent Solution film. SVR ARCHIVES

LEFT: Ivatt 2-6-0 No. 46443 is filmed crossing Victoria Bridge in The Thirty Nine Steps. SVR ARCHIVES

RIGHT: Robert Powell as Richard Hannay in the production of the 1978 film The Thirty Nine Steps, which also starred John Mills. SVR ARCHIVES

ABOVE: Ivatt 2-6-0 No. 46443 masquerading as 'No. 644' in The Thirty Nine Steps. SVR ARCHIVES

fantasy The Box of Delights. An episode of Cilla Black's Surprise Surprise that year also included the railway.

Bewdley station had a starring role in the BBC's 1987 adaptation of Agatha Christie's Miss Marple novel, 4.50 From Paddington.

LMS 'Flying Pig' No. 43106 featured in the 1987 ITV children's serial, Knights of God, while Bewdley station became 'Hilton' railway in the Merchant Ivory Productions' 1992 film of EM Forster's Howards End (film) featuring Anthony Hopkins and Emma Thompson.

The SVR was featured in the 1993 adaptation of Death at the Bar; an episode of The Inspector Alleyn Mysteries.

Between 1995-97 the railway was used for filming the sitcom Oh, Doctor Beeching! set in 1963 and featuring Paul Shane, Su

Pollard and Jeffrey Holland. Exterior shots were filmed in Arley station, which became 'Hatley' station where a false row of cottages was temporarily erected in the goods yard.

The 1998 ITV family drama Goodnight Mister Tom, featuring John Thaw, had its station sequences filmed in early spring at Arley, with trains running through without stopping for two weeks.

In the 2005 big-screen version of CS Lewis' The Chronicles of Narnia: The Lion, the Witch and the Wardrobe, GWR 4-6-0 No. 7802 *Bradley Manor* appeared with the train that brought the Pevensies to the nearest station to the professor's house. That year, celebrity steeplejack Fred Dibnah filmed scenes for his TV series Made in Britain – Engines at Work.

Dancing On The Edge, a five-part dramatisation by Stephen Poliakoff, filmed in February 2012 and aired in February 2013, featured Bewdley and Kidderminster stations and LMS mogul No. 42968 hauling the line's rake of LNER teak coaches.

In 2012, the BBC2 documentary series Great British Railway Journeys presented by Michael Portillo visited the SVR, filming one of the series' latest journeys for its fourth series, which was broadcast in January 2013. Also in 2012, the series How Britain Worked and The Golden Age of Steam Railways with Jenny Agutter, best known for her role in EMI's

big-screen adaptation of The Railway Children on the Keighley & Worth Valley Railway, were filmed on the SVR.

Los Angeles-based Indian filmmaker Kavi Raz in 2014 chose the railway and Worcestershire for scenes in his movie The Black Prince, based on the real-life story of Sikh Maharaja, the last king of Punjab and starring Satinder Sartaaj, Jason Flemyng and Keith Duffy.

Judging by its track record to date, it seems that the Severn Valley Railway will be on the big and small screens for decades to come. •

ABOVE: David Niven at the Severn Valley Railway in 1977 during the filming of Candleshoe, also starring Jodie Foster. SVR ARCHIVES

LEFT: The DVD collection of the popular TV sitcom Oh Doctor Beeching!, which was filmed at Arley station.

BELOW: The opening credits for Oh Doctor Beeching! featured Ivatt 2-6-0 No. 46521.

ABOVE: John Thaw and Nick Robinson at Arley in 1998 during filming for the TV family drama Goodnight Mr Tom. SVR ARCHIVES

ABOVE: Actress Jenny Agutter signs copies of her book, The Illustrated Railway Children, published to mark the centenary of the Edith A Nesbit children's classic, with SVR driver Don Shadwell at Kidderminster station on September 24, 2005. SVR ARCHIVES

ABOVE: GWR 4-6-0 No. 6024 *King Edward I*, which had just completed repairs at Didcot Railway Centre, gets ready to haul the Royal Train carrying the future king out of Kidderminster Town on June 10, 2008. PETER BROSTER

By royal appointment

The Severn Valley Railway is no stranger to royal guests eager to ride on the footplate.

Prince and Princess Michael of Kent were its first royal visitors in 1993 aboard the Orient Express and Princess Alexandra has also visited in a personal capacity.

However, in what is believed to be a 'first' for a heritage railway, the Royal Train travelled the full length of the line carrying the Prince of Wales and the Duchess of Cornwall on June 10, 2008.

The high-profile visit had been pencilled in for 2007, but was called off when the line was twice affected by the floods that year. Now, Charles and Camilla wanted to see for themselves the work that had gone into restoring the line following the devastation.

GWR 4-6-0 No. 6024 *King Edward I* fittingly hauled the Royal Train, which was brought to Kidderminster behind a Class 67 diesel. A collection of classic cars, usually on show during special transport galas at the railway, were lined up to greet the royal visitors arriving by car from Worcester after an earlier engagement, one car representing every decade from the Twenties to the Sixties.

After talking to people in the crowds gathered outside Kidderminster Town station, the couple entered the ticket office where

guards in old-fashioned waistcoats and flat caps were waiting to greet him, and where they were presented with complimentary tickets for the trip.

In the booking hall Prince Charles unveiled a plaque, while Camilla was presented with a bouquet by Anna Leach, the 10-year-old daughter of the line's late marketing manager, John Leach; she was among a group of flag-waving youngsters from Bayton Primary School.

Charles was also presented with a replica of LMS Princess Royal 4-6-2 No. 6201 *Princess*

Elizabeth, which was on loan to the railway for the occasion in case of breakdowns.

The Prince asked visitors if they were "all steam enthusiasts" and told them it was "important to keep the heritage railway going".

King Edward I then coupled up to the Royal Train and set off for Bridgnorth. After visiting Bewdley North signalbox, Charles, dressed in an impeccable grey suit with a light blue shirt and tie, donned an overall and gloves provided by stationmaster, Alan Longdon, and took the controls of the locomotive on its journey as far as Arley. ▶

ABOVE: Prince of Wales unveils a plaque marking his visit on June 10, 2008.

ABOVE: Princess Anne boards the footplate of GWR 4-6-0 No. 7812 *Erlestoke Manor*. BOB SWEET/SVR

ABOVE: Princess Anne, wearing a driver's overall, talks to fellow members of the *Erlestoke Manor* footplate crew. BOB SWEET/SVR

Alan said: "It went like clockwork. It really couldn't have been better. "This was the first time the Royal Train has ever been on a heritage railway."

Boarding the footplate, Charles sounded the whistle. "It's amazing what small things will please," he quipped.

The train stopped at Hampton Loade railway station where they were joined by Lord Lieutenant of Shropshire, Algernon Heber-Percy, and his wife Jane.

The Prince and Duchess greeted stationmaster, Steve Dockerty, and railway members Bill and Muriel Bennett who had lived in the station house at Hampton Loade for more than 50 years.

At Bridgnorth, the Prince unveiled a plaque to mark his visit to the station, talked of the childhood memories that the steam trip revived for himself and Camilla and also had half a pint in the station's Railwayman's Arms bar.

The train was returned from Bridgnorth between two Class 67s in top-and-tail mode. No. 67006 had been sent light engine ahead of the train in case of problems.

THE ENTHUSIAST DUKE

Its patron since 1998, the Duke of Gloucester, has visited several times, officially opening the £650,000 Kidderminster Town station extension in 1996 and the Engine House Visitor Centre at Highley in April 2009. He also visited in October 2007 to observe the rebuilding programme following that summer's floods.

He returned on May 14, 2012, to give the royal seal of approval to the line's 150th anniversary celebrations.

Renowned for his special interest in railway preservation, the Duke toured an exhibition at Kidderminster Railway Museum documenting the history of the line since the

ABOVE: Princess Anne meeting pioneers of one of the world's most successful heritage railways, Keith Beddoes, Christopher George, Columb Howell and Roger Hobson. BOB SWEET/SVR

ABOVE: The Princess unveils a plaque at Kidderminster Town station marking her visit. ROBIN JONES

ABOVE: The Princess is presented with a billy can and whistle by Nick Paul CBE, chairman of Severn Valley Railway (Holdings) plc. BOB SWEET/SVR

first public trains ran on February 1, 1862, and made the short journey to Bewdley behind the country's oldest working steam locomotive, visiting 1863-built Furness Railway 0-4-0 No 20 and unveiling a commemorative plaque, recording the 150th anniversary of the line.

Another plaque was unveiled at Bewdley to mark the 150th anniversary of the first train on the SVR line, from Hartlebury Junction to Shrewsbury.

THE PRINCESS OF STEAM

Princess Anne rekindled her love for steam when she drove GWR 4-6-0 No. 7812 *Erlestoke Manor* from Bewdley to Kidderminster as one of the major highlights of the line's 2015 50th anniversary celebrations.

Following in the footsteps of her brother, the Princess Royal captured the hearts of the railway's founder members, officials and supporters when she donned overalls and took the controls of the locomotive during her eagerly awaited visit on April 13.

Waiting in Bewdley station were children from the town's primary school who had gathered in anticipation to welcome the Princess, who arrived by car to be greeted by mayor of Bewdley, Coun Derek Killingworth and was introduced to a group of SVR pioneers and station staff including younger volunteers.

She then took up the invitation to board the footplate of the Manor to make the 15-minute journey to Kidderminster. She enjoyed her footplate experience so much that she stayed on board after the locomotive had pulled into the station, chatting to driver, Paul Fathers, and fireman, Ryan Green, about the ins and outs of driving and firing a steam engine.

Although she was making her first visit to the line, Princess Anne is no stranger to the footplates of steam locomotives. She had previously been given a private locomotive driving course along with her second husband,

naval officer Timothy Laurence at the Gloucestershire Warwickshire Railway; the closest line to their Cotswold home.

Waiting on the Kidderminster concourse to greet the Princess were four of the SVR founding members, Keith Beddoes, Christopher George, Columb Howell and Roger Hobson, along with a group of flag-waving children and teachers from Comberton Primary School.

The Princess was then asked to unveil a plaque celebrating 50 years of the SVR, but the great British weather got there first, blowing the curtain off before the official unveiling, much to her amusement.

She made a short speech congratulating the SVR on its golden jubilee and thanking all those involved in the visit for enabling her to travel on the footplate, making special mention

of the Queen's Award for Voluntary Service made to the line two years before.

Finally, she was given a behind-the-scenes tour of the carriage works at Kidderminster, to meet volunteers and some of the young apprentices of the Heritage Skills Training Academy. She was shown demonstrations of the apprentices in action in the upholstery shop, paintshop and mechanical floor.

SVR general manager, Nick Ralls, said: "She was extremely complimentary about our buildings, personnel and achievements and was more than happy to chat to volunteers about steam locomotives and 'trainspotting'. She seemed to enjoy her footplate experience so much that it looked like she could have stayed up there chatting to our volunteers for much longer if she didn't have a tight schedule to keep to!" ●

RIGHT: Kidderminster Town is home to the Coalyard Miniature Railway, a 390-yard 7¼in gauge line, which starts next to Kidderminster Station Museum and runs past the water column. Its name is derived from a coal merchant business which operated alongside Kidderminster Town until 2004, it dates from 1988. Decked out as a Royal Train in miniature for the arrival of Princess Anne on April 13, 2015 is Station Road Steam 0-4-0ST *Phoebe*. ROBIN JONES

Chapter 17

Kidderminster
Railway Museum

As a separate attraction, Kidderminster Town station has a splendid railway museum housed in a former GWR warehouse.

Few heritage lines can boast attractions of the likes of the Engine House at Highley and Kidderminster Railway Museum at Kidderminster Town station.

Although the latter was established by group of volunteers from the Severn Valley Railway in 1990, in a warehouse built by the GWR in 1878, it is a separate entity.

The museum contains a vast array of artefacts, from nameplates to signalling equipment and tickets to miniature steam locomotives. In addition, it has a fabulous archive of more than 150,000 photographs and 25,000 slides from 1880 onwards, covering not the entire SVR history but that of the entire UK network, although there is a bias towards the GWR system.

The volunteers who set up this splendid facility first had to return the building to its original appearance while making it safe.

The ground floor of the warehouse was used for the storage of grain for the nearby flour mills, and wool was kept for Kidderminster's famous carpet industries.

Served by a siding on one side, it had road access on the other. It was converted into a parcels warehouse in the Sixties, but with the rundown and closure of the line became disused and by the early Eighties it had become derelict.

Among the larger exhibits are the Midland Railway booking office from Alvechurch, a telephone exchange with working equipment and an exhibition of trackwork and associated items such as boundary and gradient posts. It has one of the biggest collections of signalling equipment in the country. The picture, magazine, book and archive collections are held in the library and are available for research, but prior booking is essential. The

museum has a Friends Club that raises money for capital projects.

Special events are held throughout the year, ranging from film shows to postcard fairs and art exhibitions.

A registered charity, it is a fully registered and accredited museum with the Museums Libraries and Archives.

The images in the archive are fully documented and are available for private research or for publication, subject to payment of a reproduction fee. Several well-known collections are now deposited in the museum, along with the early photographic archive of signalling manufacturer Westinghouse.

The museum can also be booked for private functions and corporate hospitality.

For details about opening times visit www.krm.org.uk or telephone 01562 825316. ●

BELOW: Kidderminster Railway Museum at Kidderminster Town station. A miniature line called the Coalyard Railway runs outside. ROBIN JONES

ABOVE: A miniature version of Western Region 15XX pannier tank No. 1511, a sister locomotive to the SVR's No. 1501, on display inside the museum. Introduced in 1949, the 10-strong class would never have carried this livery in service. ROBIN JONES

LEFT: Kidderminster Railway Museum general manager, David Postle, gave the Duke of Kent a guided tour during his visit to the Severn Valley Railway on May 12, 2012. ROBIN JONES

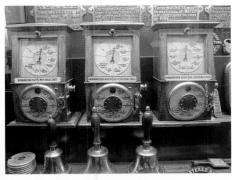

ABOVE: Block signalling equipment on display. ROBIN JONES

ABOVE: A nameplate and numberplate from SVR flagship GWR 4-6-0 No. 4930 *Hagley Hall* are among many on display. ROBIN JONES

ABOVE: Relics from lines that were not so fortunate as the Severn Valley branch: King's Heath station in Birmingham was a pre-Beeching closure while Alcester lost its services from Redditch and Evesham and was wiped off the railway map. ROBIN JONES

ABOVE: An extensive collection of historic railway mileposts and boundary posts. ROBIN JONES

ABOVE: Station totem signs both from the West Midlands and further afield. ROBIN JONES

Chapter 18

The day of the diesels

Not only a world-renowned haven of steam, the Severn Valley has a fleet of classic diesels too – and a state-of-the-art maintenance depot for them.

While steam remains the predominant image of railway preservation, and indeed was the primary reason for the origins and subsequent growth of the movement, most heritage lines now have their own fleet of diesels.

Detested by linesiders as the cause of the demise of their beloved steam locomotives, classic diesels are now a source of nostalgia for subsequent generations of enthusiasts.

Indeed, it is often forgotten that the first public trains on Britain's biggest narrow gauge line, the Ffestiniog Railway, and the Middleton Railway, which claims to be the country's first preserved standard gauge line, were hauled by diesels, in 1954 and 1960 respectively.

Diesel traction now has a firm place on the Severn Valley Railway.

Its splendid fleet includes classic examples of the Western Region diesel hydraulics, which were ousted from the national network by British Rail in the name of standardisation, with the diesel electric types preferred by the other regions becoming the norm, and other first-generation types.

Included in that category are several shunters essential for undertaking permanent way work at a fraction of the cost of firing up a tank engine to do the same job.

The railway also holds successful diesel weekends and galas, and specified dates where a set number of services are hauled by modern traction.

For many years the SVR has included a diesel turn in some of its timetables, especially Timetable C, which operates on Saturdays as well as Timetable A during mid-week running. Today around 10% of the SVR's trains are scheduled to be hauled by heritage diesel locomotives or diesel railcars.

Although there is little doubt that the majority of visitors at preserved railways expect their train to be pulled by a steam locomotive, there is increasing evidence that a growing number are perfectly happy to be pulled by a diesel, or a mixture of the two.

BELOW: The railway has enjoyed occasional visits from preserved Class 55 Deltics, which replaced the likes of *Flying Scotsman* and *Mallard* on the East Coast Main Line. No. 55015 *Tulyar* passes Eardington on May 7, 1988. BRIAN SHARPE

TWO WESTERNS ARRIVE

The Severn Valley is home to two of the mighty Class 52 Western diesel hydraulics, a classic example of a modern traction type that steam fans begrudgingly came to admire. Both are under the custodianship of the Western Locomotive Association.

The Class 52s Co-Cos, of which 74 were built by Swindon and Crewe Works between 1961-64, were designed to do what the otherwise successful Class 42s could not, including runs over the notorious South Devon banks.

D1013 *Western Ranger* emerged from Swindon on December 13, 1962 and was first based at Cardiff Canton, It was later transferred to Old Oak Common, Swansea Landore and Laira, from where it was withdrawn on February 28, 1977, with 1,300,000 miles on the clock.

One of the last batch of Westerns in service, it headed many 'farewell' railtours that year, including the 'Southern Belle' and 'Western Tribute', the latter marking the last day in service of the class.

Privately purchased by Richard Holdsworth at Newton Abbot in May 1977, it worked on the Torbay & Dartmouth Steam Railway (now known simply as the Dartmouth Steam Railway), until transferred to the SVR with sister D1062 *Western Courier* on September 29, 1978. They were the first 'big name' ex main line diesels to arrive on the SVR.

No. D1062 was outshopped by Crewe Works on May 6, 1963, and was allocated new to Old Oak Common, later serving at Cardiff Canton, Swansea Landore and Laira. Withdrawn on August 22, 1974, it had 1,096,000 miles on the clock.

Founder members of the Western Locomotive Association met in 1973 to discuss saving a Class 52, at a time when the first withdrawals of the class were taking place. At a meeting in Bristol in January 1974, the association was formally launched.

ABOVE: Class 52 diesel-hydraulic D1062 *Western Courier* passes Eardington on May 7, 1988. BRIAN SHARPE

In October 1976 the association bought D1062 *Western Courier* and had restored it to full operational condition in original maroon livery by May 1977. Richard Holdsworth placed *Western Ranger* in the care of the association before selling it to fellow member Roger Smith.

The move to the SVR greatly increased the opportunities to operate the locomotives. Over the years a considerable amount of overhaul and maintenance work has been undertaken to ensure that the locomotives remain in peak condition.

D1013 is currently undergoing an extensive overhaul, including a complete rewire, which is due for completion in 2018. D1062 remains fully operational on the line.

A DIESEL PRESERVATION FIRST

A landmark member of Britain's heritage diesel fleet is Class 42 Warship diesel-hydraulic Bo-Bo D821 *Greyhound*, because it is one of only two examples of a once-proud and distinctive main line type that is preserved.

The class was largely based on the German V2000 class of 1953, with 38 being built by Swindon and 33 by North British, as a direct result of British Railways' 1955 Modernisation Plan.

D821 *Greyhound* emerged from Swindon in May 1960, and was allocated to Plymouth Laira, with brief periods at Newton Abbot.

The Warship class appeared in 1958 and was designed for working fast services from Paddington to Bristol, Plymouth and Penzance and also from Bristol to Shrewsbury and Crewe. However, the comparatively low 79-ton total weight was not good enough to guarantee adhesion on the South Devon banks, especially in autumn when leaf fall greased the rails. Double-heading became necessary at such times – hardly an improvement on the steam era.

So, when the abovementioned Class 52 Westerns appeared in 1961, the Warships were taken off the more prestigious passenger trains, and replaced Bulleid Pacifics on Waterloo to Exeter trains from 1964 onwards. They were also to be found on cross-country traffic from Bristol and Cardiff,

with limited use from Paddington to Oxford and Wolverhampton, and miscellaneous parcels work. All of the Class 42s were withdrawn between 1968-72.

D821 was withdrawn from Laira in December 1972, having run in BR green, maroon and corporate blue livery during its career.

The year before, Colin Massingham of Modern Traction Kits models came up with the idea of preserving a diesel locomotive. At that time, although several classes of first-generation diesels had been withdrawn and were destined to be rendered extinct by the scrapman, less than no interest was shown by the majority of enthusiasts who habitually and vociferously expressed their disdain for diesels.

However, in May 1973, D821 made history by becoming the first main line diesel to be preserved by a private group, and moved to Didcot Railway Centre. The group had tried to save North British Warship D6319, but it was scrapped at Swindon.

The Great Western Society disliked the presence of diesels at the centre, and so on February 9, 1974, D821 was hauled to Reading Gasworks where it was restored to maroon livery.

In 1977, Colin along with five other enthusiasts formed the Diesel Traction Group.

In February that year, D821 was towed to

Swindon Works along with the group's Class 35 Hymek D7029 (see below).

Returned to working order, the pair were towed to the North Yorkshire Moors Railway on April 16, 1981, and D821 operated there successfully for a decade. Its owning group moved it to the SVR in September 1991. Since then, it has run in regular service and also visited other heritage lines. Between March 2001 and September 2002, it took on the identity of *Cornwall* after being twinned with a Royal Navy warship of the same name during a visit to Falmouth Docks.

ABOVE: Class 42 Warship D821 *Greyhound* was the first main line diesel to be bought by a private group. PAUL APPLETON

FOUR CLASS 50s

The last main line diesel passenger locomotive built for British Railways was the Class 50 Co-Co, of which English Electric's Vulcan Foundry built 50 works at Newton-le-Willows, near Warrington. All of them had entered service by December 1968, based at Crewe Diesel Depot, from where they worked Anglo-Scottish services north of the then West Coast Main Line electrification limit at Crewe.

As the electrification of the WCML moved northwards, the need for the 50s on their premier route was reduced, but they found

a welcome bolthole on the Western Region, replacing diesel hydraulic types between 1973-76. They were used to haul top expresses from Paddington to the west of England, and later, Waterloo to Exeter services, replacing Class 33s.

In turn, they were displaced by the arrival of Class 43 High Speed Train sets, Class 47s and Super Sprinter DMUs. As the class was relatively small, they were a target for British Rail's mid-Eighties standardisation pruning of its locomotive fleet.

The Fifty Fund was founded in 1989 in an attempt to preserve a Class 50 at a time when it seemed unlikely that many examples would be saved. The class was withdrawn between 1987-92, but 18 ended up in preservation – including four on the SVR.

No. 50031 entered service in July 1968 as D431, and in June 1978 was named *Hood* in honour of the Royal Navy ship of that name. Withdrawn from Laira in August 1991, it was bought four months later by two enthusiasts who wished to place it in the care of the Fifty Fund. ▶

ABOVE: English Electric Class 50 (formerly Type 4) No. 50031 *Hood* is one of four examples of the class in the care of the Class 50 Alliance that will benefit from the new facilities at Kidderminster. Here it takes charge of the shunt at Highley that saw 'Black Five' No. 45110 replace GWR No. 4930 *Hagley Hall* in the Engine House Visitor Centre in 2013. PAUL APPLETON

ABOVE: Three of the four Class 50s in the care of the Class 50 Alliance, stand in the yard at Kidderminster on the site of the new diesel maintenance depot. JONATHAN DUNSTER

After undergoing repairs at St Leonards depot in East Sussex, it toured several heritage lines before moving to a new permanent home on the SVR at the start of the May 1994 diesel gala.

It became the third diesel to be certified for main line running and made its comeback on the network with the 'Pilgrim Hoover' tour from Birmingham International to Plymouth on November 1, 1997. In June 1998, a regular rush-hour turn on the Cardiff to Rhymney commuter service was undertaken.

As D435, No. 50035 was allocated new to Crewe in August 1968, and was named *Ark Royal* at a ceremony in Plymouth station on January 17, 1978. It was withdrawn from Old Oak Common in August 1990, carrying Network South East livery.

The Fifty Fund bought it in August 1991 and after undergoing repairs at St Leonards, it was taken to Kidderminster by road in September 1996.

The line's third 'Hoover', No. 50044, was outshopped in August 1968 as D444. Named *Exeter* at a ceremony at Exeter St David's in April 1978, it was withdrawn from Laira in February 1991.

No. 50044 was bought by the Fifty Fund from storage at Stratford, East London, in November 1991, and moved to St Leonards for work to be carried out. It moved to the SVR together with No. 50031 after a rededication ceremony at the Exeter 150 rail exhibition on May 1, 1994.

Exeter was originally bought as a source of spares for No. 50035, in the mistaken belief that many of its components had been stripped, but during the purchase it became clear that it was almost intact. It has since run both on the SVR in regular traffic and at the head of main line excursions.

In 2006, the Fifty Fund agreed to merge its ownership and maintenance responsibilities with Project Defiance. The new combined organisation was named the Class 50 Alliance, with the Fifty Fund becaming a fundraising organisation and historical resource centre.

Built in 1968, No. 50049 *Defiance* worked its last train in August 1991 and was withdrawn that month.

The Class 50 Society bought it in December 1991. The society had been formed back in 1983 as an interest group for followers of the class, and in 1991 formed a limited company called Project Defiance to manage the locomotive. Bought from BR in working order, some restoration was undertaken by society members at Laira.

Initially moved to the West Somerset Railway, it later worked alongside *Hood* on railtours,

Following the formation of the alliance, it was moved to the SVR, where it successfully ran in traffic for several years.

THE HYMEK IN WAITING

A later arrival on the SVR yet to run was Class 35 Hymek Bo-Bo D7029, an example of what has been described as the most successful of the diesel hydraulic types. Beyer Peacock of Gorton, Manchester, built a total of 101 examples between 1961-64. Lacking electric train heating capability, all were withdrawn between January 1971 and March 1975.

D7029 went new to Cardiff Canton in April 1962, moved to Bristol Bath Road in August 1965, Plymouth Laira in August 1967, back to Bristol Bath Road in November 1967, Old Oak Common in April 1968, and was withdrawn from there after two months of storage following a mechanical failure in February 1975.

It was bought by Diesel Traction Group members and stored with the group's Warship D821 at Reading Gasworks. At Swindon Works, D7029 was returned to working order in BR green livery.

D7029 ran in North Yorkshire Moors Railway traffic for six years until withdrawn for repairs on July 23, 1987, and placed in storage.

The Hymek was taken to the SVR in March 1996, initially for tyre turning and air receiver repairs. It was moved to Old Oak Common in May 2000, and returned to the SVR five years later. It is still the subject of long-term restoration having never run on the line, but is one for the future.

SANDWELL COUNCIL'S OWN DIESEL!

A diesel with a connection much closer to home is Class 27 D5410, one of a fleet of 69 designed by the Birmingham Railway Carriage and Wagon Company at Smethwick; it appeared in the summer of 1961. The class was withdrawn during 1985-87, but in the early Eighties,

ABOVE: Three of the four Class 50s in the care of the Class 50 Alliance, stand in the yard at Kidderminster on the site of the new diesel maintenance depot. JONATHAN DUNSTER

members of Sandwell Metropolitan Borough Council decided to buy one because of its local origins.

D5410 was outshopped in August 1962 and served at Cricklewood and Kentish Town depots, before being transferred to the Wellingborough and Nottingham districts early in 1965. It was moved to Scotland in February 1969, and in January 1974, converted for push-pull operation as No. 27123. It was renumbered to 27205 after undergoing electric train heating conversion in December 1974, and 27059 when special equipment was removed in 1983. It was withdrawn from service on July 6, 1987, but visited the Severn Valley gala on October 10-12 that year, after being chosen for the council from a condemned selection at Glasgow Works.

Placed in storage at Tyseley, it had its blue asbestos content removed at Vic Berry's yard at Leicester in 1988 – hauled there by Class 31 No. 31413, which had been named *Severn Valley Railway*, and restored as D5410 at Tyseley by April 1990.

The SVR was chosen as its permanent home, and it was moved there on May 26, 1991. It took part in several galas and special workings, but has since been stored out of use for many years. In 2011, Sandwell Council appealed for help in restoring it.

ABOVE: Visiting Peak diesel D100 *Sherwood Forester* passes the former Tenbury Wells junction near Northwood on October 14, 1989. BRIAN SHARPE

AND THE REST...

The SVR's diverse range of diesel locomotives, includes seven 350hp 0-6-0 diesel electric shunters that provide vital support along the length of the railway to Bridgnorth, as yard shunters, station pilots and on engineering trains. These include Classes 08, 09 and 11, some dating back to the Fifties.

There are also two BR Class 20s, D8059 and D8188, both restored to authentic early BR green livery. A recent acquisition is Class 14 diesel-hydraulic 0-6-0DH D9551 *Angus*, owned by the SVR Class 14 Co Ltd, which is being gradually restored to operational condition at Bridgnorth.

Representing the go-anywhere do-anything Class 37 Co-Co is No. 37906.

Three former industrial diesel mechanical 0-4-0 shunters built by Ruston & Hornsby are all in full working order and can be found along the line used on lighter shunting duties, such as the carriage works at Kidderminster and for shunting the boiler works at Bridgnorth.

RIGHT: Class 20 D8059 pauses between duties at Highley in February 2015. The locomotive is a regular on both engineers' and passenger trains on the Severn Valley Railway. PAUL APPLETON

LEFT: Also based on the railway is a fully operational Class 108 DMU, with five cars operating in various permutations – currently as a four-car set while one car undergoes maintenance. Owned by the DMU Group (West Midlands), it is normally based at Bewdley, where it is seen calling at the station on a special service on February 28, 2015. ROBIN JONES

A DEPOT OF THEIR OWN

The Severn Valley Railway has for long had an open-door policy when it comes to diesel locomotives.

Since the arrival of D1013 and D1062 in 1978, its diesel fleet has grown to more than 20, yet like most other preserved railways, maintaining and overhauling them has not been a priority.

Work on diesels has been largely left to their owning groups, often in open sidings, without any protection from the elements.

At best, some railways have accommodated diesels alongside steam locomotives in their restoration and maintenance sheds, while some groups have been given permission by their host railway to erect basic steel structures, or tents, to carry out essential maintenance.

Diesels require major tasks such as engine changes, which means opening up the roof hatches and craning out the defective unit. Such jobs can involve expensive crane hire fees and also the cooperation of other groups whose vehicles are standing on adjacent pieces of track – a far from ideal state of affairs.

At Kidderminster, a dedicated diesel yard next to the railway's one-fifth of a mile-long carriage shed was established, but it was very much open plan, with groups having to work on their locomotives in all kinds of weather.

There had long been the recognition that some kind of permanent facility was required, but with the excessive demands made on stretched financial resources, a new diesel locomotive maintenance depot has never reached the top of the priority list – until now.

In December 2014, contracts were at long last signed for work to start on building a new dedicated diesel depot – a first for the heritage sector – in the yard at Kidderminster, with the erection beginning in April 2015.

The new building is a three-road shed, the centre road having an inspection pit, and will occupy a footprint of around 1000 sq m.

It will have an overhead travelling crane with a 10-ton lifting capability and there will also be a set of 25-ton synchronised lifting jacks to allow bogies to be released from beneath locomotives.

Jonathan Dunster, a director of the railway's holdings company and also chairman of the diesel committee, said: "After having maintained the entire fleet in the open air, this facility will represent a quantum leap both in terms of the engineering capabilities of the SVR in relation to diesel traction and in terms of the conditions our volunteer staff have to work in. No longer will complex technical work have to be undertaken totally at the mercy of the elements.

"Diesel traction has a broad range of uses, as well as on-service trains and driver experience turns they are also used on ad-hoc traffic such as engineering trains. Diesel shunting locomotives are in almost daily use and are critical to the operation of the SVR. Without provision of dedicated maintenance facilities for diesel locomotives now, it would be impossible to continue to provide locomotives reliably for the railway.

"In my opinion this will be the most well-equipped diesel maintenance facility yet provided anywhere within the UK heritage railway movement and will significantly improve the condition of our resident fleet of heritage diesel locomotives, the majority of which are already more than 50 years old at least.

"In the medium term we are hopeful the facility may attract commercial work from other heritage railways. This may enable us to consider staffing it more regularly and potentially even creating apprenticeships in diesel maintenance skills that are far less common in the wider rail industry following the reduction in the use of locomotives on the national network.

"Once the depot is completed it is our intention to make it available on selected days each year for guided tours as is the case with some of the other SVR facilities that are normally off limits to our visitors."

It is estimated that the total cost of the building, crane and fit-out will be more than £600,000, and is scheduled to be ready by the end of 2015. The Diesel Traction Group, Class 50 Alliance and the Western Locomotive Association have all made significant financial contributions towards the depot, while fundraising for this landmark project is ongoing, led by the Severn Valley Railway Charitable Trust, which was set up in 2012. ●

CONTRACT

The position of the new diesel depot in the yard at Kidderminster. SVR

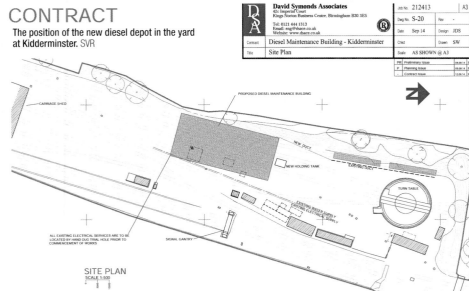

SITE PLAN
SCALE 1:500

ABOVE: The SVR has a fleet of no fewer than seven 350hp 0-6-0 diesel electric shunters, all of which have hitherto had to be maintained in the open air. JONATHAN DUNSTER

Chapter 19

A new locomotive for the
Severn Valley

Once we restored scrap engines: now let's raise the Standard!

ABOVE: BR Standard 3MT 2-6-2T No. 82030 outside Swindon Works on October 18, 1959. RL COOK/82045 SLT

Barry scrapyard has long since closed, and the only means of acquiring steam locomotives today is to buy them from other preservationists.

Yet it has always been a second-hand market: as with buying a used car, what you pay is measured according to the remaining life expectancy, before the vehicle is scrapped or expensive new parts are bought.

So why not build a locomotive from new? Many successes have been accomplished in this field, firstly on miniature railways and then on narrow gauges as with the Ffestiniog Railway, for example, having built itself two new double Fairlies and a single one.

Arguably the most popular steam locomotive on the UK main line this century has been The A1 Steam Locomotive Trust's new-build Peppercorn Pacific No. 60163 *Tornado*, which was officially launched by Prince Charles at York station on February 19, 2009. A project which started out with an idea to recreate a class of locomotive extinct since 1965. It took 18 years to build the first British main line steam locomotive since *Evening Star* was outshopped from Crewe in 1960.

During that time, other new-build groups were formed, including a scheme to build a new example of the extinct British Railways 3MT 2-6-2 tank engine; No, 82045, conceived by South Devon Railway fireman, John Besley, in 1988, during a conversation with the author.

Later taken under the stewardship of Severn Valley Railway enginemen Tony Massau and Chris Proudfoot, it took off at the end of 2008 when the finished frame plates for the new engine were delivered to the group's site at Bridgnorth.

ABOVE: BR Standard 3MT 2-6-2T No. 82031 stands in Platform 3 at Bewdley after arriving on June 29, 1957. PJ SHOESMITH/SVR ARCHIVES

The Riddles Class 3 tanks and their mogul sisters in the 77XXX class slipped through the preservation net. All of them went to the scrapyard, even though three of the tanks survived until as late as October 1968. It was a major loss to preservation, as these smart little engines would have been ideally suited to conditions on today's heritage-era lines.

The 82045 Locomotive Fund, as the group was initially called, was reconstituted as a company limited by guarantee in April 2009 and gained charitable status in January the following year, accompanied by a change of name to The 82045 Steam Locomotive Trust. Its stated aim is to build the next member of the extinct Riddles class (the BR engines finished at 82044) specifically for heritage line use and with no plans to run on the main line – unless, of course, a potential benefactor wishes to see this happen and is prepared to put up the necessary cash. When completed, it will run both on the SVR as well as visiting other heritage lines.

Project engineer, Tony Massau, a professional engineer, had considered for many years that Standard 3 tanks would be an ideal engine for average-sized heritage lines, because of their economical size.

Around the original partnership grew a multi-talented team of SVR volunteers, including three skilled engineers, a Lloyd's coded welder and a patternmaker. A set of driving wheels were cast and machined at Boro' Foundry in Lye, and were pressed on to their axles and fitted with tyres at the South Devon Railway's Buckfastleigh Works.

The chassis complete, machining of the cylinders has taken place at Tees Components in Saltburn-by-the-Sea. With the pony trucks, driving wheels, cylinders and bunker coming together at Bridgnorth during the early part of 2015, No. 82045 was beginning to look like a locomotive for the first time.

The fabrication of the locomotive's bunker was completed at the Ffestiniog Railway's Boston Lodge Works and has been painted and lined out, before being fixed to the frames at Bridgnorth.

No. 82045 will emerge from Bridgnorth Works as an identical locomotive (as far as this is still possible) to the one that should have been built by British Railways at Swindon early in 1956. The later members of the class as built had a slightly different boiler tube configuration and a larger-capacity coal bunker (the self-trimming slope at the base of the original bunker was done away with in order to allow for an extra three quarters of a ton of coal), and No. 82045 will reflect these minor changes.

The 82XXX tanks were an everyday sight on the Severn Valley line in BR days, so the engine will have the added attraction of being authentic for the heritage-era SVR.

Trust member, Paul Anderson, a fireman at Nine Elms (70A) shed from 1963-66, who regularly worked on them, said: "They were lovely, perky little engines that did everything it said on the box. Disposal was a doddle, and you could finish a shift on one without feeling all wrung out!"

An estimated date for completion of the Standard 3 tank has been given as 2017, provided money from supporters keeps rolling in. Two young Severn Valley fitters, Will Marsh and Gary Williams, raised £5000 towards the project by completing a sponsored parachute jump over Swindon.

At the start of 2015, it was estimated that another £180,000 was needed, including the cost of a boiler.

Anyone who would like to sponsor the building of No. 82045 is invited to send a cheque to Mrs Barbara Massau, 4 Southfield, Prestbury, Cheshire, SK10 4XF – payable to The 82045 SLT, or visit www.82045.org.uk

It has even been suggested that the drawings and patterns used for No. 82045 could be used to build a batch for use on other heritage lines that need an economical locomotive, which in theory, should not need expensive heavy repairs for two decades or more. ●

RIGHT: A poster, painted by Stockport artist, Stephen Millership, for sale by The 82045 SLT, shows No. 82045 crossing Oldbury viaduct with the Bridgnorth skyline in the background. 82045 TRUST

RAISING THE STANDARD

Coming Soon - The New BR Class 3MT Tank For The Severn Valley Railway.

THE 82045
STEAM LOCOMOTIVE TRUST
Practical Steam for the 21st Century
82045.org.uk

The Art of Travel
www.stephenmillership.com

ABOVE: The machined cylinder castings. TEES COMPONENTS

ABOVE: The wheelsets of No. 82045 at the South Devon Railway in September 2014. CHRIS SHIELDS

ABOVE: The bunker of new-build BR Standard 2MT 2-6-2T No. 82045 is fitted to the frames. PAUL APPLETON

Chapter 20

War on the line

Each year the SVR turns back the clock to the Forties to recreate wartime Britain, evacuation trains included.

During the Second World War, the Severn Valley route became strategically useful as a bypass around the West Midlands conurbation for troop and munitions trains, and today those dark days are remembered each summer. The Severn Valley's Step Back to the 1940s weekends are among the most popular attractions of any heritage railway in Britain.

The eagerly awaited events, normally held at the end of June and the beginning of July, attract armies of re-enactors who turn the clock back to the Forties. From the sergeant major to the spiv, traditional wartime characters are brought to life. Tens of thousands of people turn out to see the displays, exhibitions and entertainers as an intensive service of evacuation trains run throughout the weekends.

Stations along the line are transformed as re-enactment groups and replica sets provide visitors with an insight into snippets of life of Forties Britain, including replica air-raid shelters, a wartime operations room and even a Forties wedding.

Among the familiar faces regularly re-created for the event have been Sir Winston Churchill, King George VI and General Montgomery.

LEFT: Army officers chat to a footplateman on GWR 0-6-0 pannier tank No. 7714 before a morning departure. SVR
BELOW: Crowds gather on the platforms to board wartime services. SVR

Many of the visitors also dress up for the occasion. Period clothes stalls at both Kidderminster and Bewdley sell suits, dresses, trousers and hats; specially made for the growing Forties interest market.

Passengers are issued with identity cards – copies of the genuine wartime design – and they have to produce them if asked by military or plain-clothes police officers.

Bakelite radios boom out BBC home bulletins, 78rpm record-playing phonographs are wound up to play Glenn Miller 'big band sound' favourites from loudspeakers, and stalls selling all kinds of Forties memorabilia are positioned at stations along the line.

Events have included flypasts over Bewdley by the Battle of Britain Memorial Flight based at Coningsby in Lincolnshire and static displays of wartime aircraft on the ground, plus a convoy of historic and military vehicles.

In 2011, an RAF Lancaster bomber – the last example still flying – made two low-level passes over the railway, one in each direction.

Events have included simulated Luftwaffe bombing raids over Kidderminster Town station, with pyrotechnic 'explosions' and surround-sound recordings of bombers around the site.

All along the line, station windows are taped up with blackout curtains and sandbags are laid around ARP posts as the line becomes one giant film set – but one in which any member of the public can take part.

Kidderminster station becomes a living museum of the Forties, with its own resident compere, Guy Roles from Stourport, playing the big band numbers of the age.

Visitors can experience how life was 'at home' in wartime with a three-sided mock-up of a typical terraced house of the period. Its living room has flowery wallpaper and frumpy curtains, a horsehair sofa and oak sideboard with mantel clock and framed sepia photographs.

The sparse kitchen has a stone sink, with a mangle and washboard, an old vacuum cleaner and a gas stove or cooker. Re-enactors play family members peeling potatoes and boiling the kettle to make the tea.

The set even has a Dig For Victory allotment garden.

Visitors can take refuge during bombing raids in a corrugated steel Anderson shelter and also view the smaller, table-like self-assembly Morrison shelter, designed to absorb the impact of falling debris in homes without cellars.

On Kidderminster's concourse, spivs sell black-market nylon stockings, chocolate and other unattainables from their battered old suitcases.

Each station has its own attraction. Past events have seen Bewdley station yard host a display of Thirties and Forties family cars and the story of wartime US Army hospitals in an exhibition inside a Red Cross coach under the banner of Wyre Forest at War. Arley has been the site of the tented headquarters of a full Dad's Army platoon in the form of the Pitsford (Northants) Home Guard, which was formed in 2005 as a tribute to the county's 9th (Brixworth) Batallion of the Northants Home Guard.

The main attraction for many visitors is to be found at Highley, where the traditional

ABOVE: Sunday best: all dressed up for an outing in the family car. SVR

ABOVE: Soldiers guard Arley signalbox. JIM CARTER

ABOVE: Overpaid, oversexed and over here: a high-ranking US army officer gets his girl at the 2013 event. SVR

ABOVE: "We'll meet again" – a parting farewell as this solder heads out to front-line duty. SVR

ABOVE: 'Winston Churchill' aka re-enactor Stan Steather arrives to deliver a morale-boosting speech to the troops, usually delivered at Highley at 1pm each day. JIM CARTER

ABOVE: The bunting may be patriotic, but each station has to be guarded against Nazis. SVR

ABOVE: Home on leave: a typical Forties kitchen interior. JIM CARTER

ABOVE: "Read all about it" – newspapers were a lifeline for war-weary Britons anxious for every glimmer of hope that the conflict might be turning their way. SVR

ABOVE: Nylon for knickers anyone? A wartime spiv joins the action. JIM CARTER

ABOVE: A new forces sweetheart in the offing?
JIM CARTER

ABOVE: Women take over the running of trains while the menfolk are on forces duties. SVR

'battle' between German and Allied troops takes place around 1pm, aided by pyrotechnic effects and blank ammunition.

For the past few years, SS uniforms and the portrayal of senior Nazi figures such as Hitler and Himmler have been banned by the

Severn Valley, in line with Heritage Railway Association guidelines, for fear of causing offence to those who suffered from their extreme actions and policies.

The Engine House becomes a live RAF wartime operations room.

As a mark of respect to those who made the ultimate sacrifice, a bugler plays The Last Post, while the union flag is lowered and prayers said in a short ceremony at Kidderminster Town station at around 4.30pm on both Sundays. ●

ABOVE: Forties fashions to the fore. SVR

ABOVE: Donate your saucepans to the Spitfire Fund at Kidderminster Town. JIM CARTER

ABOVE: "Get me to the church on time!" A Forties wedding re-enacted. JIM CARTER

ABOVE: "We meet again"… and still have fond memories of those times past. SVR

BELOW: A jeep in action at Highley. JIM CARTER

ABOVE: "Who do you think you are kidding Mr Hitler?" The Home Guard HQ at Arley. JIM CARTER

ABOVE: A gun emplacement and military fuel supplies at the ready. JIM CARTER

ABOVE: 10-minute shuttle rides in a vintage bus run from Kidderminster Town station. JIM CARTER

HONOURING THE MAN WHO SAVED BRITAIN

A member of the Severn Valley steam fleet which takes pride of place at the Forties events is Bulleid Battle of Britain Pacific No. 34053 *Sir Keith Park*, which is on long-term loan from Southern Locomotives Ltd.

It is named after the New Zealand-born air chief marshal nicknamed 'The Defender of London' who deployed Britain's squadrons of Hurricane and Spitfire fighters against the Luftwaffe in 1940.

The son of a Scottish geologist, Keith Park was born on June 15, 1892, in Thames on the Coromandel Peninsula.

He joined the Army as a territorial soldier in the New Zealand Field Artillery but aged 19 he went to sea as a purser aboard collier and passenger steamships.

During the First World War, as a non-commissioned officer, he participated in the landings at Gallipoli in April 1915 and commanded an artillery battalion. During the conflict, he transferred from the New Zealand Army to the British Army, joining the Royal Horse and Field Artillery.

After Gallipoli, Park's battalion participated in the Battle of the Somme. On October 21, 1916, Park was blown off his horse by a German shell. Wounded, he was evacuated to England and medically certified "unfit for active service", meaning he was unfit to ride a horse. So he joined the Royal Flying Corps in December 1916 and learned to fly.

He returned to France as a major to command 48 Squadron, and went on to earn a bar to his Military Cross, the Distinguished Flying Cross and the French Croix de Guerre.

When the new RAF officer ranks were introduced in 1919, Park became a flight lieutenant. Promoted to air vice-marshal, Park took command of No. 11 Group RAF, responsible for the fighter defence of London and South East England in April 1940.

He organised fighter patrols over France during the Dunkirk evacuation and in the Battle of Britain his command took the full force of the Luftwaffe's air attacks.

Among the many air battles fought over Britain, Park personally commanded RAF forces on August 13 (Adlertag), August 18 (The Hardest Day) and September 15 (Battle of Britain Day).

Lord Tedder, Chief of the Air Staff, said in February 1947: "If any one man won the Battle of Britain, he did. I do not believe it is realised how much that one man, with his leadership, calm judgment and his skill, did to save not only this country but the world."

Battle of Britain hero RAF pilot, Douglas Bader, said: "The awesome responsibility for this country's survival rested squarely on Keith Park's shoulders. British military history of this century has been enriched with the names of great fighting men from New Zealand of all ranks and in every one of our services. Keith Park's name is carved into history alongside those of his peers."

After a distinguished wartime career, during which he was knighted in 1942 for his role in the defence of Malta, Park retired and was promoted to air chief marshal on December 20, 1946, and returned to New Zealand where he was elected to Auckland City Council. He died on February 6, 1975, aged 82.

No. 34053 was built at Brighton Works in 1947 and allocated to Salisbury shed. Sir Keith himself named the engine on September 19, 1947, at Brighton station.

The locomotive spent considerable time on loan to Stewarts Lane depot, from where it hauled the heavy continental boat expresses, including 'Golden Arrow'. Following brief spells at Nine Elms and Exmouth Junction, it returned to Salisbury in 1951 working over the entire South Western network.

In November 1958, the locomotive was rebuilt and its air-smoothed casing was removed. It returned to Salisbury shed, and a final transfer in 1960 saw it operating out of Bournemouth depot, running over the Somerset & Dorset main line at the head of the 'Pines Express' on many occasions.

Following withdrawal in October 1965, No. 34053 arrived at Dai Woodham's scrapyard in Barry during March 1966.

It became the 153rd locomotive out of a total of 213 bought from the legendary scrapyard for preservation purposes. Enthusiast Charles Timms bought it in 1979, but it did not leave the yard until the summer of 1984.

Taken to the former Hull Dairycoates depot, restoration began under the direction of Tom Tighe, who later became the locomotive engineer on the Great Central Railway.

Charles Timms died in 1992 and the locomotive was sold to Dr John F Kennedy and moved to Crewe Heritage Centre and three years later to a private site next to Thingley Junction in Wiltshire.

It was sold on to Jeremy Hosking as a source of spare parts for West Country Pacific No. 34046 *Braunton* and was duly moved to the latter's restoration base on the West Somerset Railway in January 1997.

ABOVE: Air vice-marshal Sir Keith Park at his desk.

Southern Locomotives bought the surplus-to-requirements remains of the locomotive in 2000 and moved them to its base at Sellindge in Kent, with the ultimate aim of restoring it in its own right as a memorial to the wartime hero.

Parts were restored at various heritage engineering sites and in 2008 the frames arrived at the Swanage Railway's Herston Works. Its restoration was completed in May 2012 and it was taken to the Severn Valley, which had agreed a long-term loan deal.

After weeks of testing and adjustments, it entered passenger service that August.

It was rededicated at Kidderminster Town on August 31 in front of three RAF veterans who fought in the Battle of Britain, as well as members of Sir Keith's family and Oliver Bulleid, the grandson of the engine's designer.

The guest of honour was the Right Honourable Sir Lockward Smith, New Zealand High Commissioner, who unveiled the nameplate.

A guard of honour was mounted by the 156 (Kidderminster) Squadron ATC. A flypast by a Hurricane and a Spitfire from the Battle of Britain Memorial Flight took place over Bridgnorth.

Nick Thompson of Southern Locomotives said: "The restoration of *Sir Keith Park* took a great deal of time, effort and money. Part of the incentive to restore it was its historic association with *Sir Keith Park* and his crucial role in the Battle of Britain.

"We hope that it will serve to remind visitors to the railway of the debt owed to him by Britain."

RIGHT: Bulleid Battle of Britain Pacific No. 34053 *Sir Keith Park* in action on June 29 during the 2014 Forties event. Honouring one of Britain's greatest wartime heroes, it did not carry the name during the Second World War, when it would have appeared as built with air-smoothed casing. JIM CARTER

ABOVE: Military police organise proceedings as visitors admire the locomotive that honours Sir Keith Park, the 'hands on' air vice-marshal who is credited with victory in the Battle of Britain. SVR

So where next for the
Severn Valley?

The future looks very bright for the next 50 years of the railway, but what are the options for further development?

Over 50 years, the railway has gone from strength to strength. It has achieved the goal of running the full 16 miles from Bridgnorth to Kidderminster, once beyond the founder members' wildest dreams, and has consolidated itself as one of Britain's leading tourist attractions and the world's premier heritage lines.

Could it expand further in length? There is no appetite by the current board to enter the 550-yard Bridgnorth Tunnel and extend northwards towards Ironbridge, not only because of the extensive physical obstacles,

including housing, to overcome but also because of the monumental cost. Reopening a railway with the track already down is one matter – rebuilding one from scratch is another, and where would be the business case for doubling the price of tickets to justify the expense?

No. The policy followed up to now and one that has been pursued with immense success is to consolidate, developing an excellent railway into a magnificent one, and not only that, to remain at the cutting edge of tourist attractions. Basic facilities, which

would have sufficed in the Seventies, would be considered grossly inadequate by today's far more discerning family visitor, who has access to Tripadvisor.

Steam continues to fascinate all ages and heritage diesels have their following too, but today's visitor wants much more if they are to give up a day and part with hard-earned money. The railway is aware of this, and has plighted much time and resources into attending travel shows to promote the line, with commendable results. However, there is always something more that can be done

BELOW: WD Austerity 2-8-0 No. 90733 passes Bewdley South signalbox with the 6pm from Bridgnorth to Kidderminster on March 22, 2015, the last day of the 50th anniversary gala. DUNCAN LANGTREE

ABOVE: GWR 0-4-2T No. 140 pilots pannier No. L92 through Oldbury cutting on March 20, 2015. MALCOLM RANIERI

ABOVE: LNWR coal tank No. 1054 works along the Tenbury branch wall north of Bewdley with a local gala service on March 22, 2015. JED BENNETT

ABOVE: Mount Pleasant Tunnel today.

ABOVE: In November 2013, the Severn Valley Railway took the opportunity of leasing the first floor of the modern office block at 1 Comberton Hill from Wyre Forest District council, a stone's throw from Kidderminster Town station. Its 3000sq ft accommodates Severn Valley Railway plc, the Holdings company, guarantee company and charitable trust activities. ROBIN JONES

LEFT: Puddles the Bridgnorth station cat. ROBIN JONES

to improve the visitor experience, and here is the current thrust of a horizontal expansion drive.

The question of whether to allow an outside train operator to run daily commuter services from Bewdley to Birmingham habitually arises. The big problem is the acute lack of car parking for such a venture at Bewdley, plus the need to ensure that the railway's core business – running heritage trains – is not compromised. At this point in time, it looks a non-starter.

One possibility that has been spoken about in whispers – and has also been suggested by the author – is the relaying of the stub of the Stourport line, the trackbed of which the SVR owns. As we saw earlier, it was relaid temporarily for a movie job.

You could never rebuild the line back to Stourport, and the best that could be achieved is to Burlish Halt, near where Mount Pleasant Tunnel lies in the undergrowth. However, having Bewdley become a junction again would add another string to the line's bow if only for gala and special events.

Resignalling would be the only major expenditure here. Volunteers could lay the rest of the short branch and could also raise the money to source second-hand rail,

without it costing the SVR companies a penny. Many heritage sector volunteers could join a revival scheme to lay track as opposed to run trains: such a low-key scheme would tap into that source of volunteer labour. Not only that, but it would 'claim back' another piece of the original Severn Valley line.

I've no doubt that this and many other new ideas will emerge during the next half century, as the railway continues to gather pace and reinforce its position in the market, breaking visitor records, holding many more stupendous galas and firing the imagination of many, many generations to come. ●

50TH ANNIVERSARY STEAM GALA CRACKER

The first big event of the Severn Valley Railway's star-studded 50th anniversary year was the March 20-22 spring steam gala, which proved to be a soar-away success with three days of stunning weather.

Guest locomotives included the first-ever visit of the Keighley & Worth Valley Railway's WD 2-8-0 No. 90733 and Jeremy Hosking's 2-8-0T No. 4270 on its way back to the Gloucestershire Warwickshire Railway from the Steel, Steam & Stars IV gala at Llangollen, it too making its debut at the SVR.

The other guest locomotives were both returnees; 127-year old LNWR Webb coal tank No. 1054 was making its third visit in recent years, but GWR 0-6-0PT No. 5786 in its latter-day London Transport maroon guise as L92 had not been seen on the SVR since it was one of the first arrivals there in the line's formative days, its owning company the Worcester Locomotive Society having long since relocated to the South Devon Railway.

The remainder of the cast was made up from the SVR's resident fleet, with a total of nine locomotives in operation, with a further two in steam on standby, on an intensive and imaginative timetable that saw No. 90773, No. 2857, L92 and No. 4270 on full line trains, with the coal tank Nos. 1450, 4566, 1501 – and intriguingly Bulleid Battle of Britain Pacific No. 34053 *Sir Keith Park* – on local trains, while a freight train also operated each day. Ivatt 4MT 2-6-0 Nos. 43106 and GWR 4-6-0 No. 7812 *Erlestoke Manor* were the spare engines.

The steel wheel
turns full circle

Catch Me Who Can replica is built at the SVR workshops.

While the Severn Valley Railway has worked miracles in recapturing the atmosphere of the steam and early diesel eras, it has also played a part in re-creating the locality's claim to fame as one of the birthplaces of the railway locomotive.

As mentioned in Chapter 1, Cornish mining engineer Richard Trevithick built his first steam railway engine at Coalbrookdale in 1802; and his last, *Catch Me Who Can*, which gave the world's first passenger rides near Euston in 1808, was constructed at Hazeldine Foundry in Bridgnorth by John Urpeth Rastrick.

A non-working replica of Trevithick's Coalbrookdale locomotive was constructed in Birmingham in 1987 by Task Undertakings Ltd, partially supported by the Manpower Services Commission and the Prince's Trust, and was subsequently displayed at Telford Central station. In 2012, it was moved to make way for a new £1 – million passenger seating area and relocated to the engineering gallery at Hadley Learning Community school to be used as a visual prompt to discuss local industry over the past two centuries.

The school's director of engineering, Jeff Williams, said: "It will be a constant reminder of the wonderful achievement and the importance of Ironbridge as a World Heritage Site."

Two years later, a fully working replica was built by apprentices at GKN Sankey in Telford in 1989, and is now at the Ironbridge Gorge Museum. It can be seen regularly in operation on the track at the Blists Hill site.

However, for the bargain price of £50,000, a group of Bridgnorth residents formed a charity with the aims of building a working replica of *Catch Me Who Can* and organising events including lectures, concerts and outdoor events to celebrate its bicentenary in 2008.

Under the banner of Trevithick 200, the group also built its replica in Bridgnorth – making use of the Severn Valley's workshops.

On July 19-20, 2008, the group celebrated the 200th anniversary of *Catch Me Who Can* by holding a gala weekend at Bridgnorth's Severn Park – next to the site of the Hazeldine Foundry in Low Town, fragments of which survive.

RIGHT: The replica of *Catch Me Who Can* outside Bridgnorth Works on May 14, 2012, with its wooden cladding fitted. ROBIN JONES

While the locomotive was not completed, it was nonetheless in steam at the event.

The group then displayed it, part completed but with a fire in its boiler, at a gala weekend at Barrow Hill Roundhouse near Chesterfield in September that year. It has subsequently had wooden cladding fitted.

CLOSER TO THE ORIGINAL THAN THOUGHT

A discovery revealed in 2008 showed just how much like the original the replica is. For decades, the sketch of *Catch Me Who Can* hauling two carriages around a circular track trainset-style inside a stockade somewhere near the heart of the London of 1808 graced textbooks.

However, Science Museum curator, John Liffen, has produced evidence to show that the sketch, long attributed to the contemporary illustrator Thomas Rowlandson (1757-1827), is an early 20th-century forgery.

He rediscovered a genuine picture of *Catch Me Who Can*, a colour wash by John Claude Nattes, which shows the locomotive boiler resting on wooden planks somewhere in London before its wheels were fitted for the fabled demonstration runs. The picture, found in the Guildhall Library in the City of London, shows a half-completed locomotive remarkably similar to the Trevithick 200 group's replica.

The 'Rowlandson' sketch – which had hitherto been seized upon by the public as the only indication of what the locomotive looked like – bears an incorrect date, 1809, and features buildings that probably did not exist in London until even later, including the tower of St Mary's Church in Eversholt Street, which was not built until 1826.

There are also wood pulp traces in the paper used, which suggest a later date of origin.

John decided to start afresh from the beginning and look at all the pieces of evidence.

Historians had previously suspected that the design of the locomotive in the 'Rowlandson' sketch was based on a surviving admission ticket from the 1808 runs.

John concluded that the 'Rowlandson' sketch is a forgery, dating from the first decade of the 20th century. Rowlandson's drawings and satirical cartoons experienced a renaissance in popularity in Edwardian times, which led to a surge in forgeries.

Furthermore, John said that he may have discovered the exact location on which the circular track was laid – a site now occupied by the Wellcome Trust's new building in Euston Road.

John's paper, Searching for Trevithick's London Railway of 1808, was the opening presentation of the Fourth International Early Railways Conference, held on June 12-15, 2008, at University College in London – which lies alongside the site of the demonstration track.

Nattes, who was born around 1765, was a founder member of the Society of Painters in Watercolours, founded in 1804; but, somewhat ironically in view of the debunking of the 'Rowlandson' sketch, he was expelled after two years for exhibiting other people's work as his own, yet continued to exhibit at the Royal Academy until 1814. ●

ABOVE: A coloured version of the widely published sketch of Trevithick's first passenger train locomotive, long attributed to Thomas Rowlandson, is said by researcher, John Liffen, to be a fake.

ABOVE: Revealed: the first and only surviving picture of Richard Trevithick's *Catch Me Who Can* waiting for the wheels to be fitted shortly before its public demonstration on a site near present-day Euston Road in the summer of 1808, and drawn by John Claude Nattes. GUILDHALL LIBRARY

ABOVE: Compare the Nattes drawing with the replica's boiler as pictured in Bridgnorth works. GW (SVR) ASSOCIATION

ABOVE: A fire burns inside the replica boiler at Barrow Hill Roundhouse. ROBIN JONES

ABOVE: The 1989-built 3ft gauge working replica of Trevithick's Coalbrookdale engine of 1802. IRONBRIDGE MUSEUMS

ABOVE: The *Catch Me Who Can* replica inside Barrow Hill Roundhouse in September 2008. ROBIN JONES

Chapter 23

Bridgnorth's
second railway

*Bridgnorth is famed for its steam railway but is also home
to Britain's only currently operational inland public funicular
line, linking the High Town with the Low Town…*

ABOVE: One of the two cars departing from the top station, from where the funicular railway is controlled manually. JONATHAN STONEHOUSE

LEFT: View from the top, with Low Town and the River Severn below. JONATHAN STONEHOUSE

Bridgnorth is not only home to one of the world's finest heritage lines, but has a second historic railway line, one that's been performing vital public transport for the past 125 years. It also remained way beyond the remit of Dr Beeching.

Linking High and Low Towns is the Bridgnorth Cliff Railway, Britain's only currently operational inland public funicular line, a type more commonly associated with seaside resorts, and which takes a minute and a quarter to ascend or descend Castle Hill.

It too boasts an impressive technological pedigree, dating back to 1890, when it was planned by funicular railway pioneer, George Croydon Marks.

Marks was born in Eltham in Kent, the eldest of eight children of William Marks and Amelia Adelaide Croydon.

After attending a local private school, at age 13 he became apprenticed to the Royal Arsenal in Woolwich, where his father William, a Somerset farm worker who came to London in 1855 looking for work, was a foreman, and continued his general education part-time at the Royal Arsenal School. At 17, he won a two-year scholarship to King's College, University of London and became a mechanical engineer.

In 1881, Marks married Margaret Maynard in Watford. They didn't have any children.

A great admirer of Isambard Kingdom Brunel, the following year Marks joined engine manufacturer Sir Richard Tangye's company, as a leading draughtsman for hydraulic machinery. The company also produced funicular lifts and had installed two water-powered cliff railways in Scarborough.

Marks was appointed head of the firm's lift department, and was charged with the design and installation of the cliff lift at Saltburn-by-the-Sea. Replacing an earlier cliff hoist, Marks designed and constructed a funicular with a height of 120ft and a track length of 207ft (63m), creating a 71% incline. It is said to have carried its first public passengers at the end of June 1884, and although refurbished since, and owned by the local council since the Second World War, Marks' railway has changed comparatively little ever since, and still gives sterling service today.

In 1890, a public meeting was called to discuss a new means of communication between High Town and Low Town in Bridgnorth, so that local people would not have to climb the 200 steps between the two.

Marks heard about it and, along with George Newnes, MP, his partner in the building of the Lynton & Lynmouth Cliff Railway, drew up plans for an inclined lift to ascend the sandstone cliff.

ABOVE: George Croydon Marks MP, who designed the Bridgnorth Cliff Railway and became its first managing director, pictured in 1906.

A route from the bottom of the Stoneway Steps to the end of Castle Walk was finally chosen. Accordingly, the Bridgnorth Castle Hill Railway Company Ltd was registered in 1891 to build it.

WORK BEGINS

Construction began on November 2, 1891. Initial work was hindered by the discovery of caves set into the cliff face, into which many houses had been jerry built. Station buildings were constructed at the top and bottom.

The company eventually opted for a double track 3ft 6in gauge system, 201ft long, with a vertical rise of 111ft, giving the railway an incline of 33 degrees, the steepest and possibly the shortest in England.

The sleepers were bolted into solid rock. At the upper end of the track, the hauling pulley was built on solid concrete foundations, Flat-bottomed rails were used and the entire line was ballasted with concrete to avoid any slippage. Horizontal rollers were set into the track at regular intervals to support the steel ropes. ▶

ABOVE: George Croydon Marks' Bridgnorth Castle Hill Railway Company share certificate. DR MALVERN TIPPING COLLECTION

ABOVE: The 'Bridgnorth Gang' at the completion of the railway in July 1892. 'A' denotes Edward Marks, who, as another engineer oversaw the construction while 'B' denotes George Croydon Marks. DR MALVERN TIPPING COLLECTION

ABOVE: Looking up: Britain's steepest incline railway and arguably the shortest. ANTHONY HOLLINGWORTH

Each car was mounted on a triangular frame of steel girders that housed a 2000-gallon water tank. The tank on the car at the top was filled with water from a 30,000-gallon tank mounted on the roof of the top station. When the tank was full, the total weight of the car was more than nine tons, easily enough to counterbalance the bottom car with its 18 passengers.

As the top car was being filled, the tank on the bottom car was being emptied, and the water pumped directly up to the top station tank by means of a pair of pumps driven by independent Forward gas engines.

The cars were linked by a pair of steel ropes, and were fitted with rapid gripper brakes, which automatically engaged, should the rate of descent become too great. A second manually operated brake was the responsibility of the brakeman riding on the bottom platform of each car.

The railway was opened by the mayor on July 7, 1892, and townsfolk were given a public holiday.

It was an instant success. Between July and September 1892, more than 50,000 passengers used the railway. It ran continuously for

the next 41 years, until April 1933. In May the following year, it was reopened by new shareholders.

When the gas engines were reaching the end of their working life in 1943, it was decided to rebuild the line so it could use electricity. The hydraulic system of counterbalanced cars was replaced with an electrically operated 32hp mining type motor.

The new haulage system consisted of two main ropes, one winding on to one drum as the other winds off. In addition, a safety rope connects the two cars via the original head wheel. The original emergency brake was retained, so in the event of a rope break the car would grip the rails until they came to a halt.

The speed of the cars was regulated by air brakes acting on the haulage drums, and proximity devices would act to slow the cars as they approached either end of the track.

Further safety improvements included interlocked loading doors at top and bottom, and a dead man's pedal speed controller.

Francis & JS Lane carried out the conversions, with electrical gear supplied by Metropolitan-Vickers Electrical Co Ltd. The

rebuild doubled the speed of the railway up to a maximum speed of 250ft per minute.

The official reopening on May 9, 1944, was conducted by mayor TC Pembro, who had taken office only two hours previously. The railway showed an immediate increase in traffic. In 1955, the original heavy wooden cars were replaced with a lighter modern aluminium monocoque type, with improved lighting.

Each car weighs approximately 5.5 tons when fully laden with 18 passengers. New wheelsets and car bearings were installed during 2000.

Simple sliding doors at each end of the cars run on their original ball-bearing rollers.

The rails were replaced around 1972 with the bullhead design formerly used on main line railways.

Major improvements took place in 2005-06 to form better access to the engine room, the Winding House Tea Rooms, railway offices and storage together with an apartment for letting. In 2009, the main electrical braking system, which had given excellent service since 1955, was replaced.

NEW OWNERS, OLD LINKS RENEWED

In 2011, the cliff railway was sold to the Tipping family from Suffolk, and here the wheel turned full circle.

For both George and Edward Marks were the grandsons of Michael Marks, a West Somerset farmer, and were related to ancestors of the Tipping family who were nearby North Devon farmers from the Lynton area.

Bridgnorth Cliff Railway director, Eileen Tipping's maternal grandfather, Walter Crang, was a butcher and the son of a farmer from Parracombe near Lynton. He was a third cousin of George and Edward Marks.

The Marks brothers were in turn more distant cousins of the Jones brothers who founded the Lynton & Lynmouth Cliff Railway, designed by George with Edward overseeing its construction – just as he did at Bridgnorth.

The Sladers, who remain the second largest shareholders of the Lynton cliff railway, are great grandsons of Bob Jones, one of the two Joneses who founded it. The Tipping family are therefore are distant relatives of the Sladers.

MARKS' OTHER RAILWAYS

Other funiculars built to the same Marks' design were Bristol's Clifton Rocks Railway and the Constitution Hill Railway in Aberystwyth. Marks was also involved in the construction of the cliff railway in Budapest – for which he was rewarded with a knighthood of the Ducal order of Ernest – and steep-incline tramcar systems, including the Swansea Constitution Hill Incline Railway.

Together with Newnes, he worked on initial plans for the Babbacombe Cliff Railway. Other works included the new Gothic pavilion at the Royal Pier in Aberystwyth and the resort's Cambrian Hotel, later the United Theological College.

In 1893, he completed the steep-incline cable-hauled tramway in Matlock, Derbyshire.

Marks also collaborated with Dugald Clerk, pioneer of the two-stroke engine with whom he filed various patents on behalf of the Parson brothers of Easton & Anderson in Erith.

Together in 1887 they formed a company of patent agents, Marks & Clerk, which survives today as one of the largest international legal firms dealing with intellectual property rights (a term which originated within the company).

Marks was a personal friend of Thomas Edison and set up an office with him in New York in 1911, the year he was knighted. Marks became the first chairman of the Edison Phonograph company and subsequently of Colombia and HMV and then a director of EMI.

He was a member of the Institution of Mechanical Engineers and an Associate Member of the Institution of Civil Engineers.

He was involved in engineering works at Bude, Torquay and Padstow harbour.

POLITICAL CAREER

Marks was elected as Liberal MP for Launceston in 1906 and following boundary changes in 1918, held the North Cornwall seat until 1924.

In 1914, he joined the Ministry of Munitions and in 1917 was awarded a CBE for his outstanding work as a commissioner for the dilution of labour.

In 1929, Marks suddenly declared his support for the Labour Prime Minister, Ramsay MacDonald, who led a minority government with Liberal support. Later that year Marks defected to the Labour Party and was elevated to the peerage as Baron Marks of Woolwich.

George Marks became treasurer and then president of the Sunday School Union and president of the London Sunday Schools Choir.

He died at his home in Poole, Dorset in September 1938, aged 80, without any heirs and the title Lord Woolwich died with him.

The railway operates 362 days a year, and is closed on Christmas Day, Boxing Day and New Year's Day. ●

RIGHT: Similar in design to the Bridgnorth Cliff Railway was the George Marks' underground Clifton Rocks Railway. This linked the Bristol suburb of Clifton with a station, near Isambard Brunel's Clifton Suspension Bridge at the top, to Hotwells at the bottom of the Avon Gorge in a tunnel cut through the limestone cliffs. The publisher George Newnes, who was also proprietor of the Lynton & Lynmouth Cliff Railway, funded construction. It opened on March 11, 1893, but closed on October 1, 1934. It is now the subject of preservation efforts. ROBIN JONES COLLECTION

ABOVE: Another Marks' masterpiece still running today is the Lynton & Lynmouth Cliff Railway in North Devon, a contemporary of the Bridgnorth Cliff Railway. ROBIN JONES
RIGHT: George Croydon Marks' first funicular railway was the Saltburn Cliff Lift at Saltburn-by-the-Sea in Cleveland. ROBIN JONES

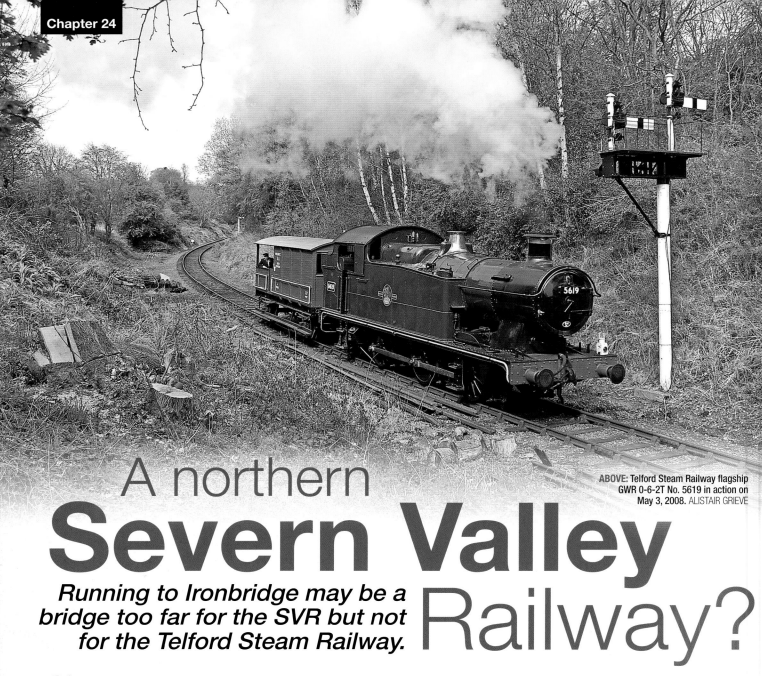

Chapter 24

A northern
Severn Valley
Railway?

Running to Ironbridge may be a bridge too far for the SVR but not for the Telford Steam Railway.

Go on, admit it. You've visited the Severn Valley Railway, and asked the inevitable question, "Why don't they extend to Ironbridge?"

Just think of it. Almost double the length of the journey; the creation of a steam highway would see visitors pour into the famous museums at the World Heritage Site.

Yes, it sounds an absolutely brilliant idea, so why haven't they thought about it before? Actually, they have.

The railway's commercial arm adopted the stance many years ago that the figures would not stack up. Never mind the cost of rebuilding the railway through and beyond Bridgnorth Tunnel and over the many pieces of trackbed which have been blocked since closure – would passengers really be prepared to pay for a ticket for a longer journey, and then buy another to get into the Ironbridge museums, especially if they have only two or three hours to spend there?

We would all love to see that line reopen, but would enough people be prepared to support it with lavish helpings of cash from their wallets?

So no, it does not look like that the Severn Valley Railway will be going to Ironbridge in our lifetimes. However, that does not mean that the gorge will not one day reverberate to the south of steam locomotives again. Far from it.

A slice of the northern end of the valley is firmly within the sights and aspirations of another, but currently smaller heritage operation, the Telford Steam Railway.

LEFT: Peckett 0-4-0ST *Rocket* heads away from the new Lawley station on April 6, 2015, following the opening of the Telford Steam Railway's northern extension. ALISTAIR GRIEVE

THE GREAT WESTERN PEDIGREE

Formed 11 years after the Severn Valley, in 1976, the line is operated by the Telford Horsehay Steam Trust Company Ltd under the trading name of the Telford Steam Railway. It is based at Horsehay & Dawley station and goods yard in Telford.

Originally on the GWR branch from Wellington to Craven Arms via Ironbridge, the section from Wellington to Horsehay was opened in 1859, with the line completed to Craven Arms by 1867.

However, the site at Horsehay has a longer history, being the site of one of the Coalbrookdale Company's first blast furnaces, dating to 1755, when a narrow gauge tramway served the surrounding ironworks and mines. Originally these were wooden railed, but from 1769 were being replaced by some of the first cast-iron ones in the world.

The furnaces gave way to steel works and later a crane manufacturer that used rail transport until the early Eighties. The housing estate opposite the main railway entrance is built on the site of this works.

The through rail link from Wellington to Craven Arms had been closed in stages, beginning with the Craven Arms to Much Wenlock section in 1951.

Horsehay & Dawley saw its last passenger train in 1962, but the route from Lightmoor to Horsehay was kept open for the transportation of bridge sections, the last regular shipment leaving in 1979.

Telford Development Corporation bought GWR 56XX 0-6-2T No. 5619 in 1974. One of nine survivors of a class numbering 200, it was built at Swindon in March 1925 and lasted in service until June 1964, working on South Wales heavy coal traffic before finishing service on pilot duties from Old Oak Common. It reached Barry scrapyard in September of that year.

The development corporation at first transported the locomotive to Horsehay for static restoration and display in the Old Loco Shed.

Dating back to the building of the railway, this structure was used as a transhipment shed to transfer goods from the internal narrow gauge tramways to the main line railway. The bricked-in narrow archways either side of the main entrance are where the original narrow lines entered the building. Outside, an original 'tiebar' can be seen set into one of the entrances.

It was also used as the works engine shed and eventually as a lorry store.

The steam trust was formed with the objective of restoring No. 5619. Members convinced the local authority to allow it to be returned to operating condition, and this was successfully completed by 1981.

ABOVE: A solitary diesel railcar comprises the 4.40pm service from Wellington to Much Wenlock on July 21, 1962, the last day of services on the route. It is pictured leaving Horsehay & Dawley. MICHAEL MENSING

ABOVE: GWR-designed prairie No. 4178 leaves Doseley Halt with the 'Beeching Special' on July 21, 1962, the final day of services. Dr Richard Beeching had been installed as British Railways chairman the year before, but at this time was largely rubber-stamping regional managers' recommendations for closures, and his landmark report, the Reshaping of British Railways, which called for widespread cuts across the network, was not published until March 27 the following year. No. 4178 was built at Swindon Works in November 1949 and had three spells allocated to Wellington shed. It was withdrawn from Oxley shed in Wolverhampton in October 1965 and scrapped during April 1966. MICHAEL MENSING

A RAILWAY BEGINS ANEW

The goods yard at Horsehay & Dawley was acquired by the trust in 1983, along with the goods transhipment shed dating from 1860.

Since then, much progress has been made. Regular trains operate on all Sundays and bank holidays from Easter to the end of September, initially along the original line as far as Heath Hill Tunnel. However, from Easter 2015, services began running through the tunnel to a new station at Lawley Village, close to the original Lawley Halt.

No. 5619 worked hard on many preserved railways until its 10-year boiler certificate expired. In 1998,

Heritage Lottery Fund grant aid was secured to commence the restoration to running condition again.

This time, a major strip-down and full overhaul of the motion and boiler was required. Initial work was carried out by the railway and Tyseley Locomotive Works Railway works.

In 2006 a major financial deal was arranged and the locomotive was completed at Bill Parker's Flour Mill workshops at Bream in the Forest of Dean, which also took over the responsibility of hiring out the locomotive until the cost of the overhaul had been recouped.

No. 5619 re-entered service in February 2008 and spent most of its time on hire to other

railways, returning to Telford for galas and special events.

In 2014, after boiler issues, No. 5619 returned to the Flour Mill for an early 10-year overhaul, with an intended return to service in 2015.

The Old Loco Shed now houses both the railway's main operating locomotives and others under restoration.

Today, Horsehay & Dawley is again a multi-gauge venue. A unique 2ft gauge steam vertical-boilered tram and trailer, built in 1979 by Kierstead Systems and Alan Keef for the nearby Telford Town Park, were relocated to Horsehay in the early Eighties. For 2015, it was extended to provide a full circular ride ▶

ABOVE: Peckett 0-4-0ST No. 1722 of 1926 *Rocket* spent its working life at the Courtaulds Co Ltd at Coventry. In preservation, it became part of the private Shropshire Collection that was stored in a field near Shrewsbury. The collection was bought in 2003 by the Somerset & Dorset Locomotive Company Ltd, which restored *Rocket* to steam that year. After only three trial steamings, No. 1722 was brought to Telford and immediately entered passenger service. It is the main service locomotive on steaming days and is now owned by the railway following a bequest by a long-term member who remembered it in industrial use at Courtaulds. It is seen at the new Lawley station on Easter Monday, April 6, 2015, the weekend of the line's latest extension. ALISTAIR GRIEVE

ABOVE: The labyrinthine lines that once ran in the Telford area. Extant Network Rail routes are in red, the current Telford Steam Railway in green and the former Severn Valley Railway in yellow.

ABOVE: The bespoke 2ft gauge steam tram and trailer at Horsehay & Dawley. TSR

ABOVE: The Old Loco Shed at Horsehay & Dawley station. TSR

at the edge of Horsehay Pool and runs on every operating day. The pool dates from the old steel works and water from it was used for cooling purposes.

The affiliated Phoenix Model Engineering Society operates a 5in gauge miniature railway system and there is also an extensive model railway display and exhibition.

Although the original station building and signalbox have long since been demolished, Railway House was built as offices for the National Coal Board and now houses the line's massive model railway layouts and other exhibits. At present the southern terminus, the track continues south from Horsehay & Dawley station almost to Doseley Halt, about three quarters of a mile away. These tracks have been used to transport waste spoil from the heritage line's northern extension to Lawley and will soon be upgraded for public use in its planned extension southwards... to Ironbridge.

ABOVE: Passengers can once again ride through Heath Hill Tunnel. The line's DMU, operating in push-pull mode, is seen exiting the tunnel on April 4, 2105, the day of the official opening of the Lawley extension. ALISTAIR GRIEVE

ABOVE: The original Horsehay & Dawley station. TSR

BELOW: A taste of better times ahead, if the Telford Steam Railway's plans come to fruition. Tyseley-based tour operator Vintage Trains ran a steam-hauled special over the Ironbridge branch on November 3, 2007, behind Western Region pannier tank No. 9466. The 'Pannier to Ironbridge' trip from Tyseley is seen passing the site of Abraham Darby's smelter furnaces at Coalbrookdale. TSR

ABOVE: *Rocket* stands at the head of a train waiting at Horsehay & Dawley station, where the Telford Steam Railway had to replace the demolished original buildings. TSR

STEAMING BACK TO IRONBRIDGE

Although one of the smaller players in the UK heritage portfolio the Telford Steam Railway has much bigger plans for its future.

Its ambition is to operate regular steam trains into the Ironbridge Gorge, providing a park-and-ride service to help alleviate the present difficulties with parking there.

These plans have their roots not in the proposed southern extension to join the existing Network Rail freight-only branch from Madeley Junction, on the Wolverhampton to Shrewsbury main line to Ironbridge Power Station, but in the completion of a northern extension to Lawley, in the opposite direction.

The original course of the railway continued to Heath Hill Tunnel, through Lawley and eventually to Wellington, but was dissected by open-cast coal mining during the Seventies. When the mining ended, the trackbed was backfilled to a height 20-30ft above the earlier level, leaving the rail revivalists facing a mountain of clay-based mud as they exited the tunnel.

However, planning permission was sought and obtained in 2000, for a small northern terminus. Part of the requirement was to move the mud bank… by rail!.

At a later date, the requirement for more housing and amenities in the Lawley area lead to wide-scale changes to the area being needed. Through negotiations with the local council, landowners and developers, the railway obtained further planning approval for a larger terminus, integrated into this development.

Volunteers moved more than 10,000 tons of spoil by rail, some with Army assistance. After changes to the station design to assist its partners in the development of Lawley, the railway had the remaining spoil removed and the area extensively regraded to allow the extension to move with more haste.

The 500-yard northern extension to the new Lawley Village station was opened on Easter Saturday, April 4, 2015. It left the railway with a Y-shaped running line, from Spring Village to Lawley and back to Horsehay, each arm of the

'Y' being just under a mile, and giving a total passenger journey of 3½ miles.

Spoil from the northern end has been used for the next stage of expansion, south from Horsehay & Dawley Station towards Doseley Halt. Some of the waste material has been disposed of just before Doseley, making the embankment less steep.

The trackwork here is temporary and suitable for works trains only. Now that Lawley is complete, the volunteers will then focus their attention on upgrading the existing railway and laying the last few hundred yards into Doseley Halt itself. At the same time the railway will be making an application for a Transport & Works Order.

From Doseley, the old trackbed is secured for the final two miles to Lightmoor. Vegetation clearance and some upgrading will be required before rails are laid.

Immediately before the point where the railway would have joined the abovementioned Network Rail route to Ironbridge Power ▶

THE IRONBRIDGE POWER STATIONS

It was in February 1927 that the West Midlands Joint Electricity Authority chose the site of the first of two coal-fired power stations on the banks of the River Severn at Buildwas. Rail access for the cost-effective delivery of coal and a substantial water supply for the cooling towers were primary factors in the choice.

The building of the first Ironbridge (also known as Buildwas) power station began in 1929, and it officially opened on October 13, 1932. It became known as Ironbridge A Power Station. The addition of extra boilers and generating sets was completed in 1939 and gave the station a total generating output of 200mW.

Following the Second World War, the Central Electricity Generating Board decided to add a new 1000mW power station, Ironbridge B, alongside the A station. Ironbridge A station was partially closed on October 27, 1980, with the decommissioning of 100mW of its generating capacity. The remainder of the station

LEFT: A saddle tank shunts the sidings at Ironbridge Power Station in 1968. F BUTLER/KIDDERMINSTER RAILWAY MUSEUM

BELOW: British Railways' main line steam ended in 1968, but steam traction soldiered on at many industrial concerns for several years, including Ironbridge Power Station, pictured in 1972. F BUTLER/KIDDERMINSTER RAILWAY MUSEUM

Station, the biggest challenge by far awaits, in the form of the Ironbridge bypass.

This major road can be bridged, but at a cost. Across the road, the freight branch to the power station awaits.

ABOVE: Lightmoor signalbox – waiting to control future Telford Steam Railway services running on to the Ironbridge branch. The heritage line leases it from Network Rail. TSR

The two routes originally joined here at Lightmoor Junction, with the two single lines becoming double track. Network Rail has now singled this double track, with negotiations ongoing with a view to the Telford Steam Railway taking over the redundant Up line and signalbox for a service to the Ironbridge Gorge, and reinstating the missing portion of the bridge over Brick Kiln bank.

This bridge was previously reduced to a single-track width when Network Rail replaced the original double-track width brick arch with a single-track width concrete section.

New stations would be constructed near the museums in Coalbrookdale, Dale End Park and near Buildwas Abbey, at the end of the line. Coalbrookdale's original station buildings survive as part of the Green Wood Centre's Woodland Experience site.

In August 2008, the heritage line concluded negotiations with Network Rail for the lease and occupation of Lightmoor Junction signalbox. Substantially intact, volunteers have begun work to replace components removed by NR and plans to return the box to Fifties

conditions. Until it comes into operational use, the Telford Steam Railway will make it available for group visits and a limited number of open days during the year.

Just imagine parking your car at Lawley, catching a steam train to Horsehay to visit the Rail Museum, continuing your journey through open countryside past Doseley, Dawley Parva and Lightmoor before moving then into the Industrial Revolution area of Coalbrookdale with its impressive viaduct.

Maybe stop here a while for the Ironbridge Gorge museums, before continuing your trip, either to Dale End with a short leisurely stroll into Ironbridge or over the River Severn on the magnificent Albert Edwards Bridge and ending your journey at the historic ruins of Buildwas Abbey, with its new station built after the closure of Ironbridge Power Station.

A pipe dream or reality? In simple terms, access to the gorge is two miles of track and one bridge away. However, much hard work remains before the Telford Steam Railway can stake a claim to being the second Severn Valley Railway. ●

ABOVE: The cooling towers of Ironbridge B power station as seen in 2014. Fuel is brought in along a remnant of the original Severn Valley Railway. JOHN MCLINDEN

ceased generating electricity in 1981 and significant portions of the station were demolished two years later.

The building of Ironbridge B began in 1963. Project architect, Alan Clark, worked closely with landscape architect, Kenneth Booth, to ensure that the station merged as seamlessly as possible into its natural surroundings. The cooling towers were built using concrete into which a red pigment had been added, to blend with the colour of the local soil, and cannot be seen from the World Heritage Site. The station's 673ft chimney is fifth tallest in Britain. It is the tallest structure in Shropshire, as well as being taller than Blackpool Tower and London's BT Tower.

The B station began supplying power in June 1969 and reached capacity in February 1970.

Up to 6000 tons of coal were delivered to Ironbridge B each day via the Network Rail branch from Madeley Junction by DB Schenker, Freightliner and Fastline. The plant consumes about 1.2 million tons of coal and 20,000 tons of oil each year. After the trains are emptied, they are usually stabled at Warrington Arpley Yard.

In 2006, Friends of the Earth claimed that Ironbridge B was Britain's second worst-polluting power station per megawatt output. Ironbridge was subsequently opted out of the European Union's Large Combustion Plant Directive, which means the station was allowed to operate for up to 20,000 hours after January 1, 2008, and must close by December 31, 2015.

In 2012, the station was modified to allow one generating unit to run on 100% biomass in the form of wooden pellets as a trial, bringing 100 new jobs to the station. The modification was undertaken to allow co-combustion with up to 20% coal for improved efficiency. In 2014, three daily trains carrying biomass chips, by then the main source of fuel for the station, were running from Liverpool Docks.

In February 2014 fire damaged one the station's 370mW generators, and three months later, operator E.on announced that it would not be repaired. E.on has said it does not plan to relicense the power station as a biomass plant beyond 2015.

A bid to have the cooling towers given listed building protection has so far drawn a blank. English Heritage has said that they cannot be protected as they do not meet strict criteria, meaning there is a strong chance they will be demolished after the station closes. The Gorge Parish Council and retired chartered engineer, Keith Newby, who himself worked on the building of eight cooling towers at Eggborough in North Yorkshire in the late Sixties, have both applied for them to be listed as local landmarks.

He argued that the cooling towers are of architectural, civil engineering and historic interest as they represent a particular type of construction undertaken in the 20th century.

He said: "I want to save the Ironbridge towers from demolition and keep them in their idyllic setting for posterity and to benefit the heritage of Shropshire and England."

However, as one door closes, another one may open, with steam trains regularly running into the gorge once more.

ABOVE: Peckett 0-4-0ST No. 1990 of 1940 spent its working life at Ironbridge Power Station until it was retired in 1980 and sold to the former Steamport Museum at Southport. tIn 1984 it was purchased by Telford Steam Railway and restored to working order at Horsehay. For 10 years No. 3 was the main steam locomotive at Telford until its firebox was found to be life expired. It remains out of service awaiting a new firebox and full overhaul. J SEARGEANT/TSR

ABOVE: The remains of Buildwas Abbey, which was dissolved by Henry VIII in 1536. It's considered to be among one of the best-preserved 12th-century examples of a Cistercian church in Britain and is now in the care of English Heritage. A terminus for an extended Telford Steam Railway would bring in visitors. STEPHEN JONES

Chapter 25

Steam driving?
You too can have a go!

Relive the great days of steam first hand.

Men may have had a monopoly on the steam age, but women are now getting in on the act. *Heritage Railway's* advertising manager Sue Keily took her cousin on a day out with a big difference… on the Severn Valley Railway.

The pair drove and fired a classic locomotive on a journey from Bewdley to Bridgnorth – and found that anyone can do it.

Generations of schoolboys wanted to be an engine driver, for footplate crews were the role models of the early to mid-20th-century.

The railways were, brief periods in wartime apart, an almost exclusively male-dominated empire. Not only that, but to become a top-link driver, you faced decades of guaranteed hard slog while ascending the ladder to join an elite 'club'.

You would start as an engine clearer at 15, and after many years may graduate to fireman, perhaps being allowed to drive a shunting engine in the yard. A long road still lay ahead if you aspired to become a fully fledged driver, and there were those who did not reach the peak of their chosen profession until their late forties or fifties.

Since the end of the steam era, a tidal wave of change has swept through society, in most cases for the better. In today's modern diesel and electric age, for example, we have female drivers in their early twenties.

Yet on today's heritage railways, locomen will still tell you that it takes many years, maybe a decade of more, to qualify as a steam driver. In layman's terms, you are taking responsibility for moving a huge and unforgiving chunk of metal on wheels weighing several hundred tons at speed, and relying on the view of the road ahead from the limited field of view offered from a cab aided by lineside signals and markers.

It is impossible to underestimate the sheer level of skills and finer techniques needed to drive a steam engine on a regular basis. However, it is nowadays possible for anyone – yes, anyone – to learn the basic principles of footplatemanship and experience, maybe if only for a day, what it was like to be at the beating heart of the steam age.

BELOW: Ivatt 2MT 2-6-0 No. 43106 heads a driver experience course special across Oldbury Viaduct. SVR

THE IDEAL GIFT

The Severn Valley is one of many railways that offers driver experience courses, and has a very wide range of packages to suit all pockets for that special occasion. Most of the experience course trips run from Bewdley to Bridgnorth.

Sue Keily, railways division advertising manager at publisher Mortons, was looking for the ideal 50th birthday present for her cousin Cathy Camp. Cathy has long been a railway fan, and admitted to following our www.heritagerailway.com page. The ideal gift, therefore, had to be something to do with steam, and Severn Valley Railway's helpful staff were happy to oblige – with a driver experience course.

Sue, who is always prepared to try her hand at anything, is familiar with footplate experience courses through our regular advertising features, but has never been on one herself. However, here was the perfect chance.

Cathy's birthday celebrations, ironically, somewhat parallels those of the railway. She was born a few months before the landmark meeting in the Coopers Arms, which led to the formation of the Severn Valley Railway back in 1965 – a call for a double celebration if ever there was one.

Cathy and Sue booked on to the most popular course, the Introductory Experience, which costs £295 per person.

For that you get a familiar briefing from the footplate crew before the journey, the chance under their expert supervision to take the controls of a steam locomotive – in this case Ivatt 2MT 2-6-0 No. 43106 – over part of a return journey from Bewdley, the starting point to Bridgnorth and also act as fireman.

Anyone over 18 can undertake the courses provided they are fit. In addition, up to four guests over the age of five are allowed to travel in a coach behind the locomotive free of charge. When you consider that the return journey costs around £20 per adult, what you get for the package compares extremely favourably with adventure experience courses in other sectors.

Not only do you get to drive the train at line speed on a fully fledged standard gauge line, but you can experience the delights of the wonderful scenery of the valley itself. Of course, it helps if the sun is out, but if it is dull and murky outside, at least you are in the warmest place for miles around.

Sue and Cathy were taken under the wing of train driver Dai Price, a charismatic character who looks straight out of the pages of The Wonder Book of Trains.

No question is too stupid to ask, no query is left unanswered – and he is right behind you all the way to ensure you get it right first time every time.

The Introductory Experience lasts around 3½ hours from start to finish, afterwards the footplate crew presents you with a certificate and souvenir SVR china mug.

LEAVING WANTING MORE

In fairness, Cathy was already bitten by the steam bug, but had never been on a footplate before. "What a wonderful 50th birthday present to remember," she beamed.

"I thought it would be very hard with all the different levers and pressure gauges but it wasn't.

"I absolutely loved it and didn't realise the speed it could go – maximum 25mph – but

ABOVE: Cathy enjoys the warmest spot in Worcestershire on February 28, 2015, before the locomotive's departure.

ABOVE: Sue and Cathy are given a crash course in the principles of steam driving.

ABOVE: Sue swaps her advertising manager's desk for the footplate.

it seemed fast for a steam train. The fire pit looked amazing.

"I drove it first from Bewdley to Hampton Loade with a chap called Peter who was also there for the experience. Each of us had a turn on the firing and driving.

"The footplate crew said I did remarkably well.

"The whole experience was amazing and I recommend it to anyone who loves steam trains."

For Cathy, the experience did not end at Bewdley, for she now hopes to find a local heritage line on which she can volunteer.

Cousin Sue enthused: "When the train rolled into the station ready for us to board, I had no idea at that point what to expect, we were told it was a 1951 tender engine called the 'Flying Pig'.

"There were six of us on the experience altogether, divided into twos, with two people driving at a time.

"I was in the third pair, so for me, travelling in the carriage attached to the train for the first part of the experience with other passengers through the fantastic countryside was great. It took me back in my mind to many years ago when these old steam trains were the normal means of transport.

"I was born in 1963, so I don't remember how wonderful these old steam trains were back then – I was too young.

"When it was my turn to drive the train, I felt nervous and excited at the same time.

"I climbed up into the hub of the fantastic locomotive. The skipper Dai Price said 'come on up here and be prepared to get dirty'.

"'Yep I'm up for that,' I said, I was paired with a lovely chap called Neville who had been bought the experience by his family.

"For the first part of our journey I was with Steve 'Ron' Chandler the fireman and Neville was with Dai driving the train, so Steve said 'grab that spade and get this fire stoked'.

▶

ABOVE: We're off! The green flag is waved, the signal raised and Ivatt 2MT No. 43106 is engulfed in a cloud of smoke as it departs Bewdley station on a trip of a lifetime for those undertaking the footplate experience course.

ABOVE: Fireman Ron Chandler explains the cab controls.

"He showed me the technique so I picked up the spade, shoveled the coal on to it, and turned round to throw it in to the big open mouth of the fire.

"I hit the metal opening of the fire and threw it all over the floor – that's how not to do it said Steve!

" I tried again, my aim was perfect this time, straight in through the hole. Once you get your balance as the train is thundering along the track it's great fun.

"Steve then said, 'Okay you're a great fireman Sue, once you got the hang of it'.

"I then swapped with Neville and had a go at driving the train, Dai showed me what to do, when to apply the brakes, when to open up the speed etc.

"One of the great things is the very loud horn. Every so often, Dai said, 'sound that horn Sue, let them know we are coming'.

"I kept calling Dai 'Casey Jones'. Not only did he look the part but it took me back to my childhood remembering it was one of my favourite programmes. Never did I think I would be driving an old steam train just like that in my later years.

"It's an experience you have to try yourself to explain the exhilarating feelings you get actually driving and firing such a fantastic steam engine.

"It might look difficult for females to do, but it is not. A lot of females probably hold back from an experience like this because they are worried about the manual work involved, but it really is not difficult.

"It was one of the most wonderful amazing experiences of my life and I would urge anyone to try it, male or female."

LADIES DAY

'The Flying Scotswoman' is the name given to a special footplate experience taster course run as part of the line's Ladies Day celebration, a new annual event held in the summer.

These courses are offered for just £125 a head, giving the opportunity to drive and fire a steam locomotive for four miles. Men too are welcome to book on the day.

During this and the line's regular Taster Footplate Experiences, one guest may travel with you in the coach behind the locomotive. Free travel tickets for the day are provided for the driver and this guest.

A further two guests may also travel in the footplate experience train free of charge.

Several other levels of footplate experience are available, including driving a diesel, right up to the Ultimate Experience, with two days, two steam locomotives, two nights' accommodation and 128 miles of driving – at £1595 per person.

For further details of the range of courses available at the Severn Valley, visit www.svr. co.uk or telephone 01562 757900 between 9am and 5pm or email footplate@svrlive.com ●

ABOVE: Sue gets to grips with the shovel – and found that it was by no means as hard as it looked!

ABOVE: Tea cans keep warm above the grate.

ABOVE: Sue rides in GWR Collett nondescript brake saloon No. 9103 alongside other guests as she waits for her turn on the footplate.

ABOVE: Cathy, Sue and driver instructor, Dai Price, at Bewdley after presentation of their certificates and souvenir mugs.